THE AWAKENED LIFE

WICCA AND WITCHCRAFT

BY DENISE ZIMMERMANN AND KATHERINE A. GLEASON
REVISED WITH MIRIA LIGUANA

ALPHA
A member of Penguin Random House LLC

Publisher: Mike Sanders
Senior Acquisitions Editor: Janette Lynn
Book Producer: Lee Ann Chearneyi/Amaranth@LuminAreStudio.com
Copy Editor: Laura Caddell
Cover Designer: Jessica Lee
Book Designer/Layout: Ayanna Lacey
Indexer: Celia McCoy
Proofreader: Lisa Starnes

Published by Penguin Random House LLC
001-313873-JUN2019
Copyright © 2019 by Amaranth

International Standard Book Number: 978-1-46548-371-3
Library of Congress Catalog Card Number: 2018960706

21 20 19   10 9 8 7 6 5 4 3 2

Interpretation of the printing code: The rightmost number of the first series of numbers is the year of the book's printing; the rightmost number of the second series of numbers is the number of the book's printing. For example, a printing code of 19-1 shows that the first printing occurred in 2019.

Printed in the United States of America

Note: This publication contains the opinions and ideas of its authors. It is intended to provide helpful and informative material on the subject matter covered. It is sold with the understanding that the authors and publisher are not engaged in rendering professional services in the book. If the reader requires personal assistance or advice, a competent professional should be consulted. The authors and publisher specifically disclaim any responsibility for any liability, loss, or risk, personal or otherwise, which is incurred as a consequence, directly or indirectly, of the use and application of any of the contents of this book.

Most Alpha books are available at special quantity discounts for bulk purchases for sales promotions, premiums, fund-raising, or educational use. Special books, or book excerpts, can also be created to fit specific needs. For details, write: Special Markets, Alpha Books, 1450 Broadway, Suite 801, New York, NY 10018.

Trademarks: All terms mentioned in this book that are known to be or are suspected of being trademarks or service marks have been appropriately capitalized. Alpha Books and Penguin Random House LLC cannot attest to the accuracy of this information. Use of a term in this book should not be regarded as affecting the validity of any trademark or service mark.

Reprinted and updated from *The Complete Idiot's Guide to Wicca and Witchcraft*

A WORLD OF IDEAS:
SEE ALL THERE IS TO KNOW

www.dk.com

CONTENTS

Part 1: Wicca Wisdom—Wiccan Way...1

CHAPTER 6: OBSERVING RITUAL: THE WICCAN WAY 61

Part 2: Being a Witch...73

Part 3: Working Magick...137

Part 4: Magickal Timing—Witches' Brew...211

Appendixes

FOREWORD

If you are reading this foreword, it is only because I have succumbed to Witches' Local Union 719 and their promise to turn me into a newt if I didn't write it. Now don't get me wrong, I have nothing against newts. I kind of like them. But it is quite difficult to type manuscripts when you are one.

Newts. Witches' spells. Love charms. Flying broomsticks and cauldrons. Halloween. It's amazing how many stereotypes still exist about Wicca and witchcraft. We are living in a time when a tremendous amount of knowledge is available to the average person, and yet there still exist a great deal of misconceptions about, and even intolerance of, Wicca. Now, I am not Wiccan, but even I get raised eyebrows over my own magickal life. I can only imagine what Wiccans and witches still experience.

Informative and fun, *Wicca and Witchcraft, The Healing Awakening*, breaks down the misconceptions and myths about one of the most ancient and empowering traditions on the planet. It is a guide for beginners and advanced alike. Never has so much information on Wicca and witchcraft been available from a single source. The authors, Denise Zimmermann and Katherine A. Gleason, aided by Miria Liguana, cover every facet in the world of Wicca and witchcraft, and they do so with simple respect, wisdom, and humor.

This book teaches the wonders of creating and living a magickal life. From simple divination to practical spell work to sacred ritual, every aspect of this reverent and magickal tradition is explored. The reader is taken by the hand and guided along the path of natural wonders with living history, practical explorations, commonsense advice, and gentle encouragement.

Wicca and Witchcraft, The Healing Awakening, will weave a magickal spell of new understanding, knowledge, and wonder around you and your life. And that's not just the newt in me speaking!

—Ted Andrews

Ted Andrews, an internationally recognized author and teacher, has written more than two dozen titles, which have been translated into more than 20 foreign languages. His books include the best-selling *Animal-Speak: The Spiritual & Magical Powers of Creatures Great & Small* and *How to Meet and Work with Spirit Guides*, the award-winning *Animal-Wise*, and the delightful *Magic of Believing* from the new series, *The Young Person's School of Magic and Mystery*.

INTRODUCTION

Right now, are you asking yourself, do witches really exist? Well, we are here to tell you, they absolutely do. Through the information in this book, you'll find out what and who witches really are. You'll also enhance your own spirituality and grow and become empowered through the wisdom of the Craft.

Perhaps you are curious and hope to learn more about a subject that has often been shrouded in mystery. Or it could be that you are looking to make a change in your life. Perhaps you are a seeker on a spiritual road. Or you are looking around for a road, a path, a direction that feels right for you. Spiritual fulfillment is one of the primary tools that help us on our journey to wisdom. Our ancestors knew this. And they have given us a way to make this change—the power of witchcraft.

How to Use This Book

Read through the first few sections of this book before you make any hard-and-fast decisions. Give yourself the time and the space to decide if a practice of witchcraft feels right for you. Before you run out and buy a lot of magickal tools, try the exercises we've provided and see how they feel. As you progress through the book, do a ritual or two. And you may want to try some of the spells. Are you ready? Hop on your broom, hold on tight, and prepare to fly!

This book is divided into four parts:

Part 1, Wicca Wisdom—Wiccan Way, introduces you to the beliefs and moral code of Wicca. We also discuss the history of witchcraft and its growing popularity in the present day and take an in-depth look at Wiccan beliefs. We also examine some of the responsibilities of being a witch and introduce Wiccan ritual and some basic magickal tools.

Part 2, Being a Witch, is where you'll learn how to prepare yourself for ritual. You'll also learn how and where to do ritual, including how to cast a circle. A Magickal Record form is also provided to use to record magickal doings in your grimoire.

Part 3, Working Magick, takes a closer look at ritual and celebrates the Wiccan holidays. You'll also learn about magickal natural objects and entities.

Part 4, Magickal Timing—Witches' Brew, shows you how to work with astrology and the calendar to enhance the effects of your magick. With potions, powders, and more, you will learn all about spells—how to write them and how to cast them. You'll also find a year-and-a-day-long plan to guide you along the Wiccan Way.

Acknowledgments

From Denise: I would like to thank Lee Ann Chearneyi and her mom, Gloria, for giving me the opportunity to do this book. I also would like to thank Katherine and her kitty for all those late-night phone sessions, lengthy conversations, and fits of laughter. To my friend and business partner, Carol, for her encouragement, and members of the Coven of the Blue Crab for their support and kindness, I thank you. Special thanks, all my love, and appreciation to my wonderful husband, Lee, for his gentle kindness, support, and belief in my abilities. And foremost, I would like to dedicate this book in loving memory to my father, who believed that all I had to do was open my arms and I could touch the stars.

From Katherine: Thanks to Denise and thanks to Denise again for staying up so late talking, for her good humor, generous and gracious spirit, patience, and also for all the magick. Thanks, too, go to Lee Ann Chearneyi at Amaranth, without whose vision this book wouldn't have happened. And thanks to Douglas Rose for making the connection, Michael Thomas Ford for all the time on the phone, and Johannes Brahms (1833–1897) for the music.

A thanks for the hard work, good sense, and good humor, Miria Liguana. Miria, a third-degree Wiccan priestess with more than 35 years of experience in the Craft, helped ensure that all information is accurate and up to date.

Special Thanks to the Illustrator

Warm thanks to graphic designer and computer whiz Kathleen Edwards for her inspired illustration work. Always professional, cheerful, pragmatic, and adventuresome, we count Kathy as a friend and invaluable talent.

Trademarks

PART I

WICCA WISDOM— WICCAN WAY

Wicca is one of the fastest-growing religions in the United States today. A faith practiced by many witches, Wicca honors the Goddess and God in the many forms deity can take, giving reverence to the Earth. Despite many misconceptions about Wiccans, witches, and their practices, Wicca and witchcraft have survived the ages and are going strong. Let Wicca's wisdom connect you to the All, the source of all things, and help you to understand the profound beauty of living in tune, responsibly with Nature. Now, as never before, humanity's future rests in addressing and nurturing its relationship with planet Earth and embracing its destiny as an explorer of the universe and its workings.

Whether practicing solitaire or with others, Wiccans believe in the healing power of magick. Following Wicca means making a serious commitment to a spiritual path. You'll learn about the ethics of the Wiccan faith, and we'll ask you to reflect on why you want to be a witch. We'll introduce you to the Wiccan Rede: "And if it harms none, do what you will." We'll talk about what witches wear and what magickal tools they use for rituals. We'll provide you with guidelines for doing ritual, and show you how to create your own Book of Shadows. Soon, you'll be ready to do magick!

CHAPTER 1

WELCOME TO WICCA AND WITCHCRAFT

Witches are all around you! Chances are that witches have been part of your life from as far back as you can remember. These were the homely, wart-nosed crones with pointy black hats who tried to turn children into a snack, who enticed with luscious apples poisoned secretly, and who imprisoned beautiful princesses in towers and dungeons. But the reality is that witches today are everywhere and look just like ordinary people. That's because they are! All it takes to be a practicing witch is a little knowledge, good intentions, and the will to make it happen.

Through the practice of Wiccan beliefs you can begin to find your inner natural power and learn to become a positive force in the world. This book can help you begin your exciting new spiritual journey, and introduce you to a magickal life.

WICCA AND WITCHCRAFT

Wicca is a religion gaining popularity in the United States, although just how many practicing witches there are is uncertain. Because many people are still suspicious of witchcraft and because there is no controlling Wiccan body as there are with other religions, trying to get an exact number of Wiccans is difficult. What most sources agree on, however, is that Wicca is the fastest-growing religion in America, and the number of Wiccans is doubling every two years or so. The practice of Wicca is taking its place alongside the practice of other established beliefs. As of 2015, the website Religious Tolerance estimated there are three million Wiccans in the United States. Rest assured, becoming a witch will put you in very good company!

What exactly is Wicca? For now, let's just say that Wicca is an earth-based or nature-based religion founded on ancient beliefs that honors both the Goddess and the God. Wicca is a welcoming religion. Wiccans do not exclude anyone based on race, color, gender, age, national or cultural origin, or sexual orientation or preference. Not all Wiccans are *witches*, and not all witches are Wiccan, but a lot of them are. Today, the term *Wicca* refers to a religion that many (but not all) witches practice. The word witch comes from the Old English words *wicce*, which means "female witch," and *wicca*, which means "wizard." A witch is someone who uses magick in her or his everyday life. Wiccans don't use the word *warlock* to refer to male witches. Male witches are witches, too. A warlock is a person who has broken an oath, and because of that has been ostracized from the group.

And what about *wizards*? What about Harry Potter? Most kids grew up reading the books and seeing the movies. It is beautiful, fanciful *fiction*. The word *wizard* has exciting and exotic connotations that the word *witch* never seemed to possess in literature and films. Merlin was a wizard people went to for help. He assisted King Arthur and kept him safe. Witches in literature and film tend to be very ugly or very beautiful, and almost always full of trickery against men. Until HP, there was a very sexist divide between witch and wizard. In reality, whether people identify as witch or wizard, they are all magick people, tapped into the energies of the Earth and walking a magickal path every day. It is common for magick people to make things a bit better wherever they go, just by their connection to the magick coming through them. This is part of the real wizarding world, and you don't even need a cloak or a flying broom for it!

There are many different traditions in the Wiccan religion. We're going to talk mostly about Wiccan witches, and in this book we will use the terms *Wiccan* and *witch* interchangeably. We'll explain more about Wicca, witches, and their history in the sections and chapters that follow. So read on, have a great time learning about Wicca and witchcraft, and welcome home!

Supernatural Abilities?

Everybody has the ability to channel energy. We all have an inherent power within us to (1) take control of our own lives and (2) make things happen. Because many of us have been taught to always look to outside authorities, we have, to a large extent, repressed this ability. Using energy, or powers, to control your life and make things happen is just as much a part of the natural world as getting up from your chair. Witchcraft can help improve your life, but you still must make responsible moral choices. When you study witchcraft, you learn more about yourself, your needs, and your wants. That knowledge will help strengthen your inborn power. But it also requires some pretty mundane efforts to make things happen.

Some people see witches' abilities as greater than ordinary and call them "supernatural," but the forces that witches use are available to all human beings and are, thus, ordinary. Witches use natural energies to enhance their lives and to heal and protect themselves, their loved ones, and the Earth.

… Or Super Abilities in the Natural?

A witch's powers may be super or, well, powerful, but they are natural. We're not talking about powers like the ones the three young sisters possess on the TV show *Charmed* (rebooted in 2018). Stopping time, moving objects with your mind, seeing black and white images of the future—those are powers conjured up by the writers' imaginations. We're talking about the natural powers you were born with. Once you start experimenting and practicing Wicca, you'll begin to understand what that force is—and that the divine natural energy is in all of us. Just like the young witch Dorothy in the classic movie *The Wizard of Oz*, you'll realize that everything you need is already in your possession.

When you learn to focus on your natural energy, you'll learn to increase it, channel it, and send it out into the world. Our natural energies make up our power, and we can use that power in the natural world to do natural things. Using your energy is not a substitute for mundane action, though. You still have to read the textbook, study for the test, and concentrate to get that "A" you want. You may think of the word *mundane* as meaning boring, humdrum, or every day. The word is often used that way. Here, "mundane" means worldly, earth-bound, ordinary, real-life, and nonmagickal.

If you use your magickal energies, too, they may just help you stay clear-headed and focused. Powers are a special blessing that we all have. Some witches believe that their powers come from the Goddess (we'll discuss this later in the chapter). Wherever they come from, just know that you have them. If you open your heart and mind, you can use your powers. And the more you work with them the better, the more powerful, you become.

Dorothy's magickal ruby slippers.

Embracing Our Magickal Energy

The abilities you have are natural and inborn, so there is no reason to be frightened of them. Some of us are more in tune with these innate energies and thus find them welcome tools to enhance our lives. Don't worry. You won't suddenly find that green sparks shoot out of your fingers every time you are annoyed. Your powers are *yours*. You will control them. You'll learn to respect your abilities and send them out to work for your own or someone else's benefit. Your powers are not to be used as party entertainment. Enjoy them, but consider them sacred!

Soon you will come to rely on your magickal powers as you learn to connect to and harness natural energies. You'll discover your place in the world, in the divine universe. Learning about your magickal abilities is a process of self-discovery. One useful tool in such a process is a journal. Witches refer to their journals as their Book of Shadows (see Chapter 6). As you learn more about witchcraft, record your changing thoughts and feelings about yourself and the world around you. Your Book of Shadows is just for you—there are no rules to follow.

WHO CAN BE A WITCH?

Anyone! You've probably met at least one witch in your life. Maybe more! Witches have all different kinds of jobs. Witches are schoolteachers, bus drivers, chefs, construction workers, computer programmers, actors, nurses, bankers, doctors, lawyers ... you name it. Witches are parents and even grandparents. Witches go hiking, play music, knit, attend baseball games, surf social media, and sing.

When you first meet someone, do you ask that person what her or his religion is? You probably don't. In most cases, the subject rarely will come up. Usually you get few clues about a person's belief system from just outward appearance. So, because witches look pretty much like everyone else, you probably have already met a witch without even realizing it. Witches not only look like everyone else, they are a lot *like* everyone else. Witches make friends, fall in love, have families, learn, grow old, and ultimately they die, just like everyone else who lives.

You can recognize some witches by the jewelry they wear. A teenage witch in a Detroit suburb was told that she could not wear her pentacle necklace to school. The American Civil Liberties Union argued in court that the prohibition violated her First Amendment rights under the U.S. Constitution. The court decided the school was wrong, and the teen returned to school wearing the Wiccan symbol.

WHAT DO WITCHES BELIEVE?

In the 1970s, the Council of American Witches, an organization that no longer exists, drew up a list of basic principles. We'll paraphrase them here to give you an idea of what they sound like:

◆ We practice rites to attune ourselves with the natural rhythm of life forces.

◆ We recognize that our intelligence gives us a unique responsibility toward our environment.

◆ We acknowledge a depth of power far greater than is apparent to the average person.

◆ We conceive of the creative power in the universe as both masculine and feminine. We value neither gender above the other.

◆ We recognize both outer worlds and inner psychological worlds, and we see in the interaction of these two dimensions the basis for paranormal and magickal exercises.

◆ We do not recognize any authoritarian hierarchy.

◆ We see religion, *magick*, and wisdom-in-living as being united in the way one views the world and lives in it.

◆ Calling oneself a "witch" does not make a witch, but neither does heredity itself, or the collecting of titles, degrees, and initiations. Witches seek to control the forces within themselves that make life possible in order to live wisely and well, without harm to others, and in harmony with Nature.

◆ We acknowledge that it is the affirmation and fulfillment of life, in a continuation of evolution and development of consciousness, that gives meaning to the universe we know, and to our personal role within it.

◆ Our only animosity toward Christianity, or toward any other religion or philosophy of life, is that its institutions have claimed to be "the one true, right, and only way" and have sought to suppress other religious practices and beliefs.

◆ We are not threatened by debates on the history of the Craft. We are concerned with our present and our future.

- ◆ We do not accept the concept of absolute evil, nor do we worship any entity known as "Satan" or "the devil" as defined by Christian traditions.

- ◆ We work within Nature for that which contributes to our health and well-being.

Basically, Wiccan witches try to live in harmony with Nature and take responsibility for the environment. Wiccans believe that the Goddess is in everything and is not some force standing "out there" watching us. In the faith of Wicca, we believe in one deity—the All. We divide that into a male spirituality and a female spirituality, the God and Goddess, or Lord and Lady. Neither the male nor the female is stronger, or better, or more important. Wiccans also work with the demigods, different, smaller aspects of the All. The All is so big that most witches find it helpful to visualize it in a more personally comprehensible form. For example, a witch might keep on her or his altar a statuette of the Venus of Willendorf. This Goddess, with her big hips and enormous, full breasts, is the epitome of fertility and motherhood, but at the same time is part of the All.

Wiccans honor teachers and leaders, but do not recognize authoritarian hierarchies because no one is intrinsically better than anyone else. You can become a witch through solitary study, study with a family member who is a witch, or by joining a *coven* where you will be taught. A coven is a group of witches who practice their religion together. *Coven* probably comes from the Middle English word *covent*, which means "a gathering." The English words *convent* and *convene* come from the same root. Witches are not anti-Christian, nor do they harbor negative feelings about other religions.

Wiccans believe in the morals that are common to most faiths. But Wiccans do not believe in the Christian concept of original sin. Wiccans live in the now. While some Wiccans believe in reincarnation, life is to be lived for what it is in the present so that we may learn from this lifetime on Earth. As Wiccans, we do not deny ourselves pleasure or put up with unnecessary pain. We are not waiting for some reward that we will get only after we are dead. We enjoy life's pleasures so that we can learn what it means to be on this Earth and to be part of life on Earth. Wiccans believe that we all have a job to do, or a lesson to learn, or maybe a debt to pay from the last lifetime. Once we have succeeded in our mission, we must move on to Summerland, where we can reflect and choose our mission in the next life.

Venus of Willendorf.

We believe that we are put on Earth to live in harmony with Nature, never to abuse it. While Wiccans don't believe there is a hell to punish sinners, Wiccans do believe there is a universal law, called karma, that puts our behavior on display so that we can learn from it. Karma doesn't punish us; it operates like a feedback system and makes us think about our past actions.

Wiccans believe that people are basically good. A person's behavior might be unacceptable, but that person is not inherently bad. We are all made in the image of the Lord and Lady. Nobody is born evil. Some people may act that way or harbor those energies, but the evil or negativity is not inborn.

In 1986, a federal appeals court ruled that Wicca is a legal religion. That means that the practice of Wicca is protected by the U.S. Constitution. Ever since the ruling, more and more Wiccans have "come out of the broom closet."

Three Times Bad and Three Times Good

Witches know that whatever energy or actions they send out, whether they are negative or positive, will come back to them threefold. If you punch someone in the eye, that does not necessarily mean that you will get punched in the eye three times, but you may fall down the stairs and break your ankle. And that fall will be three times worse than the punch you sent out. You may get temporary pleasure out of ratting on someone at work, but in the end, you could be the one who loses your job even though you had more seniority. That's how karma works. The negativity might not come back to you right away, but it will come back. Usually it gets you at the most inopportune time. And hopefully you will remember what you did to deserve the payback and not repeat the same mistake!

If you send out positive energies, you will get positive energies in return. In this way, your life will continuously expand and improve. Think about the many ripples that tossing a pebble into a pond causes. Every positive ripple you send out has the potential to affect many, many people for the good.

And If It Harms None, Do What You Will

Because there are many different types and traditions of witches, witches believe a variety of things. If you ask 200 witches a question, you will probably get 400 different answers. But there is one core belief common to all Wiccan witches that none will deviate from. This central principle is called the Wiccan *Rede*, and it is expressed, in somewhat archaic language, like this: "An it harm none, do what ye will." If you think about it, this statement covers many of the Christian Ten Commandments in one phrase. *Rede* is an archaic word that means "advice" or "counsel." It can also refer to a narration or story. In this context, a rede is a good rule to live by!

Wiccan witches do think about the Rede and about its implications. Just like Christians, Wiccans know it is wrong to kill, deliberately hurt, steal, or bear false witness. Because the Rede does not list all the things you should avoid, you must take personal responsibility for right living by its rule.

"How can I cause the least harm?" This is a question that Wiccans ask themselves all the time (especially when doing magick). For some people, this may mean avoiding recreational drugs, alcohol, or cigarettes because these substances hurt the body and thus cause harm. Everyone agrees that inflicting pain on animals for fun is wrong. Wiccans believe strongly in the integrity and freedom of the animal kingdom. Some witches believe in vegetarianism, although it isn't a requirement. Wiccans who do eat meat give thanks to the animal that gave its life for others to eat. They don't take an animal's life carelessly, such as swatting a honeybee in the garden when it's in search of a bloom. Wiccan witches try to cause the least harm to all living things in Nature. Many Wiccans have become serious environmentalists.

Witches do not believe that negativity or evil is an organized force. Most of the time, negative beings act simply out of self-interest to affect their own personal gain; therefore, they're more like independent contractors. Neither do Wiccans worship Satan or believe there is a hell where the damned or the evil languish and suffer. And as we said earlier, witches do not try to gain power through the suffering or misfortune of others. Wiccans hold the complete pure energy of the All, of the Goddess and God most high, and have a great reverence for life.

ARE YOU READY FOR WICCA'S MAGICK?

Performing magick makes you feel good. It's a healthy form of self-expression because the magick in witchcraft comes from the power that is already within you. If you are ready to make your life better, to take control of yourself, to empower yourself, to explore who you are and who you want to be, if you are ready to look at the world in a new and different light, then you are ready for magick.

Here goes: go outside, if possible, and find a quiet place where you can be alone in Nature. Close or cover your eyes, and take a deep breath and hold it in briefly. Release your breath and say:

> *All that I am is magickal.*
> *All that I see and hear is magickal.*
> *All the world is magickal.*

Before opening your eyes, take another deep slow breath in, hold, and release. Now open your eyes and begin to look slowly around you at your surroundings. In the rush of tasks and needs and everyday responsibilities, it is easy to see with everyday eyes. We let ourselves become inured to the beauty around us. And yes, there *is* beauty in all of the mundane details of our world, from the ground we stand on to the sky above us all. Look again slowly at your surroundings. Notice all the sounds and smells and textures. Notice the taste in your mouth. Feel. Experience what is beautiful about this moment.

In our haste, we often miss our experience altogether as we push through a blur of objects, surfaces, and environments. When that happens, stop and perform this lovely ritual to center yourself where you stand and remember to see and experience the magick of your everyday world. Learn to aim your attention toward the divine magick in the everyday. Welcome to Wicca.

CHAPTER 2

MILLENNIA OF WICCA AND WITCHCRAFT

Many, many people practice Wicca and witchcraft, and you can be among them. Witches practice in a variety of traditions and follow various teachers. In this chapter, we'll tell you about the different traditions and talk about solitary witches—witches who practice alone—and those who join covens.

As you read, you may get ideas about the kind of witch you want to be. We'll give you some tips about learning more and finding a coven or a teacher. Whatever you decide to do, you'll want to do additional reading and research before you make any type of commitment.

ALL KINDS OF WITCHES

You probably already have a sense of some of the history of Wicca and witchcraft. You may have read novels such as *The Witch of Blackberry Pond* or the play *The Crucible*. You've watched shows and read books featuring characters that hold magickal powers like *Game of Thrones* or the Harry Potter books and movies. Or you may have visited Salem, Massachusetts, the town whose name has practically become synonymous with "witchcraft." Some of the history of witchcraft is not pretty—accusations, trials, torture, imprisonment, and burnings at the stake. But how did witchcraft start? Why did so much persecution and misunderstanding happen? And where does all this troubled history leave the modern witch today?

Just as there are many different denominations of Christians, today there are various kinds of witches. Some witches practice rituals in covens. Some follow a prescribed set of traditions, while others work alone and make up their own rituals. Some witches draw their practice from a number of different traditions. And some witches find their traditions within their own families.

The Witches' Coven

Simply put, a coven is a working group of witches. Covens usually have one or two leaders who are known as the High Priestess or High Priest. The number of witches in a coven runs between 3 and 20. Some covens keep their membership to 13 or fewer because 13 people is the largest number you can comfortably accommodate in a 9-foot circle—a size that is considered traditional by some witches. Covens perform magick together and engage in religious rituals, according to the tradition that they follow. Every coven is autonomous, so each coven gets to make its own decisions.

Some people believe that the coven was an invention of the Inquisition. Because the inquisitors saw witchcraft as a parody of Christianity, they decided that witches must be organized in the same way that Christian monks were. At the time, monks were grouped into "convents" of 13 in honor of Christ and the 12 apostles. Other people believe witches have worked in covens since time immemorial. Either way, modern covens do exist!

Of Popes and Pagans

Before Christianity, before the Roman and Greek empires and their pantheons of deities, before recorded history, humanity honored the life-giving spirit of each thing—trees, grass, plants, animals, rivers, streams, mountains, and deserts. The spirits of the wind, rain, fire, Earth, Sun, and Moon also were important.

In 371 C.E., the Roman Empire adopted Christianity as the official state religion. Roman soldiers spread the official state religion and their interpretation of it wherever they went. Often this meant killing the priests of the local religion; this slaughter included the Druids. The Christian Church gained religious, political, and economic power. Pope Gregory I (540–604), also known as "the Great," is credited as being one of the major forces in consolidating the power of the Catholic Church and Christianizing Europe. Gregory had 10,000 baptized in England alone and built churches on the sites of pagan temples.

In many areas, people developed a hybrid religion—in outward appearance they were Christians, but deep down they still believed in the old faith. You can see this phenomenon functioning today in many parts of the world in the cult of the Virgin Mary. For example, in Europe many churches dedicated to her are called "Our Lady," another name for the Goddess.

After Gregory's death, the pope and the Catholic Church continued to gain power. Inquisitors hunted down and imprisoned heretics. In 1484 Pope Innocent VIII wrote a bull, or letter, in which he complained that no one took the threat posed by witches seriously enough. Pope Innocent's bull paved the way for the *Malleus Malleficarum* in 1486, a book credited with starting the mass hysteria of witch persecutions in Europe.

Pope Innocent's bull and the *Malleus Malleficarum* led to the deaths of many people. Witches today refer to that horrible period of history as the Burning Times. Some scholars estimate that 50,000 people were killed in Europe during the Burning Times. Other people place the number as high as nine million. No one knows for sure how many people were hung, burned at the stake, or died as a result of the tests they endured.

Enduring and Surviving the Crucible

Despite persecution, witches and their beliefs survived the crucible, or severe trial of the Inquisition and the Middle Ages, although the trouble was far from over. Repression continued into the seventeenth century with King James I's Witchcraft Act of 1604, but it was less widespread.

Under this act, the punishment for using witchcraft became hanging. Previously in England, this crime entailed one year in jail. This act also associated witches with the devil and made any act of consorting with the devil a crime punishable by death. But James went one step further. He actually is said to have changed the Bible. Where the text once read, "Thou shalt not suffer a poisoner to live," in his translation it says, "Thou shalt not suffer a witch to live." King James I's Witchcraft Act of 1604 was used to prosecute individuals who were accused of witchcraft in Salem, Massachusetts.

For those of you who don't know the story of the Salem trials, several girls and young women, ranging in age from 9 to 20, started accusing certain citizens of Salem and nearby Salem Village of bewitching them. The accusers had fits during which they cried out in pain, as if being pinched or strangled. Sometimes they were violent and disrespectful. The first four people they accused of tormenting them were a female slave; a poor woman; a widowed, disabled woman; and the mother of an illegitimate, mixed-race child. But soon more accusations flew and the trials began.

By the time the Salem witch scare was over, almost 150 people had been arrested and 31 people tried. Eventually, 19 people, 13 of them women, were hanged, and 1 old man was crushed to death with rocks. The five women who confessed to witchcraft at their trials were given reprieves. An additional two people died in jail. Fourteen years after the trials, Ann Putnam, the youngest accuser, admitted that the people she had accused were innocent.

After Salem, practitioners of witchcraft stayed hidden in the shadows and kept their knowledge and powers secret. An oral tradition became a written one with rituals and spells recorded safely between the covers of beloved Books of Shadow passed down from generation to generation.

In 1951, the English Parliament repealed its surviving laws against witchcraft and the practice slowly emerged from the shadows. Two years later, Arthur Miller's play *The Crucible* was a hit on Broadway. Historically and culturally, this was a turning point for witches. Not only did witchcraft reemerge into public discussion, but the witch hunts were seen for what they were—persecution for no good reason.

Wicca and the World We Live In

Wiccans and witches can now practice their faith in the open. A 1986 Fourth Circuit Court of Appeals, ruling reaffirmed that Wicca is a religion deserving First Amendment protection. Since that time, Wicca has received recognition from the United States Internal Revenue Service and has tax-exempt status as a legal religion. In the Netherlands, students of Wicca are allowed to write off the cost of schooling on their Dutch tax returns!

And just in case witches do encounter discrimination, there are organizations around the globe to help. In 1986, Laurie Cabot founded the Witches' League for Public Awareness. The Witches' Anti-Discrimination Lobby (now known as the Alternative Religious Education Network), the Earth Religions Assistance List, and several other organizations also are active on the behalf of witches. Still, it's often prudent not to openly broadcast your status as a witch. Spirituality is, after all, a personal affair. If friends are curious, answer their questions honestly but stress the positive aspects of your religion: harm none; live as though the Earth and all of its inhabitants are sacred; strive toward the positive. You will find doubters, but there is no need to turn them into adversaries. Your exemplary behavior toward others might just turn some skeptics into believers.

THE TRADITIONS OF THE CRAFT

Today, witches follow a variety of traditions, or practices. Many witches work skyclad; skyclad means to work nude or "clothed by the sky." Other witches practice Wicca robed. Here are descriptions of some of the different Wiccan traditions:

♦ **Gardnerian Wicca.** In the 1950s, after England repealed its witchcraft laws, Gerald Gardner went public about his practice of witchcraft. In 1954, he published his *Witchcraft Today.* Gardner, a longtime student of religion and magick, believed that information handed down in his coven's Book of Shadows was inaccurate and incomplete. He rewrote the rituals of the coven he belonged to so they would be more accurate. Some people see Gardner as the founder of modern-day Wicca. Gardnerian covens have a degree system in which one learns about the Craft. Individuals must be initiated by the coven and cannot initiate themselves through self-study. Gardnerian covens work skyclad. In addition, some covens try to have equal numbers of men and women in the group.

♦ **Alexandrian Wicca.** Alex Sanders founded this tradition in the 1960s. Originally based in England, practitioners work skyclad and much of their ritual is similar to Gardnerian practices, although the Alexandrians place more emphasis on ceremonial magick. Sanders called himself the "king" of his witches.

♦ **Georgian Wicca.** George Patterson founded the Georgian tradition in Bakersfield, California, in 1970. The followers of Georgian Wicca also are known as the Georgian Church. Their rituals are drawn from Gardnerian and Alexandrian traditions, with other elements added as the coven members see fit. In some covens, members write their own rituals. Some Georgian covens work skyclad, and some do not.

♦ **Seax-Wica.** In 1962, Raymond Buckland, a protégé of Gerald Gardner, moved to the United States, where he founded this tradition. Buckland taught the Gardnerian tradition for a number of years. Because of problems that he saw in the practice of the Craft, he started his own tradition in 1973. Seax-Wica is based on Saxon traditions, but as Buckland admits, he made it up alone. Covens decide for themselves if they will work skyclad or robed. Witches of this tradition can be initiated by the coven or through self-study.

♦ **Feri.** There are a number of ways to spell the name of this tradition; you'll also see Fairy, Faery, and Faerie. Victor Anderson is credited with bringing the Feri tradition to the United States, where he has taught in the San Francisco area since the late 1960s. Feri teachers tend to add something of their own when they teach, so there is a strain of eclecticism in this tradition. Feris are usually solitary, or they work in small groups.

♦ **Reclaiming.** Starhawk, the popular author of *The Spiral Dance*, received her training in the Feri tradition from Victor Anderson. In 1980, she and some of the women in her coven went on to cofound the Reclaiming Collective. Reclaiming focuses on linking spirituality and magick with political activism. The teachings of the tradition, which is nonhierarchical, have spread from the San Francisco Bay area and are disseminated by individual teachers and at witch camps, weeklong programs that are offered in the United States, Canada, England, and Germany.

♦ **Dianic.** The Dianic tradition focuses on the Goddess with little talk about a God. The Goddess is worshipped in her three aspects—Maiden, Mother, and Crone. There are different varieties of Dianic witches. Since the 1970s, the Dianic Tradition has been seen as the feminist movement of the Craft. Some, but not all, Dianic covens are women only.

♦ **British Traditional.** There are a number of different British traditions, all of which are based on what people believe to be the pre-Christian practices of England. Many British Traditional groups follow Janet and Stewart Farrar, who have written a number of influential books about witchcraft. The groups tend to be structured, with training for neophytes (beginners) following a degree program under the supervision of the coven. Their practices are said to be a mix of Celtic and Gardnerian traditions.

♦ **Celtic Wicca.** This tradition looks to ancient Celtic and Druidic deities and beliefs with an emphasis on the magickal and healing powers of plants, minerals, gnomes, fairies, and Elemental spirits. Some of the rituals are derived from Gardnerian practice.

♦ **Strega Witches.** This type of witch follows traditions from Italy sometimes known as *La Vecchia Religione* (The Old Religion). Some people trace *Strega* teachings back to a woman named Aradia in the fourteenth century. The Strega tradition is rapidly gaining popularity in the United States today. *Strega* means "witch" in Italian. Remember Tomie dePaola's children's books about Strega Nona? That's Grandma Witch!

♦ **Black Forest Clan.** The clan practices a tradition known as Euro-witchcraft, which includes the Caledonii Tradition of Druidic Wicca, Gardnerian, German, and Celtic witchcraft. This is a lineage that includes Gerald Gardner, Raymond Buckland, Lord Serphant, Silver RavenWolf, and Pow-Wow practitioners such as Gertie Guise and Preston Zerbie. Training in this tradition prepares one as a licensed member of the clergy. The High Priests and High Priestesses do not hive off. Instead, they multiply by forming new covens while remaining part of their original coven. This makes the clan both strong in numbers and in unity.

This list, of course, is not complete. There are many other forms of witch religions, and new ones are created frequently. Some of the different traditions are based on a particular national heritage. If you meet a Strega, there's a good chance that she'll be from a Mediterranean background. But this does not mean that only individuals with this heritage can learn the Strega teachings. If you are drawn to a tradition, explore that tradition, whatever your background.

Solitaire

A solitaire, or solitary witch, can practice witchcraft in a variety of traditions or in no particular tradition. As solitaires, these witches can design a system of worship that works best for them. Some traditions—Gardnerian and Alexandrian, for example—say that a witch must be part of a coven to *really* be a witch. Some people believe that most witches throughout history have been solitaires. Others see this as a more recent development in the Craft.

The proliferation of books and websites about witchcraft has led to a rise in the numbers of solitary witches. In the past, before so much information about witchcraft was available, people seeking knowledge about the traditions had to find a coven or an individual witch to teach them. Now, all the neophyte needs to do is head to the local metaphysical bookstore or log on to the internet! Solitaires act and learn on their own. To some this might seem lonely. To others it means great freedom and personal empowerment.

The Hereditary Witch

Hereditary witches inherit the Craft from older relatives who teach the family traditions. Some people believe that the traditions passed down within families represent an unbroken chain of beliefs and traditions that date back to the Old Religion of prehistory. Other people are sure that, while some family traditions can be very old, the forms of their practice are relatively recent. In rare cases, a hereditary witch might adopt someone from outside the family and teach that person the family Craft.

Witches portrayed in entertainment media often are hereditary witches. Sabrina of *Sabrina the Teenage Witch* is a hereditary witch, as are the characters played by Nicole Kidman and Sandra Bullock in the movie *Practical Magic*. And, of course, Samantha Stevens, portrayed by actress Elizabeth Montgomery in the classic *Bewitched*, was a hereditary witch, too. And who can forget Sam's powerful mother witch Endora, played by Agnes Moorehead!

SOLITAIRE OR COVEN LIFE?

Choosing between becoming a solitary witch or joining a coven can be a tough decision. Denise originally became involved in the Craft as a solitaire. She read books and took a Wicca 101 course. While taking the course, she hooked up with a local coven. She had been in the coven for six months when she realized their energies and her energies did not mix. She left the coven, returned to a solitary practice, and buckled down. She got serious and read everything she could. Despite her seriousness, she felt there was something missing. Seeking answers, she wrote to an up-and-coming Wiccan author, Silver RavenWolf. Silver wrote back: "Turn it over to the Goddess, for she always has a plan." And what a plan it was! Some years later Denise opened a metaphysical bookshop, joined Silver's coven, and became an author. Now Denise is a third-degree High Priestess with her own coven, the Coven of the Blue Crab.

In making your own decision about joining a coven or practicing as a solitaire, you'll want to keep a number of factors in mind. What kind of witch do you want to be? Do you live in an area where there are covens? Are there covens of the tradition that appeals to you? Do you feel comfortable in a group? Do you have the time to commit to coven activities? Are you more comfortable doing things on your own? These are important questions. The kind of training you look for will depend on your answers.

Discover what's out there in your community. Visit your local metaphysical bookshop. Check out the books and take a good look at the store's bulletin board, too; stores often display interesting advertisements and announcements. And scope out their newsstand. Try to attend a pagan festival in your area. There you will get a taste of what it's like to work in a group, and you'll probably meet people who share your interests. You may even find information about a local coven. Perhaps the coven will be practicing an open ritual that you can attend. And use the internet. There's a lot of information on the web. Your first step, though, will be to read, read, read, and read some more! If you're still having trouble determining your path, why not do what Denise did? Turn it over to the Goddess, and see where she leads you.

TRAINING IN A COVEN

What actually happens in a coven? Perhaps you have heard stories about scary rites or mandatory sexual performances. Let us dispel the negative myths. Coven life can be an empowering gathering of Goddess energy, amplified by the participation of strong, dedicated women (and men, too). Read on!

Dedicated to the Craft

Each coven is different, but the process usually follows these general lines.

After you have told the coven you are interested in joining, they invite you to attend their open rituals. If a coven approaches you and asks you to join, steer clear. A good coven will not ask you—witches do not try to convert people to their religion. When you visit the coven's open circle, you get to check out the coven, and they get to check you out. After a few visits, if all goes well, you tell the coven members that you still want to join. The coven meets and decides if they want you as a dedicant, or a witch in training. (In all likelihood, if you are under 18 years old and do not have your parents' support, the coven will not take you. But never fear! You can still continue to learn as a solitaire, read as much as you can, and when you are of age you can begin your formal training.) Then, in many covens, someone agrees to be your teacher. As a dedicant, you study the Craft for a year and a day before earning your First Degree Initiation and acceptance into the coven as a member. Witches study for a year and a day because the Celtic goddess Cerridwen is said to have stirred her brew in the cauldron of knowledge for that same amount of time.

The coven will probably give you a list of expectations that may include attendance and study requirements, promises to uphold the Wiccan Rede, and an oath to keep the identity of other coven members private. (Some witches are not "out of the broom closet" and their families and/or coworkers do not know they are witches.) The list should *not* include sexual favors for the High Priestess, the High Priest, or any of the coven members. If it does, this is not a true Wiccan coven, and you do not want to be part of it.

The coven will hold a dedication ritual for you. While you are a dedicant, the High Priestess, High Priest, and coven members will watch you closely to see if you are serious and if your energies mesh well with the group. You may do everything right and still not be asked to join the coven because your energies don't mix well with the other coven members. There must always be love and harmony within the coven. Each member has to enter the circle in perfect love and perfect trust. If personality conflicts rear up, that trust will be destroyed. A coven is not just a club. It is more closely a very tight-knit spiritual (and magickal!) family.

Initiation: Earning Your Degree

Many covens follow the steps below in the granting of degrees. Of course, there is some variation from tradition to tradition and from coven to coven.

- ◆ **First Degree Initiation.** A year and a day after your dedication, after study and hard work, and provided the High Priest and Priestess feel you are ready, you take part in a ritual in which you are reborn into the Wiccan Path. At that time, you earn your First Degree Initiation, you gain the official title of Priest or Priestess, and you become a member of the coven and a First Degree witch! You receive only one initiation. When you advance to higher degrees you receive elevations.

- ◆ **Second Degree Elevation.** At least a year and a day after earning your First Degree, and after more study and hard work, you can earn your Second Degree Elevation—if the High Priest and High Priestess feel you are ready. You will also earn the title of High Priest or Priestess. At this point, you usually can start teaching, writing, and leading ritual. In some cases, depending on the laws of your tradition, you will be able to start your own coven.

- ◆ **Third Degree Elevation.** At least a year and a day from the day you earned your Second Degree, you can get your Third Degree Elevation, provided the High Priest and High Priestess feel you are ready. Sometimes this degree takes a little more time to earn because there's a lot to learn and a lot of responsibilities that come with this title. At this point, you can earn the official title of clergy. Once you have your Third Degree, you are also given the title of Lady or Lord. Denise is known as Lady Shaharazad in the Wiccan community. Once you have your Third Degree, you are a Third Degree High Priest or Third Degree High Priestess, and you can break away from the mother coven, or hive off and form your own coven. If you do that, you will be the High Priestess (or Priest) and the leader of the new coven. If you don't want to start your own coven, you can stay in your mother coven with the rank of High Priest or High Priestess. Depending on the coven's bylaws and the tradition of the coven, you may share the responsibilities of leadership. In some traditions, coven members vote on the leadership of the coven, and those leaders serve the coven for a year and a day. A few traditions go to four degrees, with the Fourth Degree representing training to be a High Priest or High Priestess.

Priests, Priestesses, and Elders

Most covens have a High Priestess and a High Priest. Within the Gardnerian tradition, a coven must have a High Priestess. The High Priestess is seen as the Goddess incarnate and is the spiritual center of the coven. She leads the coven in ritual, usually teaches, and guides coven members on their spiritual paths. The High Priest assists the High Priestess and is seen as the God incarnate. Elders are people who have all their degrees but have chosen not to be High Priestesses or High Priests. Within the coven, they function as mediators and spiritual resources. Elders don't necessarily have to be old. They just have to be experienced in the ways of Wicca and magick.

TRAINING AS A SOLITAIRE

Solitary witches either have to train themselves or find a teacher outside of the coven structure. This can seem a daunting task at first, but it is also an enjoyable process. Remember, learning is fun! But where do you start?

A great place to find workshops and courses about Wicca and witchcraft is at pagan festivals. Festivals are also great places to meet people and to network. You might find a teacher at a festival, or you might hear about one from someone who lives in your area. While there is no centralized Wiccan spiritual body, the Covenant of Unitarian Universalist Pagans is a good safe place to start to meet people who practice Wicca.

Wicca, Social Media, and the Internet

Social media and the internet have made life as a solitary witch much easier. Now, you can practice as a solitaire but still have the benefits of community—the online pagan community. Do be cautious in your interactions, though. Exercise good common sense in navigating the Wiccan online community, as you would in all your online activities. You may choose to use only your Wiccan name online, to protect your mundane identity. However, always maintain your Wiccan truth online and beware of any individual or group who does not and who may be presenting a false identity for fraudulent purposes. Do your research, and go slowly in establishing online contacts and relationships.

People also teach Wicca and witchcraft classes online, and there are many online videos, podcasts, and vlogs. If you find a class or an online source you're interested in, remember to ask questions to make sure the teacher will meet your needs. If you do take an online class, be aware that even if you have completed your First Degree, a coven may not recognize your degree status.

A Mentor in Magick

To seal your intent to attract a magickal mentor, write your intention in an affirmation and place it into a bowl. Cover the affirmation in the bowl with sand, and then cover the bowl with a cloth. Say these words over the bowl: *this bowl represents my spiritual life and into my life will come the right person to teach me the Wiccan Way.* You cover your intention so its focus will be held in your life and won't scatter into the world where the teacher cannot find you. Place the bowl on your altar, or, if you don't have an altar, choose a special location for your ritual bowl. In the meantime, don't stop your efforts to learn about Wicca as a solitaire, or to find the right Wiccan group for your practice—Nature is alive, growing and moving and learning always, and so should you be!

CHAPTER 3

HONOR THE GODDESS, THE GOD, AND THE ALL

In most faiths, you worship, or honor, the Goddess(es) or God(s) of that faith. There is no choice. In Wicca, you choose which deities you will work with. Sometimes, deity chooses *you!* You can choose which aspect of the deity you are going to work with because all deities from all cultures and spiritual traditions are seen as facets of the All. So you can work with Cerridwen and Herne from the Celtic tradition, or you can pay homage to the Hindu deities Durga and Ganesha. Wiccans have very personal relationships with deities. But let's slow down and start at the beginning.

IN THE BEGINNING, THE ALL

Before the creation of the Earth, there was the All. The All existed in knowing, stillness, and silence. The All, a female spirit, was alone. She created her other half, the male spirit. They intertwined. Even though there were now two spirits, they were still one: two halves of a whole. Together they gave birth to the universe. Then they made the stars, moons, and planets. On Earth, they made water, land, air, fire, plants, animals, and humans.

The All is both female and male. No one part is better than the other. The two parts are twins of equal form. From their union came the seeds of life. The God and Goddess chose physical symbols to remind us of their presence. The Goddess chose the Moon, radiant and calm, yet changeable. The God chose the Sun, fiery and bright. These celestial bodies remind us of the Goddess and God.

Honoring the Lord and Lady

In witchcraft, you pay homage to both the Lord and Lady, or the God and Goddess, as manifestations of the All. Many Wiccans choose to focus primarily on the Goddess. As Denise explains it, Wiccans are more into the Goddess because she is nurturing and compassionate. Many Wiccans make the Goddess their focus to make up for the hundreds of years of domination by male-centered religions.

Who Is the Lady, and Where Is She?

The Lady is the Goddess, the female essence of the All. She is the nurturing part, the essence of motherhood. She is there to love us, shield us, help us to learn and to grow. She is the one you'd call on for female spirituality because she understands the pain of childbirth, nurtures our spirits and our bodies, and encourages growth and family.

The Goddess is immanent. Immanent refers to something that exists or remains within. It can be something inherent. The Goddess is in everything and is everywhere. She is not some force that looks down on us from above. The Goddess dwells in every single thing—in every tree, in every dog and cat, in every grain of sand and drop of rain, and inside you.

Who Is the Lord, and Where Is He?

The Lord is the God, the male essence of the All. He is the wild, playful, and lusty aspect of deity. He is there to protect us. He is the one you may want to call for if you suddenly need physical strength and agility. He can help you bear what life has thrust upon you by lending his speed, agility, and ability to adapt to change. Just as the Lady is, the Lord is immanent. He exists in everything.

HOW DO YOU RELATE TO THE LADY?

You work with, respect, and honor the Lady. You can see her as a Goddess from an ancient culture, or you can work with her as an abstraction. Many people feel more comfortable giving her a face and a personality. The Lady nurtures your growth. You don't beg for favors from her. She is the abundance that the Earth has to give. She has that hidden, inner knowledge, or sixth sense, that all women have. You can pull upon that part of her to guide you and help you grow. She will teach you, nurture you, and provide for you. In return, you give her your love. Out of that love, you do your best to take care of the Earth.

Luna: Maiden, Mother, Crone, and Enchantress

Luna is the Roman Goddess of the Moon. The Goddess's three phases—Maiden, Mother, and Crone—represent the three stages of a woman's life. The Maiden is an innocent young girl. To her everything is new. She is health, sweetness, and tenderness. As the Mother, she has matured. She is all-loving, protective, and nurturing. When humankind takes actions that hurt the Earth, she can get angry. And yet she still loves us, however badly we behave. She sends us signs so we, her children, can learn from our mistakes. The Crone, an old woman, holds all the things we have learned throughout our lifetimes. She can be stern, but she is a great teacher. She takes us back into her, into the Goddess, in death. These three aspects of the Goddess correlate to the phases of the Moon—new, full, and waning.

The Enchantress is that part of the Goddess, and of all women, that seduces. She is that sexy playful spirit that we get from the All. She is both Maiden and Mother, and as such relates to the Moon when it is new, waxing (growing bigger in the sky), and full.

In your journal, jot down a few words about your own conception of the Goddess. You don't have to write in sentences or worry about spelling. Just write down whatever comes to mind. What does she look like? How does she dress? What's the first thing that you notice about her when you see her? Does she have a scent? What does her voice sound like? Give yourself at least 10 minutes, then read your words. Highlight any passages or ideas that you particularly like.

The Charge of the Goddess

"The Charge of the Goddess" is an invocation that is frequently used in Wiccan ritual. There are many different versions of the charge. Here is the most widely known one:

> *When I have departed from this world,*
> *Whenever ye have need of anything,*
> *Once in a month, and when the Moon is full,*
> *Ye shall assemble in some desert place,*
> *Or in a forest all together join*
> *To adore the potent spirit of your queen,*
> *My Mother, great Diana. She who fain*
> *Would learn all sorcery yet has not won*
> *Its deepest secrets them my mother*
> *Teach her, in truth all things as yet unknown*
> *And ye shall all be free from slavery,*
> *And so ye shall be free in everything:*
> *And as the sign that ye are truly free,*
> *Ye shall be naked in your rites, both men*
> *And women also: this shall last until*
> *The last of your oppressors shall be dead:*
> *And ye shall make a game of Benevento,*
> *Extinguishing the lights, and after that*
> *Shall hold your supper thus.*

"The Charge of the Goddess" was first published in *Aradia: The Gospel of the Witches*, by Charles Leland. In 1897, a witch named Maddalena is said to have given him the text. "The Charge of the Goddess" has been adapted several times by a variety of authors. If you like, you can adapt the charge so that it suits you. Or try this one that Denise wrote:

High Priest: *Listen to the words of the Great Mother, the ancient one of ageless time. She was known by many among those who worshiped her. Artemis, Diana, Morrigan, Aphrodite, Venus, Cerridwen, Isis, Mary, and by many other names.*

High Priestess: *Whenever you have need, come to me. Assemble in a place of secret, better it be when the Moon is full and give praise to my spirit.*

I am Queen of the Witches and those who seek the knowledge of the Craft of the Wise. From me flow all its mysteries and its darkest secrets. I will teach those who gather in my honor and seek to know all its sorcery. There in my place of worship you shall sing, dance, feast, make music and love in my praise. For to do this in the presence of me shall truly set you free from bondage. In my spirit you shall feel ecstasy and joy on Earth.

In striving for your highest ideals keep your heart and spirit pure. Let no one stop you or turn you aside from me.

Enter the Land of Youth through my secret door and drink from the Chalice of Life Eternal. It is there that you will find the Holy Grail of Immortality and the Cauldron of Cerridwen. Drink in the gifts of joy, knowledge, and eternal spirit that I have bestowed upon humanity.

Upon death you will receive my gifts of peace and freedom. You shall be reunited in the spirit of love with those who have passed over before you. I demand no sacrifice in my name, for to do so would dishonor the spirit of me. I am the Mother of all living things. Give reverence unto me by honoring all that I have bestowed upon the Earth.

High Priest: *Hear the words of the Great Moon Goddess, she whose light illuminates the heavens and whose spirit weaves the tapestry of the universe.*

High Priestess: *Cherish and protect the Earth's beauty, which holds the gateway to the entrance of my temple. Call my name when you gaze upon the white Moon that stands alone in the night sky amidst the stars of heaven. Learn the mysteries of the waters and hold tightly to the desire in your hearts.*

I who gave life to the universe give my soul to Nature, therefore rise up and give your soul to me. Always know that from me all things proceed and unto me all things must return. Through me, let my beauty, compassion, strength, power, humility, and the honors of my spirit reside within you. Let my rituals of love and pleasures remain in the heart that rejoices in my worship.

To those who seek to know me, understand that all of your yearning will be in vain unless you know the mystery. If what you seek is not found within you, then you shall never find it without. For behold I am alpha and omega, the beginning and the end. I have always been and always will be with you.

If you use "The Charge of the Goddess" with a group, you want to have the person in the role of High Priest read the sections marked for him. The High Priestess reads the rest of the charge. During "The Charge of the Goddess," the High Priestess is seen to become the Goddess incarnate. You do not, however, have to be a High Priestess or, for that matter, even a woman to pull the Goddess into you. We all can fill ourselves with her energy, because she is the mother of the All.

HOW DO YOU RELATE TO THE LORD?

You work with the Lord in the form of a God or as an abstraction. He is the essence of fatherhood. He is kind, gentle, and protective, but he can also show his wrath. You look to him with honor and respect and gain from him his guidance, wisdom, protection, and strength. You pull on this aspect of the All to protect and strengthen your life, in order to do what you need to do, so you can protect your family. The Lord is representative of the playfulness and heavy sexuality we all have within us.

Nature's Royal Prince, King, and Elder

Just as the Goddess can be seen in three phases (Maiden, Mother, and Crone), the God has three phases as well. As Nature's Royal Prince, he is a youth, full of wonder, curiosity, and playfulness. As the King, he has matured into a man—noble, protective, and just. And as the Elder he is an old man—wise, weathered, and strong.

The Charge of the God

Like "The Charge of the Goddess," "The Charge of the God" is an invocation. Here's a version that Denise wrote:

High Priestess: *Listen to the words of the God who is son, lover, and consort of the Lady. He is the ancient one of time eternal, the great father who of old we know as Ra, Osiris, Zeus, Thor, Pan, Herne, Luke, and by a thousand other names.*

High Priest: *I am the radiant Sun, King of the Heaven. Come to me whenever you seek haven in my spirit. Assemble in some secret place, most notably at the eight sacred days of the wheel, and give praise. Set aside the restrictions of cultural laws and, like the beasts of the forest that are of hoof and horn, run naked and free in my presence. Sing and dance, make love, and celebrate. Delight in the moment.*

My law is harmony. My love is the seed that fertilizes the earth. My rapture is of the mind. In the grain that bursts forth and grows, I am life abundant. In the fall harvest when the grain is cut down, I am death, the gentle reaper, king of the underworld, where the living may not venture. And in spring, I am rebirth, the hidden seed of creation that bursts forth into being.

High Priestess: *Hear now the words of the great horned one whose song stirs the astral winds and whose music changes the season from one to the next, flowing in a smooth rhythm.*

High Priest: *I, who am the Sun, the keeper of the lamp that sends out the light to warm the earth, the lord of the hunt, the master of the winds that spread the seed of life, I call upon you now to arise and come unto me. Show respect for the wonder of me. Give love to others as I have given love to you. Let there dwell within you the magnificence of life, tenderness of heart, the glory of the spirit, mastery of emotions and merriment and pleasure. Keep me always in your heart, for I am the giver of peace, the source of life, the father of all things, and my protection blankets the temple of life, the body of the Lady and the Earth.*

Just as male and female practitioners can pull down the Moon, male and female can pull down the Sun.

THE PANTHEON: GETTING THE BIG PICTURE

While you are learning the Craft, work with deities from one pantheon. Don't mix and match Gods and Goddesses from different cultures at first. Discover all you can about one pantheon. Later on, you can branch out and start to learn how deities from one system relate to deities from another.

Working with Deities: Sometimes Light, Sometimes Dark

The deity you want to work with on a given day will depend on what you want to do. If you are working with the Celtic pantheon and you need healing and inspiration, you may want to call on Brigid. Within the Egyptian system, you might invoke Bastet to renew your sense of play and help you look on the bright side. You can work with any God or Goddess.

Some deities encompass a light energy, and others are darker. Be aware of the qualities of the deity you are working with. Know that Hecate is wise *and* that she is associated with the underworld. Athena is also wise, and she is a warrior. She does not have as dark an energy as Hecate does. Resist the temptation to pick a very dark Goddess or God just because you can. Remember your work with a deity should benefit you, not scare you. And what you do is for the good of All: "An it harm none, do what ye will."

Let's explore some of the major Gods and Goddesses from a number of different pantheons.

Greek and Roman Gods and Goddesses

Aphrodite (G) Venus (R)	Goddess of sex, love, beauty, and reconciliation. Often emerging from the sea. When working magick with her, every pleasure has a price.
Apollo (G), (R)	God of healing and the arts, the Sun, logic, and reason. With Artemis/Diana, his twin, represents the Lord and Lady in ritual.
Artemis (G) Diana (R)	Goddess of the Moon, the hunt, and women. Twin of Apollo. Demanding and temperamental, her strength gets magickal results.
Ares (G) Mars (R)	God of war and agriculture. Gives strength and courage.
Athena (G) Minerva (R)	Goddess of wisdom, commerce, poetry, and medicine. A warrior Athena emerged full-grown from the head of Zeus, her father.
Demeter (G) Ceres (R)	Goddess of agriculture, grain, the harvest, seasons, and motherhood. Wife of Hades/Pluto and mother of Persephone/Proserpina. Established the Eleusinian Mysteries.
Dionysus (G) Bacchus (R)	God of wine, the life force, impulse, and hedonism. In ritual his party-wild spirit must be handled with care.
Gaia (G) Terra Mater (R)	Ancestral mother of all life; Primal Goddess of Earth. Often called in ritual.
Hades (G) Pluto (R)	God of the underworld and wealth; judge of souls.
Hecate (G) Diana Trivia (R)	Goddess of magick, the Moon, doorways, and the underworld. Three-headed Maiden, Mother, and Crone. Patron of witches; queen of the underworld.
Hera (G) Juno (R)	Goddess of married women and childbirth. Volatile, strong, mature, and determined. Wife of Zeus/Jupiter.
Hermes (G) Mercury (R)	God of communication, thought, and travel. Winged, carries a caduceus.
Poseidon (G) Neptune (R)	God of water and the sea. Often called in rituals on the beach.
Zeus (G) Jupiter (R)	God of the sky and king of the Gods. Carries a thunderbolt. Married to Hera/Juno but unfaithful.

Hindu Gods and Goddesses

Durga	Mother Goddess
Ganesha	Elephant-headed God of beginnings, success, travel, and prosperity. Overcomer of obstacles.
Hanuman	Winged Monkey God, sings the name of the Divine. A fierce warrior, strong and mischievous.
Kali	Goddess of Earth, Nature, creation, destruction, and renewal, with a necklace of skulls. Wife of Shiva.
Krishna	Blue-skinned God of love, an ancient Christ-like figure.
Siva or Shiva	God of change, transformation, and destruction. Husband of Kali.

Egyptian Gods and Goddesses

Amun, Amon, Amen	God of creation, fertility, reproduction, and sexual power. Associated with pharaohs and the Sun, the one supreme God. Often seen as a ram.
Anubis	God of the dead and transformation, with the head or body of a jackal. God of the underworld.
Bastet, Bast	Goddess of the Sun, pleasure/sex, play, the East, childbirth, the Moon, healing, music, and fire. Protector of animals with a human body and the head of a cat.
Hathor	Goddess of love, beauty, and pleasure. Depicted as a woman with the head of a cow.
Horus	Solar God and avenger of evil.
Isis	Supreme Goddess of fertility, woman/motherhood, the Moon, magick, healing, and resurrection. Holds the powerful magick in the universe.
Nephthys	Goddess of magick, dreams, metamorphosis, and intuition.
Nut, Nuit	Goddess of the sky. A popular goddess called often in circle.

Osiris	Goddess of commerce, success, religion, civilization, arts, crafts, law, and resurrection. Brother or husband to Isis.
Ra	Sun God. Source of all life, truth, rituals, spells, and prosperity.
Sekhmet	Lion-headed Goddess of war. When called upon in circle, keep red beer on your altar for this once blood-thirsty goddess.
Thoth	God of mysteries, secret wisdom, intellect, mathematics, the Moon, divination, and magick.

Celtic Gods and Goddesses

Brigid	Goddess of healing, inspiration, and craftspeople. Associated with fertility and childbirth.
Cernunnos, Kernunnos	Horned God, the universal Father. Consort of the Lady, called often in pagan ritual. Wild, untamed virility, associated with snakes.
Cerridwen	Goddess of the Moon, harvest, and inspiration; stirs the cauldron of knowledge for a year and a day.
The Dagda	God of knowledge, life, death, and plenty. Controls passage of the seasons. Use in spells for prosperity and abundance.
Herne	God of the underworld and change. Leader of the phantom hunt.
Lug, Lugh, Lugas	God of magick, art, music, healing, strength, beauty, courage, intelligence, war, and the Sun. A Sabbat bears his name.
Morrigan	Goddess of war, fertility, and vegetation. Three-faced queen of demons. She takes care of wrongdoing someone has done.

Calling Scantaku of the Oglala Sioux to Start Your Day

The Native American deity Scantaku is constantly in motion, always bigger, always more. In the Native American tradition, Scantaku represents the energy of divine connection, the energy of All that is. In the morning before your daily doings, before you connect to social media or have your first cup of coffee, call to Scantaku to guide your daily path:

> *I am the whirlwind. I am the calm.*
> *I am the sword. I am the balm.*
> *I am the force. I am the will.*
> *I am strength. And I am still.*

CHAPTER 4

TO BE A WITCH, HONOR THE WICCAN REDE

Wiccan witches live their lives according to the principles and moral code of their religion. These principles are not rigid, and yet they are not always easy to follow. Abiding by the Wiccan faith can require a good deal of thought and good actions.

In this chapter, we'll help you look at the reasons you want to become a witch. Committing yourself to the Craft is a serious step that you don't want to enter into lightly. You may want to take some time to mull over the issues raised in this chapter.

WHY DO YOU WANT TO BE A WITCH?

Do you want to live in tune with yourself and Nature? Do you want to grow spiritually and gain a greater understanding of the divine? Witchcraft could be the path for you. Keep in mind that being a witch is more than saying chants, doing spells, and knowing cool stuff. Wicca is a spiritual path. It's important to look at your motivations before you set off on your journey.

A Self-Exploration

Take some time and meditate on each question. Be entirely honest with yourself. Write down your thoughts in a journal you dedicate to your exploration of Wicca, or in your new Book of Shadows (BOS), if you are ready to begin one. (See Chapter 6 for more on creating your book.)

1. Are you attracted to Wicca because it seems really different? Does it strike you as totally different from the religion you were raised with? If your grandmother knew you were investigating Wicca, would she freak out?

2. Do you like the idea that you could cast a spell to change the dynamics between you and your friends or family? Do you like the idea that spells operate in secret? That you could cast a spell and no one would know?

3. Do you think Wicca and magick can improve your social life?

4. How much of a draw is all the cool magickal stuff—wand, pentacles, athames, altars, and cauldrons?

5. Does having a reason to dress up in unusual outfits make Wicca sound fun? Do you often dress in clothes that set you apart from others and cause people on the street to take notice? Do you like feeling different? Or do you enjoy scaring people?

6. Are you attracted to Wicca because it will make you stronger? Is that sense of power really important to you? In your normal everyday life, do you feel strong or weak?

7. Are you considering Wicca because your friends are into it? Or did you just learn that this really awesome person you recently met is Wiccan so you want to be Wiccan, too?

If you answered yes to any of these questions, stop now. Time out! Do not pass Go, do not collect $200. Please go back and read this chapter a few times, let it really sink in. And then start with Chapter 1 and begin reading this book again from the start to examine whether you are ready to learn about Wicca and dedicate yourself to the Craft. But first let's look at each set of questions one by one:

1. Wicca, like all religions, has a strong moral code. If you think Wicca is super different, think again. Sure, there are differences between Wicca and, say, Presbyterianism, but when you boil it down, faiths of any stripe have more similarities than differences. (And please be nice and don't scare your grandma!)

2. First, remember the Wiccan Rede? Remember the whole idea that you treat others the way you yourself would like to be treated? And what about the Law of Three? Everything you do will come back to you threefold! And besides, casting spells on your friends and family without their knowledge and permission, even if those spells are designed to make your (and their) life easier and more harmonious, would be unethical. You cannot manipulate someone else's free will. Now, if you want to cast a spell on yourself so that you become more agreeable and easier to get along with, well, we won't stop you.

3. Again, casting spells on other people without their permission is unethical and an all around bad idea. So, you would not want to cast a spell to make new friends. Okay, it is true that joining a coven could bring new and like-minded people into your life. But the primary point of a coven, the primary focus of Wicca, is to honor the Goddess and the God.

4. Okay, we will fess up, that we really like magickal stuff, too. But, that said, if the cool stuff is a major reason you want to be a witch, then you may have a problem. Being a witch involves commitment. Being a witch means you have promised to act for the greater good and will actively work to make the world a better place.

5. Do we have to tell you that scaring people is not a good thing? Remember the Wiccan Rede and harm none! Dressing the part of a witch and being a witch are not the same thing. We know witches who wear nothing but jeans and t-shirts. If you really want to be different, walk the walk—live an ethical life, take care of the Earth and all of her children.

6. Hmmm … well, actually, a practice of Wicca probably will make you stronger. Hunger for power, though, is something you'll want to examine in yourself. If you've been ground down, a desire to get the upper hand is natural. But having power, the power to control your own life and confidently make decisions, is not the same thing as having power that means control over someone else. You can work to control your own fate and actions, but not to control others' lives.

7. It's nice to share activities with your friends. But becoming a witch is about your relationship with the God and Goddess, and sharing that commitment with others who practice the Wiccan faith with devotion and commitment. In being Wiccan, you may meet a lot of cool people (and a lot of cool people *are* Wiccan …) but Wicca is more than an after-school club or social group; it is a religion.

Is Wicca the Right Path for You?

We hope that when you look more deeply, you like what you see. You understand that Wicca and witchcraft involve self-knowledge, ethics, and morality. You also know that being a witch means you have made a commitment to the Goddess and God, to Nature and the All. Do you feel confident that being a witch is the right path for you? Many, many people do feel that way. They feel confident, as we do, that witchcraft is their right path because witches hold not only to their beliefs, but to their strong moral principles.

Even if you have discovered that you are not ready to practice Wicca, read on! You can learn a lot (and grow a lot) from finding out more about various religions. Wicca's Nature-based belief system may be just the thing to help open your mind and heart.

FOLLOWING THE WICCAN WAY

You're probably understanding that being a witch is not just about casting spells and wearing cool outfits. Neither is it a hobby or a pastime. Being a witch means that you are walking on the Wiccan path. It's a lifestyle, and it is more than that. Being a witch is about commitment and responsibility—to yourself, to your coven (if you have one), to your community, and to the Earth.

The Wiccan Rede

Remember the Wiccan Rede from Chapter 1: "An it harm none, do what ye will"? Well, what follows is the full text of a poem from which the Rede is drawn. There are other versions of Rede poems and a search of social media and the internet will reveal and interpret many of them. While there is no universally accepted Rede poem that all Wiccans observe as a sacred text, the core belief, the Rede itself, *is* held universally. You even can write your own Rede poem, as long as you stick to core principles. Whichever version of the Rede poem you prefer, you must agree that it contains a strong moral code and you must adhere to the core belief central to the Wiccan faith: "An it harm none, do what ye will".

The Rede of the Wiccae (Being Known as the Counsel of the Wise Ones)

1. Bide the Wiccan laws ye must
   in perfect love and perfect trust.

2. Live and let live
   fairly take and fairly give.

3. Cast the Circle thrice about
   to keep all evil spirits out.

4. To bind the spell every time,
   let the spell be spake in rhyme.

5. Soft of eye and light of touch—
   speak little, listen much.

6. Deosil go by the waxing Moon—
   sing and dance the Wiccan rune.

7. Widdershins go when the Moon doth wane,
   and the Werewolf howls by the dread Wolfsbane.

8. When the Lady's Moon is new,
   kiss the hand to her times two.

9. When the Moon rides at her peak,
   then your heart's desire seek.

10. Heed the Northwind's mighty gale—
    lock the door and drop the sail.

11. When the wind comes from the South,
    love will kiss thee on the mouth.

12. When the wind blows from the East,
    expect the new and set the feast.

13. When the West wind blows o'er thee,
    departed spirits restless be.

14. Nine woods in the Cauldron go—
    burn them quick and burn them slow.

15. Elder be ye Lady's tree—
    burn it not or cursed ye'll be.

16. When the Wheel begins to turn—
    let the Beltane fires burn.

17. When the Wheel has turned a Yule,
    light the Log and let Pan rule.

18. Heed ye flower, bush and tree—
    by the Lady blessed be.

19. Where the rippling waters go,
    cast a stone an truth ye'll know.

20. When ye have need,
    hearken not to other's greed.

21. With the fool no season spend
    or be counted as his friend.

22. Merry meet an merry part—
    bright the cheeks an warm the heart.

23. Mind the Threefold Law ye should—
    three times bad and three times good.

24. When misfortune is enow,
    wear the blue star on thy brow.

25. True in love ever be
    unless thy lover's false to thee.

26. Eight words the Wiccan Rede fulfill—
    an it harm none, do what ye will.

Honoring the Wiccan Rede

So that's a common version of the Wiccan Rede poem. We think it's quite beautiful. But what, you ask, does it mean? Let's take a look, line by line:

1. You must keep the Wiccan laws with an attitude of perfect love and perfect trust. If you don't completely agree with what Wicca is about, you might want to rethink your choice to follow the Wiccan path.

2. Respect people and Nature. Treat them both as you want to be treated.

3. Witches generally create a circle around them when preparing to do magick. The circle is cast, or made, three times because three is a very magickal number. It stands for the three phases of the Goddess and God, and it's the number of creativity. The Threefold Law says events usually happen in threes.

4. Witches speak their spells in rhyme because it gives the conscious mind something to do. While your conscious mind is busy listening to the words, your unconscious can tap into your energy and the energy of the God and Goddess—and magick is done.

5. Be gentle. Sit back and listen. Wise people don't blab; they listen.

6. When the Moon is waxing, or getting bigger, move around the ritual circle deosil, or clockwise, to bring good things toward you.

7. When the Moon is waning, or getting smaller, move around the circle widdershins, or counterclockwise, to dispel negativity or disease. Wolfsbane is dreaded because it is a poisonous plant.

8. When the Moon is new and has just become visible in the sky again after being dark, salute the Lady and welcome her by kissing your two fingers.

9. When the Moon is full, go after your heart's desire. At that time of the month, you can ask anything of her.

10. through 13. These couplets describe various elements associated with the four directions.

14. and 15. There are nine different kinds of magickal wood that are often burned in the cauldron during rituals—apple, birch, fir, hawthorn, hazel, oak, rowan, vine, and willow. But never burn the elder (that's a kind of tree, too). Elder trees are the Lady's trees, and in honor of her they are always spared.

16. and 17. The turning of the wheel refers to the cycle of the Wiccan year. Beltane is one of the year's major Sabbats, or holidays. It occurs in the spring. Yule, another Sabbat, sits on the opposite side of the wheel of the year, at winter solstice.

18. Take care of Nature, and respect it for the Lady's sake.

19. Watch what happens when you throw a stone into water. The ripples spread out from where the stone landed. Your actions, like the stone, send out ripples that affect everyone and everything around you.

20. Don't allow the idea of profit to sway you. Don't take money for your magickal work.

21. People will associate you with the company you keep. If you hang around with fools, you may be seen as one, too.

22. Basically, it's good to be with friends.

23. Pay attention to the Threefold Law. Whatever you do, good or bad, comes back three times.

24. When you are in trouble, visualize a blue *pentagram* on your forehead. The pentagram will protect you.

25. Be loyal in love, but if the person isn't loyal to you, forget about him (or her)!

26. Eight words sum it up—if it harms none, do what you will.

IN TUNE WITH MAGICKAL ENERGY

You really don't need much to put yourself in touch with magickal energy. Remember, magick is in *you*. Imagine yourself as Tarot's Magician, the Major Arcana card that represents harnessing infinite energies for creative power. There are three great vortexes shown in the card to express that power: the divine force of the All; our own human bodies, minds, and spirits (the Magician); and the Earth. Today, now and always, *you* are the conduit for those magickal energies of creation.

Stand tall. Reach your right arm and hand up through your shoulder blade toward the sky. Stretch your open-fingered hand beyond to the stars in the cosmos, reaching up through the lovely garden trellis blooms. Plant your feet shoulder-width apart on the ground. Stretch your left arm and hand down through your shoulder blade toward the Earth, reaching your open-fingered hand down through the lovely garden blooms to the rich loam below. As you reach, stretching through your body above and below, feel yourself connected through your own human being to the Earth and to the All, the ultimate blossoming Source. Feel the magickal energy of creation flow through you. Know this. Internalize this knowledge in your mind, body, and spirit: the magickal energy of creation flows through *you!*

CHAPTER 5

WHAT YOU NEED TO DO MAGICK

If you love "stuff," especially magickal stuff, you'll have a great time reading this chapter. You'll also want to plan to do some shopping. Or use your creativity, and make some of your tools. But we'd like to suggest that you read through the chapter before you start making lots of online purchases and visiting your city's or town's cool metaphysical stores. You want to be prudent. You don't need to go broke to be a witch! Remember, the magick is within *you*. Really, *you* are all you need to do magick!

SECRETS OF THE WITCH'S MAGICKAL CABINET

Do you want to see all the secret stuff that's in a witch's magickal cabinet? Of course you do! Well, we can't show you everything, but we will give you a good idea. You can practice your visualization skills (they're important!) to see what it all looks like. You're not going to find any eye of newt, toe of frog, or fillet of snake, but you will see amulets and candles and chalices and herbs and wands and ….

Use your intuition. Let magickal tools come to you slowly. You don't need to have every item we discuss in this chapter. But if you are absolutely drawn to an object and believe you must have it, well then, you'll want to explore that object's purpose and how you might use it for magick. Look around you as you go about your daily activities. You never know what you might find on the street, on a hike in the woods, or on the beach, and those things that you find by "accident" are there just for you.

What Are Magickal Tools?

Magickal tools are any objects used during ritual or while doing magick. They are used only for magick and ritual and for no other purpose. Magickal tools can be fancy items—objects inscribed with magickal symbols or set with stones or crystals—but they don't have to be ornate. In ritual, each tool has symbolic significance. For instance, the athame, a ritual knife, symbolizes the male, and the chalice symbolizes the female. Any object charged with energy to do magick becomes a magickal tool. Because tools are charged to help you do magick, they are not to be used for any other purpose.

How Do You Use Magickal Tools?

Each magickal tool has its own use. The way in which you utilize a given tool depends on the tool and on what kind of magick you want to do. Magickal tools help you to focus your attention and energy. And because the subconscious works with images and symbols, magickal tools tell your subconscious mind to get to work, too. When using tools such as herbs, powders, magickal dolls called poppets, oils, candles, and cords, you focus your magickal energy and put it into the tool. You can then use the tool to hold energy, or you can use the tool to send energy out.

If you made a poppet for a child who is ill, you'd put healing energy into it, then you'd give the poppet to the child. The poppet holds your healing energy and helps the child get better. If you put your energy for finding a new job into a candle, when you light the candle your magickal energy is sent out to the universe to work on your behalf.

Ritual tools—such as the athame and the chalice—are used in celebrating the Wiccan religion. Ritual tools are used during ritual to cast a circle, to represent the Lord and Lady, to welcome deity, to cleanse, to make sacred space, and to cut energy. Ritual tools are not used in the act of magick. Because they represent the Lord and Lady, ritual tools take on great symbolic significance during ritual.

Storing Magickal Tools

You can store your tools in a closet, a wardrobe cabinet, a desk with big drawers, or even a cardboard box. You don't need something fancy. But you do need to keep your tools for magick and ritual in a safe space—a place where other people won't handle them or find them by accident. Make sure that your magickal tools are not used for mundane purposes. For example, here's one way to make sure no one uses your magickal broom to sweep out the garage. Instead of keeping the broom under lock and key, disguise it. Buy a cinnamon broom, decorate it with dried flowers, herbs, ribbons, or stones. Tie a bow around it, and then hang it on the wall. People will think you have discovered a great piece of folk art! And who would take your wonderfully handcrafted object down from the wall and muck it up? Only you need to know that this fancy broom is one of your magickal tools.

So besides protecting people from your tools, you need to protect the tools from other people. Because your tools will absorb energy from whoever touches them, only you and the people who have your permission should touch them. It follows that you should always ask permission to touch or handle someone else's tools for magick and ritual, and that you show the fullest care and respect for their tools if you do. Before you put your tools away, make sure they are clean. Cleaning will get rid of any dust, dirt, or fingerprints. Before using them again, also make sure they have been charged—more than just cleaning, charging will clear old and unfocused energy from your tools and refocus and reenergize them for making magick and doing ritual. (See the end of this chapter for more on how to charge tools.)

A BASIC MAGICKAL INVENTORY

As you meet people and learn magick, your collection of supplies will grow naturally. You'll acquire what you need as you need it. Don't worry about having the "right" stuff right away. You can always use simple things. If you don't have an athame for ritual, you can use a wand. You can draw a pentagram on a piece of paper for your altar, or create one with special items found on a Nature hike or on a day spent cycling the local trails on your mountain bike. You will need candles and bowls for salt and water. You should have a broom to sweep out the energy in your ritual space. If you don't have a censer for burning incense, you can use a small cauldron. Or use a ceramic dish with some sand in the bottom. Over time your magickal cabinet will fill with special tools you'll find unique to you and irreplaceable.

A Beginner's List of Ritual Tools

Witches often start out with one object to represent each Element or direction and objects to represent the God and the Goddess.

♦ An **athame** is a double-edge knife, approximately six inches in length, used in ritual to represent the God. Originally, athames were not forged from metals, but were wooden and taken from trees. Athames are usually dull because they are never used to cut anything but energy. Traditionally, athames had black handles. Some are plain, and some are very fancy. The athame is often associated with the Element Air.

♦ A **Book of Shadows** is your personal magickal book. Record your spells, magickal information, dreams, chants, or any other material that has to do with your workings in the Craft.

♦ The **cauldron** represents the womb of the Goddess and is used for cooking or for burning incense in, as well as holding water for scrying and holding safely other things to be used in ritual or magick. Scrying is a kind of divination: to look at an object so that the conscious mind quiets and in the quiet is able to see things that haven't happened yet.

♦ **Chalices** are cups or fancy mugs that represent the Goddess. They are also associated with the Element Water. A chalice is used in doing the great rite—a symbolic unification of the male and female in which an athame is lowered into a chalice, blessing the wine or water. Many witches own more than one chalice.

- ♦ **Incense** comes in stick, cone, and powder form. It is used in Air Element magick and to cleanse magickal tools and sacred space.

- ♦ A **pentagram** can be used as jewelry. It is also placed on the altar for protection. It is associated with the Element Earth.

- ♦ A **wand,** which can be made from a variety of materials, is used to direct energy. It often is associated with the Element Fire.

Useful and Fun Magickal Objects

You can be a witch and do magick dressed in street clothes and with no special equipment at all. As you get more experience in the Craft, you may want to have more magickal supplies to enhance your practice.

- ♦ A **bell** is used in ritual when calling in the quarters and deity (asking the four directions and the God and Goddess to join you). At the end of ritual, the bell is rung to let the Elements return to their realms.

- ♦ A **censer** is a container used to burn incense. Censers often have feet so the heat they contain will not scorch the surface upon which they rest. Some censers have chains attached on top so that you can lift them easily and spread the incense smoke around the room.

- ♦ **Cords** of different thickness and colors are used to do binding magick.

- ♦ **Divination tools** such as Tarot cards, runes, pendulums, astrology charts, and the *I-Ching* are used to look into the future, to aid you in decision-making, and to do magick. It is best to learn more than one type of divination.

- ♦ **Herbs** are used in healing and in magick, and can include dried plants or spices, dried corn, and even tobacco.

- ♦ A **magick mirror** has been cleansed, treated with herbs, and charged to help you see things as they really are, or as they should be.

- ♦ **Statues,** to represent the God or Goddess you are working with, are placed on the altar.

The more you work with magick, the more you become adept at working with Spirit. The more you work with Spirit, the more connected to Spirit you will become. Spirit will start to guide you in your magickal workings and in your life. As your magickal work gets deeper, you will come to write your own spells, rituals, prayers, and Esbat and Sabbat celebrations. You will create your own talismans and magickal tools and focus your energy in the blink of an eye.

WHAT DO WITCHES WEAR?

Do clothes make the witch? Well, clothes certainly do have a function in witchcraft. And they do more than just keep you warm. Just like magickal tools, magickal clothing can help you to focus your mind. Clothes can also help create a mood and enhance energy; they can add formality, and they can be fun, too.

From High Priests and Priestesses to Covenmaids

The High Priest and Priestess of a coven may often wear crowns. Sometimes the other members of the coven wear jeweled headbands and sometimes not. In some covens, the High Priest and Priestess change the color of their robes to symbolize the change in the seasons, while the rest of the coven wears the same color robes throughout the year. They also may have special robes for performing special ceremonies, such as initiations, Wiccanings (child blessings), or handfastings (Wiccan weddings, see Chapter 23).

A coven that wears robes usually decides what kind of robes all of the members are going to wear. The robes all may be identical, or they may just all be the same color. In some covens, the color of the cord around the robe denotes the magickal degree an individual has attained. As a solitary witch, you can decide what to wear and when and how to wear it.

Doing Magick in Regular Clothes

Experienced witches can do magick and even ritual in regular, street clothes; they know how to ground themselves in the moment and summon the needed magickal energies and entities. As a beginner, it will be really difficult for you to keep your mind properly focused for magick while you find yourself surrounded by mundane things. When you become more adept, you will be able to maintain your concentration and have greater success performing magick in regular clothes, or in the moment.

WITCH'S WARDROBE CLOSET

Remember how we said that you don't want to use your magickal broom for a mundane purpose like sweeping out the garage? Well, the same is true of your wardrobe. Okay, we know you probably wouldn't go clean the garage in a silk dress. The point is, when you put on an article of clothing from your magickal closet, it tells your subconscious mind you have magick to do. So keep your magickal clothes special and separate from the clothes you wear in your everyday life. That way you'll be sure that your subconscious acts upon the right message at the right time when you slip into that felted cape.

A Cloak of Stars: Skyclad

As we first mentioned in Chapter 2, some covens and solitaires prefer to practice magick and ritual skyclad, or naked. Many witches feel that clothing restricts their energy, so they feel better working without clothes. Working skyclad can also help you get to know your body and to accept your body as part of Nature. Once you get used to it, just seeing your body and feeling the air on your skin can be very liberating. Some covens go skyclad for the same reason that middle-school kids might wear uniforms—it emphasizes that everyone in the circle is equal. Skyclad is a way to celebrate the human body, in union with mind and spirit. Sometimes witches paint magick symbols on their bodies while doing magick and ritual skyclad to increase their energy. Sometimes witches will get tattoos to commemorate a magickal rite of passage in their lives; the tattoo need not be a magickal symbol but could represent Nature.

Before you attend a coven meeting, find out if they practice skyclad or robed. If they do practice skyclad, bring along a robe; you may want something you can slip into and out of quickly. And you may have to walk some distance from where you leave your regular clothes to the spot where the ritual will be held. If the coven practices robed, ask what you should wear. Chances are you can pull out that little black robe you've been saving!

Robes, Dresses, Hoods, and Shoes

Many solitary witches like to wear purple because it is a magickal color. During the summer, you might wear green to symbolize the Goddess and Earth all in leaf. You can pick a color to correspond with the type of magick or ritual you are going to do. Or you can pick a color just because it looks good on you. Whatever you wear, remember to keep that outfit (or outfits) for magick and ritual only. Keep your magickal clothes magickal by keeping them special. Keep in mind as well when dressing that you will be working around candles and open flames. If you decide to wear robes, you can dress them up by sewing on magick symbols or embroidering them. You can even make your own robes. Some witches like to wear robes with hoods. The hood is really useful when you work in a group. If you're having trouble concentrating, pull your hood up, and like a horse with blinders on, you'll be able to see only the thing you need to focus on and won't be distracted by the people on either side of you. The cord that you wear as a belt around your robe can be the same color as your robe or a contrasting one. The cord at your waist can also hold your athame, pouches, charms, or medicine bags. Many witches do not wear underwear under their robes. (Say that three times fast!) Witches also typically do not wear shoes when doing magick or ritual. Being barefoot gives greater access to Earth Element energy and helps you get more grounded.

Jewelry

Like your magickal clothes, you want to keep your magickal jewelry for magickal occasions. You should not wear magickal jewelry for your regular day-to-day activities. The jewelry should be worn only during ritual or when doing magick. Resist the temptation to touch someone else's magickal jewelry. Just as you don't want people to touch your magickal tools, another witch doesn't want you to touch her necklace. Touch someone else's things only if that person has given you permission.

As we know, in a coven, usually only the High Priest and Priestess may wear crowns. As a solitaire, you are the Priestess or Priest, so you may wear a crown. Witches often wear magickal rings, pendants, or barrettes to hold back their hair. Medicine bags or pouches worn around the neck are also popular.

The metals you choose can be important. Gold jewelry represents the Lord, while silver stands for the Lady. Some witches wear both kinds for a balance between the Lord and Lady. Others choose to wear only gold or only silver. The designs you choose in jewelry also have significance. Images of the Moon are Goddess images. The Sun represents the God.

CHARGE YOUR MAGICKAL TOOLS

Charging magickal tools is a way of waking them up and enlivening their positive energy. Before charging magickal tools, they must always be cleansed and consecrated (see Chapter 8). One of the easiest ways to charge your tools is by laying them out under the full Moon at night. If you can, spread your tools out in the light of the full Moon for a couple hours, or even overnight. After some time in the moonlight, the energy of the Goddess will penetrate your tools and they will be ready to use. If you want to add the God energy, you can spread them out under the Sun.

In an apartment, you can place cleansed and consecrated items for charging on your balcony, or on your windowsill where a patch of moonlight filters in through your windows. Alternatively, you can hold your tools up toward the full Moon on a night when she is shining and ask the Goddess to bless them.

CHAPTER 6

OBSERVING RITUAL THE WICCAN WAY

Most religions use ritual in some way. Wicca is no exception. In Wicca, as in many other faiths, you do ritual to honor deity. But in Wicca you can do magick as part of your ritual, and you can even write your own ritual. As you practice ritual and become more familiar with the steps involved, your sense of spirituality will grow and expand, and you will come to feel more and more connected to the All.

WHY DO WICCAN RITUAL?

Ritual is special, and it gives you a safe, sacred space to do magick and to work with the energy of the Goddess and God with people you trust. Ritual puts you in a state of mind in which you can relate on a personal level to deity. It creates the necessary conditions for you to perform magick. It also allows you to connect with others in a spiritual way. Within the ritual circle, individuals use the time to share thoughts and feelings, but anything said within the circle must be held confidential.

Performing Wiccan ritual creates order and harmony in your life. It is a way to nurture and heal. It also helps you live by a moral standard. Doing ritual will enable your energy and allow you to pull upon the energy of the God and Goddess. Ritual will help you focus and keep things in perspective.

When to Do Ritual

Wiccans perform ritual in circle in honor of the holidays—the Esbats, which are celebrated once a month, and the Sabbats, which occur about every six weeks. (Read more about Esbats and Sabbats later in this chapter, and more fully in Chapters 12 and 13.) Witches also get together in circle for ritual any time they want to formally honor the God and Goddess, or when the group wants to do major magickal work. Witches perform rituals to ground themselves, to celebrate, to honor ancestors, or to perform magick spells—to name a few occasions. But ritual does not have to be confined to special occasions. You can do ritual alone or with others, when you have a problem you need to work out, when you want to connect with something larger than yourself, when you're feeling empty, or when you need to heal.

In a circle is a perfect place to meditate. If you do ritual alone as a solitaire, it also gives you a great opportunity to sit back, look at your life, and get some clarity. There's no hiding between you and deity. The Goddess and God can really enter now and help you figure out what you need to do.

It's a good idea to do a small 10-minute meditation ritual every day to honor the God and Goddess. After your morning shower, light a candle and sit in meditation in front of it. Remind yourself every day that deity is in your life. And you can remind deity that you are here, too! Then you can go about your day's happenings with less stress and anxiety.

When Not to Do Ritual

Avoid participating in ritual when you are sick. If you are working with other people, you will be in close quarters and will just give them the bug you are harboring. Doing ritual when you aren't feeling well, even when alone, isn't a good idea. We all tend to be cranky and distracted when we are sick. You want to be able to keep the full force of your attention on the ritual work with which you are involved. Ritual demands a lot of your energy. You want to be able to give 100 percent. If you can't, then it's best to wait until you're feeling better.

It's also not a good idea to do ritual when you are very tired or in a hurry. Ritual needs your undivided attention. It's hard to stay focused when you are nodding off or worrying about running out to pick up the kids after ballet practice.

Another time to avoid doing ritual is when you are angry. Anger can send your energies off in undesirable directions or just take your focus away from the work at hand. It also puts a strain on the other members of the circle. They won't be able to relax when there are negative energies zipping about. You also want to make sure you are comfortable with all the people in the ritual circle. If you are in the middle of a feud with one of them, don't do ritual with that person. Or if you feel you don't share the same beliefs with other people in the circle, don't participate. You want to be in the ritual circle in "perfect love and perfect trust."

Before you start ritual, make sure that you feel okay, that you're well rested, and that you don't have issues with any of the people with whom you are going to be doing ritual. This will help to keep your focus where it should be and help to ensure that everyone has a good ritual experience.

ALL KINDS OF WICCAN CEREMONIES, RITES, AND RITUALS

Because Wicca is a religion, there are many different Wiccan rituals and ceremonies to mark sacred passages. There are rituals for death, for entering the faith, for joining people together in love, for child blessing, for initiation, for magick, for healing, and for celebrating Esbats and Sabbats. You can do ritual solitaire or with a coven—your choice.

Performing Ritual as a Group

In a coven, the High Priest and Priestess lead ritual. Often coven members are assigned individual jobs—calling down the quarters; lighting the candles; ringing the bell; or bringing the cake, wine, candles, or incense. Calling down the quarters is another way of inviting the four directions—North, East, South, and West—and the Elemental powers—Earth, Air, Fire, and Water—with which they are associated into your ritual space. If you get together with a group of solitaires to perform ritual, usually someone will take on the role of the High Priest and someone will act as High Priestess. Group members usually take turns helping to set up or clean up.

Covens meet to perform ritual together regularly—for the 13 Esbats, Moon celebrations, and the 8 Sabbats, the Wiccan holidays (see Chapters 12 and 13). Some may work together at other times as well. Groups of solitaires can work together if they have something they all want to do. Some solitaires meet for the holiday rituals as well. Or they can do ritual together for a common purpose—a healing, some magick that needs to be done, or to celebrate a Wiccaning or handfasting. But most of the time they work alone, hence the name "solitaire."

Ritual Solitaire Style

As a solitaire, you design your own ritual for specific purposes and can emphasize the parts of the ceremony that appeal to you. And you can wear whatever you want—robes, a fancy outfit, or you can go skyclad. Working on your own, your ritual will not be as elaborate as one performed in a group. Because you are on your own and must do everything yourself, you need to be organized. When you are planning your ritual, make a checklist so you can be sure you have everything you will need. Go over the list before you start your ritual and gather all your tools together. You don't want to keep cutting holes in your magick circle to go find things. (Read more about entering and leaving a magick circle in Chapter 10.)

ALL THE PARTS OF A WICCAN RITUAL

There are many parts that are common to all Wiccan rituals. We'll list them in order here and tell you about each in greater detail in upcoming chapters.

To perform Wiccan ritual, you …

- Decide to do ritual.

- Cast a magick circle. Here only good enters and only good leaves; the circle is the sacred space in which your magick ritual takes place.

- Ground. Center your attention on your desire, and focus on your reason for doing ritual.

- Calling down the quarters—the Elements and directions.

- Call in deity.

- State out loud your intent to do ritual.

- Work magick, if that is what you need to do.

- Say farewell to the quarters and deity.

- Take down the circle.

- Partake of cakes and ale or wine. Cakes in the context of ritual doesn't necessarily mean big gooey confections. You, or the coven you visit, could use cookies, crackers, or bread as a ceremonial snack to give thanks to the Goddess.

- Relax and communicate with others who participated in the circle.

Inviting Friends and Family to Share

Covens usually work in a closed circle. In other words, only members of the coven can attend their rituals. Some covens occasionally hold open rituals in which others can participate. A ceremony such as a handfasting (wedding) or Wiccaning (child blessing) might be conducted in an open circle so friends and family of the people involved can be there.

As a solitaire, you can invite a special friend or family member to join you in your ritual circle. You might want to do that if you are going to be doing healing work. Before you do invite your special person, make sure he or she is of like mind and really understands what Wicca is all about. If you are going to do magick within your ritual, chances are your friends and family will not understand. In such a case, it is probably better not to invite anyone to join you.

Animals Join In

When you do ritual, animals can move in and out of the circle as they please. Because animals have pure energy and they enter the circle in "perfect love and perfect trust", they can join you at any time in any ritual. If you have a familiar—animals or even plants with which you can psychically communicate—it will want to participate. One cat familiar we know won't leave the circle till someone cuts a door for him! (For more about familiars, see Chapter 14.)

BEYOND THIS LIFE

Are you afraid of graveyards? Witches usually are not. Some even use gravesites in magick. There are two schools of thought about graves. Some witches believe there is no point in working with graves because the person buried there is not really there. Spirit has reincarnated; nothing is in the grave but an empty shell. Other witches believe cemeteries have special energy because people visit them to remember their dead. Also, the ground of a graveyard has been consecrated and is a sacred space.

To make yourself more comfortable, you might want to spend some time visiting historic graveyards. Pack a picnic. Read the headstones and learn about the people buried there. If you find a stone you particularly like, make a gravestone rubbing to take home. (First check that rubbings are allowed—some cemeteries forbid them because of possible damage to old stones.) Soon you will feel comfortable and will see graveyards as simply the place where the body goes after death. Unfortunately, many graveyards today can be lonely and unfrequented places. Be safe if you are unsure and call ahead to the office of the cemetery to ask for the best times to visit and whether it is safe to walk the grounds alone.

Summerland Beckons

What happens when a witch dies? Where does the spirit go? Summerland is not heaven and it is not hell. Witches who believe in the Summerland think of it as a place of reflection for the spirit. After death, spirits think about the lives they have just lived and plan where they will come back next. Some spirits decide not to reincarnate, but to remain and act as spirit guides for those they love. Ultimately, each spirit, after it has learned all it needs to learn and taught what it needs to teach, is reunited with the All. So in each lifetime, the spirit advances.

When you enter Summerland, sometimes you sleep and reflect for a long time to recover from difficult life experiences. Some witches believe Summerland is where spirits dwell in the company of the God and Goddess, and where they decide how they are going to reincarnate. Other souls don't spend much time resting, anxious to continue their journey on Earth.

Reincarnation: Rebirth

After the soul has rested in Summerland, it decides when to reincarnate. Each soul chooses who it will be and what lesson it will learn in its new lifetime. Once it has reincarnated, it doesn't remember what its lesson is, but must find out by living through all the experiences of its new life. If a soul doesn't wish to reincarnate right away, it may become a spirit guide. Or if it does not need to reincarnate, it will reunite with the Goddess.

WRITING THE STORY OF YOUR MAGICKAL LIFE

Now, in this life, you will want to keep records of your rituals. Writing down what you have done and when you did it will allow you to keep a written exploration, of your magickal life. Remember there are no rules to follow in creating your journal. The book needs to speak to you and you alone.

Your Book of Shadows and Your Grimoire

A witch's journal is called a Book of Shadows (BOS). A witch's recipe book is called a grimoire. It's best to have two books, especially as you're starting out, but it isn't required. If you choose to use just one journal to encompass everything, you will want to keep it private. Your Book of Shadows is for your eyes only—it is your witch's diary. Your grimoire can more readily be shared with other witches. Think of your Book of Shadows as a place to record your private thoughts and concerns as well as ritual outcomes. As you grow spiritually, this record can remind you how far you've come. Your grimoire is a sort of how-to book. In this book you list recipes, spells, potions, how to prepare magickal tools, and the mundane aspects of ritual like dates, Moon phases, and who else participated. It can also contain lists of angels, spirits, and the magickal properties of objects found in Nature. The content of your two books will certainly overlap but you want to make sure that your most private spiritual thoughts are in the book you don't share. Most witches use the term Book of Shadows generically to refer to both types of books. A Book of Shadows can be anything from a hardbound leather book to a spiral notebook or a sheaf of papers—it can even be an electronic notebook (with a strong password to keep all information within from being shared).

Witches' Knowledge: Your Book of Shadows

If you've kept a diary in the past, you may think of it as a chore. Or, you might look at keeping a Book of Shadows as a daily way to explore your feelings or to meditate and ponder what's important to you about Wicca and being Wiccan. Consider writing in your BOS a joyful task as you record your journey down the new spiritual path of Wicca. Don't forget to include photographs, bits of poetry, chants, or even pictures cut out of magazines. Write in different colored ink. Tape in dried flowers or grasses so your book becomes art, magick, not just a mundane record. There are no rules to follow. Just plunge ahead and see what works for you.

Writing About Ritual in Your Book of Shadows

Samhain Celebration, 10/31/2019, Waxing Crescent Moon, Visible: 15%

I offered to host our annual bonfire, which made me very nervous! I'm not the world's best hostess, and I've been so busy lately and pre-occupied with mundane matters, but everyone pitched in to help and I looked forward to connecting again with spirit and remembering that life is about more than what happens on the Earth plane. Guests started arriving at 6:00 p.m. Sylvia, Mary, Starshine, and Wick arrived first and helped set up the pyre. We used the rock circle to contain it and made sure there was no dried brush around it. Because I live outside the city limits, we don't need permission to have an open flame, which is why everyone likes it when I host. But it's fine not to build a fire when we're in the city. We usually just light candles instead. (Note: next time, have more water on hand to put out sparks!)

Other guests: Greg, Storch, Meena, Capris, Blythe and friend (don't remember his name...), Alice, and Simon.

We cast a traditional circle that included the altar, but we left the bonfire outside the circle. We called down the quarters and stirred the ancestors to welcome them in. Each guest to the circle placed a token on the altar (actually an oak tree stump) to honor the spirits who crossed over to be with us during this Samhain celebration. I used Martha's embroidered handkerchief along with Uncle Sam's key to the house that used to stand on Paca Street.

We used this incantation:

> Into this circle of friendship
> we invite friends and family who have gone before.
> May they join us in this joyous celebration,
> Goddess and God, enter in and bless our endeavors
> this night and around the Wheel of the Year.
> So mote it be.

I felt very close to Uncle Sam but I didn't really feel a connection with Martha this time. Maybe she was visiting a different celebration. (P.S. Two days later, my aunt gave me Sam's gold pocket watch! She said she just felt like he would want me to have it. It's what he carried as a young man, and what he used to help teach me as a child to tell time. I'd always wanted the watch to keep his spirit close to me, but we all thought it had been lost when the Paca Street house was torn down so I never mentioned anything about it to anyone. Now my aunt found the watch had been tucked into the pocket of an old suit vest with some things she'd been about to donate!) Afterward we each reclaimed our tokens and thanked the spirits.

We didn't have a magickal intention other than celebrating the Sabbat so the ceremony was a short one. Meena talked about her mother who just passed a few weeks ago and we asked the Goddess to bless her spirit. Meena said she could smell her mother's face cream and felt comforted she had joined us. We released the spirits and took down the circle.

I could see there was some lingering tension between Greg and Sylvia. I'm afraid I'm going to have to talk to them about bringing their differences into the circle. Maybe *it's time for those two to do a friendship ritual together. I'll suggest it to them. If Sylvia and Greg can bond spiritually their mundane differences won't matter. I felt distracted throughout the ritual, and I'm sure others did, too.*

For cakes and ale we had pumpkin bread, sesame crackers topped with black olive pate, and hot apple cider. (We had agreed a full-fledged feast was too time-consuming to prepare this year.) Afterward, Wick pulled out his fiddle and we danced around the bonfire. Sylvia made witch scarves for each of us as gifts, so we knotted them together for the dance.

The weather started out clear and balmy, in the upper 60s, but around 9:30 p.m. the starry sky clouded over and it started to sprinkle. For one brief minute, I wondered if my cloudy feelings caused the weather change. Then, Capris said the same thing out loud, and about four other people chimed in, "Me, too!" We all laughed, so the evening ended on a high note as we let the light of the bonfire shine through the mist and clear our hearts and minds. Here's the extra Water we needed to quench our Fire!

Recording the Ritual in Your Grimoire

The corresponding grimoire pages would most likely include the date and place of the ritual or meal, the Moon phase, the ritual names of the guests and the recipes for the cider, the pumpkin bread, and the pate. You might want to include the magickal correspondences for the spices and ingredients you used. The spell would be recorded and perhaps a list of the items each person placed on the altar. If the altar was special for the celebration, a description of it would be included.

When you record something in your grimoire, you will want to be extra careful about naming names. Many witches have a ritual name they use during meetings or for spellcasting to protect their identities. There are still prejudicial people in the world who frown upon Wiccans. It's best to keep your fellow witches' mundane names secret.

If you always cast a magick circle the same way each time you do Wiccan ritual, it isn't necessary to record how you did it in your grimoire each time. (See Chapter 10 to learn how to cast a circle.) You might want to have a section of the grimoire that includes your standard rituals. It's also handy to number the pages of your grimoire and keep a running index. This is most easily done on a computer so you can add entries, but if you don't have access to a computer, use note cards. Put each recipe page number on a card, and also each ritual, each Sabbat, and each spell. Use a recipe box to sort your cards. This way you can find what you need at a glance.

Any other details that would help you remember how to recreate a celebration would be appropriate to include. Remember this is a book you might want to share so comments about your guests or your own feelings would not be included in your grimoire. Private thoughts should be recorded in your Book of Shadows for your eyes only.

Where to Keep Your Book of Shadows and Who Can See It

Because your Book of Shadows contains information about your magickal workings, it is a special and sacred object. Give it a place of honor, the way you would for a family Bible, Torah, or Koran. Most people keep their Book of Shadows hidden in the cabinet with their magickal tools. You want to be sure your book is safe, that no one will make fun of it, play with it, deface it, or destroy it. Your book is private, and only you or another witch whom you trust should see it. You want to be sure that whoever does see your BOS won't disclose its contents or do anything to harm the book or you.

Blessed Be

Here is a blessing for your Book of Shadows:

> *I call this Book of Shadows a holy book*
> *May God and Goddess know it.*
>
> *And anyone who takes a look, their spirits*
> *Grow to know the wisdom I write here.*
>
> *I focus all my power to feel*
> *The energy from my words.*
>
> *Blessed be.*

PART 2

BEING A WITCH

It's almost time for magick. By now, you know that magick is all about preparation, concentration, and focus, focus, focus. Before you start casting spells, though, you may want to commit to your Wiccan faith by dedicating yourself to the Craft. We'll show you how to do that and explain how to prepare and ground yourself for ritual, and how to create a sacred space. We'll share instructions for how to cleanse, consecrate, and charge your magickal tools so you can do ritual with them. You'll learn about taking a magickal name, casting magick circles, working with the energy of pentacles and pentagrams, creating an altar, and more.

CHAPTER 7

DEDICATE YOURSELF TO THE CRAFT

If you're serious about Wicca and witchcraft, dedication is your next step. Dedication is an exciting and serious commitment. It means you have chosen to walk the Wiccan path. When you dedicate, you make a personal commitment to the Lord and Lady.

You can dedicate as a solitaire or as part of a coven. If you dedicate within a coven, that action does not necessarily make you a member of the coven. In many covens, you do not become a member until you have passed your First Degree Initiation. Whether you dedicate on your own or in a coven, dedication is a serious step. You'll want to meditate on this commitment and spend some real time thinking about it before you set off on the Wiccan path.

FIRST, TAKE YOUR MAGICKAL NAME

A name can say a lot about a person. In the past, names such as Miller, Cooper, or Smith indicated the individual's profession. These days, a name doesn't tell you that, but it can still divulge a lot. From just a name you can probably discern a person's gender, ethnicity, and even their religion.

A magickal name can be one word, two or more words, or names combined. Examples of this kind of name include those of two popular authors—Starhawk and Silver RavenWolf. Compound names actually have an ancient tradition. The modern English name "Roger" comes from the Anglo-Saxon Hrothgar, which literally is the words fame and spear combined.

When you become dedicated to the Craft, when you are ready for your First Degree Initiation, you get to choose your magickal name, or take a magickal name given to you by your magickal mentor. This will be the name other witches and members of the Pagan community will call you. Your magickal name is also the name by which the Goddess will know you.

The Significance of a Magickal Name

Your name should have real significance to you. You want it to reflect your goals, dreams, ideals, and aspirations. Your magickal name should give others an idea of who you are and what you stand for. It can also serve to remind you of these things and provide inspiration to you on your path.

Why Take a Magickal Name, and When?

Some people feel limited by their names. Janes can feel plain or ordinary. And Christophers can feel like a dime-a-dozen because there are so many of them. When you become a witch, you open up a new universe of possibilities. You don't want preconceived notions of who you are to hold you back from your limitless potential.

Having a magickal name can protect your privacy. For some people, keeping their status as a witch private is important. Others like that their magickal names are known only to members of the Pagan community because it makes the community feel more special and magickal. Usually you take your magickal name upon dedication. This is a signal that you are committing to the Wiccan path.

CHOOSING YOUR MAGICKAL NAME

You can choose a name because it gives you a special feeling. You might pick the name of a God or Goddess to whom you are particularly drawn, and whose energy you want to work with or draw upon as a part of your lifework. Or you might like the name of a famous Druid, such as Merlin. Your name could come to you in a dream, or it can be one that you have always dreamed of using!

Resist the temptation to grab the first "witchy" name that pops into your head. Yes, Samantha, Sabrina, and Tituba sound cool. And one of these names may be right for you. But don't settle for the first name you think of. Maybe there is another, more significant name just waiting for you to find it. Turn to your teacher, if you have one, for advice and inspiration on the right magickal name for you.

One witch we know took the name Summoner because she summons things. Denise lived in the Middle East for a number of years, and because she was very moved by the lives of the women she met there, she chose the name Shaharazade. You may remember Shaharazade (or Sheherazade) from the *Tales of the Arabian Nights*. To save her own life, Shaharazade told her new husband, who was in the habit of killing his brides, a story every night. Her husband was so mesmerized by her tales that he kept putting off the hour of her death. By the time she told him a thousand and one stories, he had fallen in love with her and no longer wanted to kill her. Denise particularly likes this heroine because her story emphasizes a woman's creativity and her ability to take care of herself.

Alternatively, you can choose a name from something in Nature for which you have an affinity—Tree, Forest, and Willow are examples of such names.

What Your Magickal Name Says About You

Some magickal names conjure up strong images—Raven, Bear Heart, Hawk. Others are more gentle—Moon Feather, Ash, Snow Blossom. Consider what your name is going to say about you. You want your name to go with you—your body, mind, and spirit. This is not to say that if you are a small woman you can't take a strong-sounding name. And if you are a big muscle-bound guy, you don't have to stick with rough, tough names like Thor.

Coming to Your Magickal Name: A Self-Exploration

You don't have any ideas for a magickal name? Get out your notebook and spend some time writing about each of the questions below. You may want to meditate on your answers. Or think about them before you go to bed, and you might find an answer in your dreams. You can work on one question at a time. Or scribble out answers for them all, come back, and add more thoughts as they occur to you. There are no wrong answers!

1. Do you have an affinity for a particular God or Goddess?

2. Do you have a favorite myth or legend? What is it? Who are the characters? With which one do you identify most strongly?

3. Is there a species of animal that is special to you? What qualities does that animal have?

4. Are you particularly drawn to one of the four Elements—Air, Fire, Water, or Earth? What about other natural substances such as different types of wood, crystals, or metals?

5. What is your favorite plant? Favorite flower? Favorite tree?

Your magickal name probably won't jump out and grab you, but if you're patient, we believe it will come to you. To help you determine your magickal name, write each name you are considering on a slip of paper. Keep your pen and notebook handy, and put the slips into a paper bag. Give the bag a good shake. Imagine that the name that you draw will be yours forever. Draw out one slip. Then, without thinking too much about it, write down whatever feelings come up for you, even if they sound silly. Put the name back into the hat and draw again. If you keep getting the same name, consider that to be significant. Does seeing the name over and over annoy you? Or do you find comfort in the repetition?

The Name of Rebirth

When you dedicate and take your magickal name, you are reborn. A new you emerges and your magickal personality is born. In many faiths, now and throughout history, people take a new name to show they have undergone this transformation. Their new name also indicates they have made a commitment to their beliefs and to the laws that embody those beliefs.

Numerology: Your Destiny and Life Path Numbers

Many people use *numerology* to help select their magickal names. Numerology? Isn't that about numbers? Well, it is, but numerology is not just math. Numerology relates letters of the alphabet to numbers, and as such it's concerned with names, addresses, and other significant personal information. Each number (and its corresponding letter) has its own energy and meaning.

Numerology is the metaphysical science of numbers. Numerologists study the significance of names and numbers and relate them to each other to learn about the human condition. Numerology can help you discover who you are, where you're going, and who you will be.

Pythagoras, the sixth-century B.C.E. mathematician who came up with that formula about the hypotenuse of a right triangle, is considered to be one of the fathers of numerology. Like many people do today, he believed that the numbers one through nine were symbolic representations of the stages of human life.

Numbers and Their Meanings

Number	Meaning	Archetype
1	Independence	Leader, warrior
2	Harmony	Peacemaker
3	Self-expression	Artist, joy bringer
4	Building	Builder, worker, manager
5	Change	Risk taker, innovator
6	Nurturance	Caregiver, teacher
7	Inner focus	Researcher, seeker
8	Power	Chief, the boss
9	Service	Mystic, healer
Master Numbers		
11	Illumination	Spiritual messenger
22	Enterprise	Master builder
33	Healing love	Master of healing

The first step in using numerology to help select your magickal name is to determine your Destiny Number. Your Destiny Number is derived from your birth name, the name that is on your birth certificate. Yup, that means you have to include that hideous middle name that no one knows about except members of your immediate family. Among other things, your Destiny Number reveals your life purpose, your spiritual mission, and the target you are aiming for.

For some, their birth name may be a source of pain and difficult memories. To ease the pain of the past, they sometimes have chosen a new name and identify in the world by that chosen name. Maybe they've even moved to have the change made on their birth certificates or plan on doing so. In this case, if this sounds like you, please use the new birth name—the name you've chosen to be reborn with into the mundane world. This is your true identity, the true birth name, the new Destiny being followed. You must always use the name that is your own. Only you know what name that truly is. The magickal name you choose will only deepen and add resonance to your true birth name—the one you've chosen to identify with in the world.

To calculate your Destiny Number, write down your full birth name and assign each letter a number based on the following chart. Add up the numbers for each name. Reduce the numbers for each name. Then add all the reduced numbers together, and reduce the final number to a single-digit number. Whew!

Numbers and Letters

1	2	3	4	5	6	7	8	9
A	B	C	D	E	F	G	H	I
J	K	L	M	N	O	P	Q	R
S	T	U	V	W	X	Y	Z	

We'll calculate Denise Zimmermann's Destiny Number so you can get the hang of it.

D	E	N	I	S	E		Z	I	M	M	E	R	M	A	N	N
4	5	5	9	1	5		8	9	4	4	5	9	4	1	5	5

First, add all the digits of the first name:

$$4 + 5 + 5 + 9 + 1 + 5 = 29$$

Reduce 29:

$2 + 9 = 11, 1 + 1 = 2$

Now, 11 is a special number, but we will get to that in a minute.

Then add the numbers of the second name:

$8 + 9 + 4 + 4 + 5 + 9 + 4 + 1 + 5 + 5 = 54$

Reduce 54:

$5 + 4 = 9$

Now add the two reduced numbers:

$2 + 9 = 11$

As we said, 11 is special. It's a Master Number and as such is not reduced at the end of a calculation, but is written 11/2. (The 2 is there because if you did reduce 11, you would get 2.)

Both the 11, which represents the Spiritual Messenger, and the 2, which represents harmony and peacemakers, are represented in Denise's Destiny Number. Now let's look at Denise's magickal name: Shaharazade. Once again, we get 11/2 as the result. When choosing among a few possible magickal names, you might want to pick a name that shares your Destiny Number and its special energy. Whatever magickal name you choose, embrace its numerological energy, whatever it may be, as a guide to what you will learn and express on your magickal path.

S	H	A	H	A	R	A	Z	A	D	E
1	8	1	8	1	9	1	8	1	4	5

Add it all together:

$1 + 8 + 1 + 8 + 1 + 9 + 1 + 8 + 1 + 4 + 5 = 47$

Reduce the total:

$$4 + 7 = 11, \text{ so } 11/2.$$

If the magickal name you have selected produces a number other than your Destiny Number, you can change the spelling of the name or alter the name by adding or taking away a letter.

Your Name in a Magickal Alphabet

Some witches use *Theban Script* to write their names on talismans and amulets. Some believe Theban Script arose during the Middle Ages; others believe it is a recent development. Gardnerian witches frequently use it. It is sometimes called Honorian Script or the Honorian Alphabet. It can also be referred to as the Witches' Alphabet, but many people consider that term to be a misnomer. Using this special system of writing can help you to focus your energy and send it into the object that you are inscribing. You can even try Theban Script for spells and rituals.

Practice writing your magickal name (or your mundane name, if you don't have a magickal one) in Theban Script, or use Theban Script when you make entries in your diary. If you use the script a little every day, pretty soon you'll know it by heart.

Can You Change Your Magickal Name?

In some traditions, a witch first takes his or her magickal name upon dedication. Then, a year and a day later, at the time of First Degree Initiation, he or she takes another name. A witch may also rededicate under another name if the magickal name chosen no longer fits. When you first enter the Craft, you'll learn and grow a lot. Because of all that change, it is not unusual to need a new name. As a solitaire, you can change your name when you want. But it is probably not a good idea to do it frequently. You don't want to give yourself an identity crisis!

A NEW PATH IN AN OLD WAY OF LIFE

In many ways your life will change when you dedicate yourself to the Craft. And in many other ways it won't. You will still have the same family and friends. You will probably live in the same place and hold the same job, or you will continue to go to school. For many people, their external lives do not look much different, but inside they feel the change.

What It Means to Dedicate

Dedication means just that—dedication. When you dedicate yourself to the Craft, it means that you have looked at the Craft, studied, and made a decision to walk the Wiccan path. When you make your dedication, you let the Lord and Lady know that you welcome them into your life, that you have chosen the Craft, that you will follow the path of the witch and will observe the Wiccan Rede—"An it harm none, do what ye will." You also are making a promise to respect the Lord and Lady.

When you dedicate, you don't just take your magickal name, you take an oath that you will live by the Wiccan Rede. In a coven, you usually also promise not to reveal to nonmembers any of the information you learn about from the coven.

Taking Your New Name in Dedication

At your dedication ceremony, you'll take your magickal name. In a coven ritual, the High Priest or the High Priestess will ask you by what name you will be known in the circle. From then on, that will be the name the coveners call you.

As a solitaire, you can self-dedicate. During your self-dedication ritual, you can tell the God and Goddess what name you are taking.

HOW TO DO YOUR OWN SELF-DEDICATION RITUAL

You can write your own self-dedication ceremony or use the one that follows. Look at a few other books for ideas, and don't forget the internet. Make your dedication ritual a special time for you.

Dedication Ritual

While you may enjoy reading this dedication ritual, keep in mind that ritual is primarily designed to be experienced, not read about. In other words, try it out! Read the ceremony aloud and consider how you feel about making a real dedication to the Craft. This self-dedication is designed to deepen your commitment and set you on your path.

1. First decide if this is truly what you want to do. Look deep within yourself and meditate on the question. Ask yourself, "Is this the path I want to walk?" If you decide that Wicca is truly your calling, proceed with your ritual.

2. Set up your altar. To do this, place the following objects on the surface you have chosen to work on:

    ♦ A pentagram for protection

    ♦ One silver candle for the Goddess

    ♦ One gold candle for the God

    ♦ One illuminator candle (you will light all the other candles from this one)

    ♦ One bowl of holy water

    ♦ One bowl of salt

    ♦ One Fire candle

    ♦ Your athame

- ♦ A censer

- ♦ A candle snuffer

- ♦ A chalice

- ♦ A bottle of wine or juice and some cakes

- ♦ A libation bowl

- ♦ The words of the dedication that follows (unless you want to improvise what you want to say to the God and Goddess)

You will also need a lighter or book of matches to light your illuminator candle and incense.

3. Lay out your ritual robe (if you plan to wear one) and your magickal jewelry.

4. Draw your bath. To the water add:

   - ♦ 1 tablespoon sea salt

   - ♦ A couple drops jasmine essential oil

Light your bath candles. Play meditative music. Get in the tub and relax.

Breathe in the essence of the jasmine. Think about the ritual you will be performing and what it means to you. Meditate on the changes you will be making within yourself and your life. Think about your relationship with the Lord and Lady. Cleanse your mind as well as your body.

5. After bathing, drying, and dressing for the journey you are about to take, go to the altar and prepare your sacred space.

6. First consecrate the tools on your altar (see Chapter 9).

7. Now take your water and walk the circle deosil (clockwise) and say:

   As I walk this circle round
   I cleanse and consecrate this ground.

8. Next sprinkle salt around the circle and say:

   First with Water then with Earth
   With negativity banished there's joyous rebirth.

9. Take the incense censer and walk the circle saying:

   Next with Fire, then with Air
   Leaving us only with purity fair.

10. Take your athame and mark the boundaries of the circle, pulling up the circle as you go. (For details, see Chapter 10.)

11. Stand in front of your altar and light the illuminator candle. Welcome the God and Goddess and thank them for coming.

12. Begin your dedication to the Goddess by saying the following:

    Goddess, I stand before you in this sacred place of power.
    I open my heart to your spirit.

    I open my mind to your wisdom.
    I dedicate myself to learn your mysteries.
    I dedicate my life to the Wiccan path.

    O Great Mother, take me into your fold.
    Protect me, teach me, heal me, and empower me.
    Breathe your spirit in my body and make me complete.
    Teach me to see through eyes that are wise.
    Teach me to feel through a heart that is compassionate.
    Teach me to drink through lips that speak of kindness.
    Teach me to hear through ears without prejudice.
    Teach me to live in oneness with the earth.

    Great Goddess, Queen of the Craft of the Wise, I come to you as your [daughter or son]
    [magickal name].

    From this day forward, I will follow your light and strive to learn the mysteries.

13. Light the silver candle with the flame of the illuminator candle.

14. Begin your dedication to the God by saying the following:

    God, I stand before you in the sacred place of power.
    I open my heart to your spirit.
    I open my mind to your wisdom.
    I dedicate myself to learn your mysteries.
    I dedicate my life to the Wiccan path.

O Great Father, take me into your fold.
Protect me, teach me, heal me, and empower me.
Breathe your spirit in my body and make me complete.
Teach me to see through eyes that are wise.
Teach me to feel through a compassionate heart.
Teach me to drink through lips that speak of kindness.
Teach me to hear through ears without prejudice.
Teach me to live in oneness with the earth.

All-powerful Lord, consort and protector of the Lady, I come to you as your [daughter or son] [magickal name].

From this moment forward I will follow your light and strive to learn the mysteries.

15. Light the gold candle from the illuminator candle.

16. Pour the wine in the chalice and get your cakes.

17. Before you eat and drink, pour some of the wine and break off some of your cake into the libation bowl for the Lord and Lady.

18. Now drink wine, eat the cakes, and reflect on this ritual and how you have taken the first big step in changing your life.

19. When you are finished eating and drinking, thank the Lord and Lady for attending your dedication and snuff out the gold and silver candles.

20. Take your athame and walk widdershins (counterclockwise) around the circle to take it down (see Chapter 10 for directions).

21. Snuff out your illuminator candle and clean up. Make sure you take the contents of the libation bowl, the Lord and Lady's portion of the feast, and give it back to the Earth. Go outdoors and pour it on the ground.

Congratulations! You have dedicated yourself to the Wiccan way of life.

CHAPTER 8

PREPARING TO DO RITUAL

Ritual is an important part of the Wiccan faith. In ritual you honor the God and Goddess. You can also practice magick within ritual. Because ritual is such a central aspect of the faith, you want to make sure you are properly prepared for it. To make yourself ready for ritual, you'll need to cleanse, consecrate, and charge your magickal tools as well as prepare your mind, body, and spirit. Both components are needed before you'll be able to call on the sacred Source energy of the All with the clarity and focus necessary to make magick happen. When you prepare for magick, you are showing respect for the Goddess and God, for your Wiccan faith and fellow practitioners, and, of course, for yourself. We'll show you how.

CLEANSE, CONSECRATE, AND CHARGE

In Chapter 5, you learned about ritual tools. Your tools are special as they are a physical manifestation of your sacred energy. Over time, your tools become infused with a mix of your energy and the divine energy of the All. Your tools become your expression of divine energy. You are likely to begin your magickal life as a solitaire, practicing on your own or with the help of another witch to mentor you. You may desire in time to join a coven and practice the faith with other witches by your side. Accept invitations to holiday and lunar rituals. Welcome opportunities to see how witches perform magick and how they use and care for their own magickal tools.

As you grow in the Wiccan faith, the magick you do will be enhanced when you prepare and use your ritual tools properly. Remember the Threefold Law? When you put in the right effort to work with your magickal tools, you increase their power threefold—and your intent connects more strongly to access divine energy. When preparing your tools, use this power of three: cleanse, consecrate, and charge. All three should be done to do magick and ritual to best effect. If your tools are not prepared, your magickal intent may not reach its goal and your ritual won't be successful.

First Cleanse Your Tools

So, you ask: is cleansing more of a spiritual event rather than actually cleaning an item? Cleansing is both spiritual and physical; it is the first step toward preparing a tool for ritual. Remember, the macrocosm reflects the microcosm, and vice versa. The purpose of cleansing is to strip away old energies held by the object. You'll need to focus your intent on what your tool is meant for, and how you will use it for magick. Cleansing lays bare the mundane nature of your tool and opens its potential to receive the Goddess and God through your ritual magick.

Let's say you've found a great old glass oil lamp at an estate sale that you want to use to light your work in circle. And you've purchased an athame at a Wiccan festival that you're eager to use to cut energy during ritual. Before trying out either of these tools in a ritual context, you need to cleanse, consecrate, and charge them. Begin by choosing a soft cloth, perhaps a fine microfiber, that you will use only for cleaning a new ritual tool. Gather the folds of the cloth together in your hands and pray: *may this cloth cleanse away old energies and make way for the Goddess and God to enter.* Dampen the cloth with distilled or filtered water (for water preparation, see below) and gently rinse the tools, in this case the athame and oil lamp, and dry well. If the tool will be damaged when cleaned with water, then simply hold your hand or microfiber cloth over the object and imagine every particle of the tool cleared of old energies.

The water you use to clean your tool should be holy water. Mixing in only a few drops of holy water will make your cleansing water holy, too. Don't know how to get hold of some holy water? Ask at Wiccan festivals or talk to the proprietor of your local metaphysical shop or bookstore. You may be gifted holy water by a Wiccan friend or teacher. But you can also create your own holy water by preparing a small batch of infused water and offering it to the Goddess and God. Mugwort water is good for seeing clearly and is often used to cleanse crystals. Rose quartz yields rose water and is for self-love. A few sprigs of rosemary make rosemary water for self-healing.

Once you have physically cleansed your ritual tool, you are ready to spiritually cleanse it by saying: *bless you instrument of my magickal practice.* With this prayer, your tools are ready for consecration and charging for use in magickal work.

Consecration: A Means of Empowerment

After you cleanse your magickal tools, you need to consecrate them. To consecrate something means to bless or make it sacred. Consecrating your tools before you use them rids the tools of any negative energy they may be harboring. It is also a way of dedicating your tools to the Goddess and God, to the good of All, and empowering them with positive energy.

The five Elements are Air, Fire, Water, Earth, and Spirit. In Wicca, each Element is associated with a direction in the ritual circle. Earth's direction is North, and Air is East. Water is West, while Fire is South. Spirit encompasses all directions because it surrounds and is part of everything.

Let's consecrate your athame and oil lamp. First light your incense. While you say these words, pass your athame and lamp through the smoke from your lit incense three times:

> *With the Element of Air, I blow away any negative energies from this athame and lamp so that only positive energies remain. This is my will, so mote it be.*

Pass the athame and lamp over the flame of the lit candle three times. Then say:

> *With the Element of Fire, I burn away any negative energies from this athame and lamp so that only positive energies remain. This is my will, so mote it be.*

Place the tip of the athame in the holy water on your altar. Sprinkle a few drops of holy water on your lamp. Then say:

> *With the Element of Water, I wash away any negative energies from this athame and lamp so that only positive energies remain. This is my will, so mote it be.*

While you say these words, sprinkle salt from your altar over the athame and lamp:

> *With the Element of Earth, I bury any negative energies from this athame and lamp so that only positive energies remain. This is my will, so mote it be.*

Hold your athame and lamp up to the Goddess and God one at a time and say:

> *O Lord and Lady, may you consecrate and protect this athame and lamp from any negativity. May your blessing be upon these tools as I dedicate their work for positive purposes only so as it bring harm to none. This is my will, so mote it be.*

Go through this same process with all of your altar instruments and with anything that you plan to place on your altar, use in ritual, or make holy. As you probably can imagine, the first time you set up your altar and stock your magickal cabinet can take some time! You don't need to reconsecrate all of your tools after the first time unless someone else has touched them or you feel they need to be re-cleansed and reconsecrated with positive energies.

After you've consecrated an object, no one should touch it but you. If someone does touch one of your consecrated things, you will have to reconsecrate it to get rid of that person's energy. Make sure you consecrate everything that you're going to use in ritual, including your magickal jewelry. You can consecrate your clothing in the same way, if you like, but you don't need to. It is enough just to know that your clothes are clean. (You don't need to consecrate your clothes because you don't use your robes or other clothing to do magick. They just serve to dress your body, mind, and soul for ritual work.)

Charge Your Magickal Tools

Charge magickal tools when they are new to you after cleansing the old energies that may be stuck within and after consecrating the tools to the Goddess and God. As you learned in Chapter 6, you can charge tools by laying them under the full Moon for Goddess energy and under the Sun for God energy. You can also re-charge tools you've had for a while to boost their energies. In this way, tools become more powerful and easier to use for magickal purposes. It's like putting in new batteries to get the most energy possible flowing through your tools.

To hold its power, for example, magickal jewelry often needs to be recharged. The simplest way to do this is to wear the jewelry regularly for ritual, especially if there are several people participating. The jewelry will begin to soak up the magick of all the shared energy of the witches who are there; for this reason, you want this only to be magickal people you know and trust—another reason only to go into magick work in "perfect love and perfect trust."

You can quick charge reflective tools, such as your athame, using moonlight. Harness your own spiritual powers to do this: let the moonlight hit your eyes as you focus on your intent of charging your athame. Feel the light inside you and then envision your strongest flow of magickal energy traveling along the beam of light and back into your athame. Use candlelight to quick charge your lamp by following the same flow, directing energy from the candle flame to your eyes to your lamp.

While it is essential to cleanse and consecrate your tools, it is never *absolutely* necessary to charge your tools of the Craft. However, a little time and effort in this way can increase your magickal effectiveness and can create a better bond between yourself and the tools you use in your practice.

Charging with the Elements

You can also charge your tools with the energy of a specific Elemental power. It's nice to start this process on a night when the moon is shining. For each Element, you will use a slightly different technique.

♦ **Air:** To charge one of your tools, or any other object, with Air, place it in the branches of a tree, where Air will be able to surround it. You may need to tie the object to the tree so it remains secure. Allow it to absorb Air's energy from moonlight to moonlight, then take your charged object down and use it well.

♦ **Fire:** Place the object you want to charge with Fire inside a box. Put a candle on top of the box. Light the candle and let it burn for one hour. Then snuff out the flame. The next day, at around the same time, light the candle again and let it burn for one hour. The two periods of candle burning symbolically represent a full day, from moonlight to moonlight. So, if you first lit your candle at 7 P.M. and let it burn for an hour, you may want to relight your candle the next night at 8 P.M.

♦ **Water:** If the item you want to charge can get wet, place it in a bowl of water. If the object in question cannot get wet, put it in a plastic resealable bag, seal it, and place it in water. Allow your object to absorb Water's energy and become charged from moonlight to moonlight. If submerging your object seems too cumbersome (or you risk damaging it), stand in moonlight and sprinkle the object with water while saying a few words to call up Water's power.

♦ **Earth:** You will also need a plastic resealable bag to charge an object with Earth. Place the object in the bag and seal it. Then bury the neatly sealed object in your yard or garden. Let it rest and become charged from moonlight to moonlight. If you do not have a yard, fill a bag with sand or soil. "Bury" the object that you want to charge with Earth inside the filled bag and let it drink in Earth's energy.

PREPARING BODY, MIND, AND SOUL

Preparing yourself, body, mind, and soul, is a core part of doing ritual successfully. When you are at your best, your magick reaches farther, resonates more soundly with the All, and honors the Goddess and God with respect and love for self and for Nature. Ritual baths, grounding and toning, fasting, meditation and visualization, are all some of the tools you can use to prepare yourself for ritual.

A Cleansing Ritual Bath

The ritual bath is important much the same way as cleansing, consecrating, and charging your magickal tools are important. The cleansing bath helps you let go of negativity and distracting thoughts and focus your mind. It gives you the opportunity to reflect on your self and your intentions with soulfulness. Let the water soothe you, and allow yourself to feel nurtured. Place a few drops of an essential oil that complements the ritual you will be doing into your bath water. Wash your body with care and mindfulness, slowly and with loving kindness for your body.

Enjoy a luxurious ritual bath.

A chant for your luxurious ritual bath:

> *Now my body is reclaimed,*
> *Now my body is reborn.*
> *Now my spirit is reclaimed,*
> *Now my spirit is reborn.*
> *Now my magick is reclaimed,*
> *Now my magick is reborn.*

Can't take a bath before ritual? All you need to do is touch blessed holy water with your fingertips and then touch your fingertips to your third eye, located on your forehead. Or touch your fingertips to each chakra in prayerful blessing. Meaning "wheel" in Sanskrit, chakras are round spinning wheels of energy that lie along your spine from your tailbone to the top of your head. See Chapter 16 for more on chakras.

Ground Yourself Before Ritual

If you don't ground yourself before doing ritual, your energies will not flow the way they should. Your energy will be erratic, and your magick may not do what you want it to. When you ground yourself, you align the chakras, or energy centers of the body. (See Chapter 16 for more on chakras.) In addition, grounding allows you to receive the natural flow of energy from the Earth and enables you to become one with the Earth. It also helps to prepare your subconscious to do the work it needs to do.

Grounding Techniques You Can Use

There are many different techniques you can use to ground yourself.

Foot Stomp. Do this fun grounding exercise outside. While standing, slowly stomp your feet on the ground. Feel the vibration caused by your foot landing. Feel the sensation of your foot in contact with the solid force of the Earth. Keep stomping and let yourself feel the vibrations throughout your entire body. Imagine your feet merging with the Earth until you become an extension of the Earth.

Harpoon. Picture your center, the center of your body at your third chakra, which is located in the solar plexus. Your third chakra governs the will, the energy that helps you make decisions and act upon them with confidence. When your third chakra is centered, *you* feel centered. From your centering third chakra, feel a pull that shoots down into the earth moving now through all your chakra energy centers and aligning straight down through the bottom of your spine toward the center of the earth. It moves like a harpoon on a line that goes down, down, down through the ocean so deep, and then stops to embed itself on the ocean's floor.

Once your energy reaches the ocean depths, picture yourself pulling upward on the line until the harpoon opens and you know that you are floating above yet totally attached to the ground. The extra energies that might build up within your body travel down into the Earth along that line. And the energies of the Earth on the ocean floor also come up to greet you. So you have an even flow, but nothing will become overexerted as the energies move along the line because you are anchored to the Earth that holds all of the extra, excess energy and protects you.

Fasting Before Ritual

Almost all religions use fasting to some extent. Fasting can be the total abstention from food and drink, or it can be more moderate. Many Wiccans fast before doing ritual. Some will eat breakfast, skip lunch and dinner, and drink only fruit juice and water during the day. Others eat lunch and then have nothing but juice later, and still others will have lunch and a light dinner. Whatever you do, don't eat a big meal before ritual. Do not fast if you have any medical condition that might be aggravated by such an action. Consult your primary care physician before undertaking any kind of fast.

There are several reasons why people fast on ritual days. When you eat, especially a large meal, your blood pressure goes up. Your blood pressure also rises when you raise energy during ritual. So if you eat a huge meal before ritual, you put your heart on double duty. A large meal also might make you sleepy. Hasn't that happened to you before? You eat, and, because all your energy is going into digestion, you have to lie down for a while. You don't want to feel like you need a nap when you're trying to build power!

If you decide to fast, make sure that you drink juice and plenty of other fluids. If you are diabetic or have another illness, you may not be able to fast. And that's okay. Fasting is not necessary. Healthy people should be able to refrain from eating for a short amount of time before ritual.

Magick Music, Chanting, and Drumming

It's great to use music before ritual—when you take your ritual bath, for instance. You can also play music during ritual. Look for Wiccan music, podcasts, and live streaming radio on the web. Many Wiccan artists market their music through social media. Listening to chants is a great way to get you in the mood for ritual. There are all kinds of chants—from Gregorian to Sanskrit to Wiccan. Try listening to a few different types and see what appeals to you.

Within ritual, you can use chants to build your cone of power. Just the way you would with drumming, you start out slow then you build the pace and raise the volume. For a kind of chanting without words, try toning. Toning is good for grounding and also for directing energy through a cone of power into a ritual tool. (We'll tell you more about how to build a cone of power and how to do toning in Chapter 15.)

Know that you can chant even if you don't like the sound of your own voice. When chanting, you don't need to sound like a grand diva. The point is to focus on the chant and its intent. The Goddess and God want to hear from you. So, try chanting—even if your singing makes your family shriek and the dogs howl!

When you are building a cone of power, you might want to beat a drum or tambourine. Drumming is an excellent way to build up energy. It's a scientific fact that when people listen to drums, their heart rates speed up as the tempo of the drumming increases. You'll want to start out soft and slow. Then increase the speed and volume. Keep drumming, getting faster and louder and faster and louder. Pretty soon you will notice that your heart is beating faster, too. You'll feel your energy rise up.

Hummingbird Welcome

Here in the United States, most people know drumming forms an integral part of Native American traditions. Drums are made typically from deer hide on cedar frames and are painted to depict Nature and mythical stories. The tone of drums can fluctuate with temperature and humidity. For this pre-ritual exercise, create in your imagination the image and story painted on your drum. Choose imagery and deity relevant to the ritual you will be doing. For now, picture a drum showing four hummingbirds as the four Directions, each pulling back the brilliant blue field of sky to reveal divine light.

As you drum a slow and steady beat in rhythm to your breath and heart, face North and welcome the hummingbird. Now face East and welcome the hummingbird. Now face South and welcome the hummingbird. Now face West and welcome the hummingbird. Turn in a slow circle as you continue to drum and say this prayer:

> *Welcome, hummingbird. Bring good luck and friendship to this (place/house/circle). May the sound of your beating wings beat in our hearts and fill our breast with your joy. May sweet nectar nourish us with your joy.*

CHAPTER 9

ALTARS AND SACRED SPACES

There is a time and a place for everything. But what kind of place do you need to do ritual and magick? Do you have to find a secluded tower in an ancient castle ruin? Or an isolated mountain crag fringed with toadstools? Those sound like locations with some magickal potential, but actually many witches do their magick and ritual at home in their living rooms or outdoors in their gardens.

Magick happens in sacred spaces—these are cleansed and consecrated areas you can use for ritual. Whether you are in a darkened indoor alcove illuminated by candles or outdoors under the stars, your perfect choice of sacred space will help you perform your ritual with more power and purpose. Altars, whether fixed, portable, or created for a special ritual occasion, are important magickal portals. Altars contain your magickal tools and house the deities, energies, and objects you are working with in your magick.

Whether magick ritual takes place around a back deck fire pit on a summer night or on a deserted, windswept beach at sunrise or sunset, remember that a sacred space is an intimate space. Sacred space is intimate because it holds the personal power and intent of all that you bring to create it. However ordinary or exotic, a sacred space is made so by cleansing and consecrating it, and when you cast a circle for your magick.

SACRED RITUALS NEED A SACRED PLACE

You should hold ritual in a sacred place to keep ritual sacred. We've already begun exploring what makes a place sacred and discovered that mundane spaces can be made sacred when prepared properly. However, some very special places naturally hold extraordinary sacred energy. When an altar is placed in such energy, or a building is raised in such energy, its power is enhanced.

Make a Sacred Place Sacred

In many respects, because the Goddess and God represent the All and so live in all things, you could argue that the whole Earth is a sacred place. But most witches would agree that to really make a specific area sacred, you need to cleanse the space of negative energies and consecrate it. A place that has been made sacred in such a way is a great space in which to spend time. It may not be as dynamic as hiking to the Everest base camp in Nepal, doing a walking meditation around Stonehenge in Great Britain or through the labyrinth at Chartres Cathedral in France, or standing among the ruins of Peru's Machu Picchu. But a sacred space you make is a place you can relax, focus magickal energy, or communicate with deity.

Sacred space is safe space—somewhere you feel not just comfortable, but welcome. In ancient times, altars often offered literal sanctuary for those seeking safe harbor. Your altar can be just as real a sanctuary for your spiritual life and magickal self today.

How Is a Sacred Space Different from a Magick Circle?

Sacred space is space that has been cleansed and consecrated. A magick circle is also an area that has been cleansed and consecrated, but it is more than that. A magick circle is an area of protection. Before you pull up a magick circle in which to do your workings, you need to cleanse and consecrate the area. Then you make your circle inside the consecrated space. (For more about magick circles: how to cleanse, consecrate, and cast them, see Chapter 10.)

Coming to Your Sacred Wicca Space

But how do you pick the spot for your private religious and magickal activities? Some witches consider the principles of feng shui, the ancient Chinese art of placement. Simply put, feng shui involves arranging your space to help you create the most healthful and harmonious flow of energy. Clutter, dirt and dust, broken objects, and dead plants are all seen as traps for energy. Clearing out and cleaning up are the first steps in opening the energy flow. (And, of course, you want to make the area you are going to use fit for your honored guests—the Goddess and the God, as well as other entities invited to enter your sacred space.)

Feng shui associates different areas of a house or a room with different aspects of your life. For example, as you enter a room, the prosperity area is ahead of you to the left. So keeping feng shui in mind, when working magick to increase your prosperity, you may want to do your workings in your Abundance and Prosperity area. Alternatively, you could set your altar up within your circle in the circle's Abundance and Prosperity area.

Study the feng shui diagram, which is called a bagua, and see if there is an area of your life/space that is calling out for attention. While you are developing your relationship with the Goddess and the God, why not focus on Family and Grounding Relationships and let the power of feng shui help you get closer to deity?

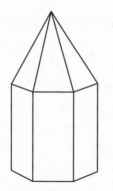

Tuning into the ancient art of feng shui can help you connect to the energy of a sacred space.

Setting and Respecting Sacred Boundaries

You should cleanse the whole area that you will be working in. It can be as small as the space around you—usually a nine-foot circle is big enough to work in. Or if you are working with a group, the space you cleanse may have to be very large—say, a quarter of an acre.

Once you have made a magick circle in which to work, you should stay inside the circle. If you need to leave, you have to cut a door in the circle to do so. Many witches believe it is best to create a door in the circle in the North or East. To make a door, you cut the energy field of the magick circle with your athame.

If you are working alone, leave your broom to guard the door while you are out of the circle. (Many witches leave their brooms by the door of their house or apartment for the same purpose.) If you are working with a group, the person who cuts the door stands by as guardian. When you return and have reentered the circle, remember to seal the door. With your athame, close up the space that you have cut by moving in the opposite direction than you did when you cut the door. In other words, if you cut the door from left to right, you will seal the door by moving from right to left. When you cut a door, you draw energy from the circle and leave a void. The energy is drawn into your athame. When you seal the door, you take the energy out of the tool and make the circle complete again. Should you forget to seal the door, you risk being visited by entities that you probably would rather not meet.

Once, a few years ago when working with a large group, Denise pulled up a circle, but then cut a door to get something from outside the circle. When she came back, she got distracted and forgot to seal the door after herself. Twenty-four hours later, she got sick, and she stayed sick for two and a half months! None of her doctors could figure out what was wrong with her. One day, as she was growing weaker and weaker, she remembered the day that she hadn't sealed the door. She knew that a negative entity would go after the person who had pulled up the circle. She called a friend, and they did a magick healing ritual. Within 12 hours Denise was back to normal, and she never forgot to reseal the door again.

The moral of the story? Remember to seal the door if you have cut one! If you keep in mind that the circle is there to protect you and that you need to honor and respect sacred space, you shouldn't have any problems. Stories about witchcraft mishaps can be frightening, but avoid dwelling on your fears. Remember that every worthwhile activity carries some risk. Behave responsibly in your Craft activities, just the way you do when you drive a car, go cycling, or cross the street, and you'll be just fine.

CRAFTING AN ALTAR

In many religious traditions all over the world, people keep altars in their homes. Some of these altars are devoted to a single deity, others to an individual's ancestors, and still others to a group of Gods and spirits. Altars are often created according to time-honored designs and traditions, or they can be just a modest corner of a room. Indeed we've seen both. An outdoor pagoda built in the twenty-first century stands among the remains of a Buddhist monastery in Hue, Vietnam. Before the Vietnam War, monk and peace activist Thich Nhat Hahn practiced there. Meanwhile, in Oaxaca, Mexico, a clay artist crafts a statue of the Virgin for a handcrafted altar, which is studded with rose petals and brightly colored creations, in the corner of her studio.

As a Wiccan, you get to create your own altar. An altar is a working surface, such as a tabletop, that is to be used only for magickal or religious purposes. The English word comes from a Latin word that meant "material for burning sacrificial offerings." Your altar becomes a highly personal reflection of your spiritual intent. Need some help to get thinking about where your altar should be and what should be on it? Try this: cleanse, consecrate, and charge a glass Pyrex bowl that you will be able to use in performing magick. Write on slips of paper words or phrases that resonate with you spiritually and to the spiritual practice you'd like to have as a witch. Fill the bowl with the slips of paper.

When you are ready, place the bowl before a lighted candle. Carefully burn the slips of paper in the fireproof bowl as a sacred offering to the Goddess and God. Sit in quiet meditation and let the image of your altar come to your body, mind, and soul. Imagine yourself working at your altar. When the ash from the offering is cool, bury it in your garden with these words:

> *Oh Mother Moon and Father Sun as above so below. Nurture my spiritual intent and guide me to the sacred space. Give expression to the altar for my practice. With Divine faith in the All, so mote it be.*

ALTAR SPECS

Your altar can be a regular table. It can be round or square. It can be triangular or oblong or oval. Your altar can be of any shape, size, or height that you like. You can use what you have or make something especially for your purposes. You can use a crate with a cloth over it. Or you can go a more natural route and use a large flat rock out in the woods or the cut surface of a tree stump in your backyard. All you have to do is cleanse and consecrate the surface you have chosen, add an altar cloth if you have one, and presto—there's your altar.

Public or Private?

If you have privacy concerns, your altar does not have to scream, "A witch lives here!" Some people use the mantle over the fireplace as an altar, and to the naive visitor it just looks like they have an interesting and creative sense of interior design. If you need to disguise your altar, there are many ways to do so, even in plain view. You may decide to have several altar spaces—one for storage, one for meditation and prayer, one for working magick, and one that is portable. Or you may be able to multitask, using your altar for several functions at once.

Location, Location: North, South, East, West

Usually a permanent altar is placed in the Northern or Eastern section of a room, but if your space constraints don't allow for such a placement, you can put it where you have to. Within a magick circle, whether you are indoors or out, you also should try to set up your altar in the North or East. Keep it oriented so that when you stand to work at it, you are facing one of those directions. If that simply isn't possible or practical for the area in which you will be working, set up the altar in such a way that you are comfortable. During ritual, you also can keep the altar in the center of your magick circle. Some witches prefer to have the altar centrally located because the center of a circle is the spot of strongest energy. The circle gives all participants a unique view, or perspective, on the ritual.

Don't practice an impromptu ritual in a park or other public place. Children playing or joggers running by will distract you. What's more, you may attract unwanted attention to yourself. You could even find your magickal workings being recorded on a smartphone and uploaded to social media by curious onlookers. You may even draw the attention of the police (especially if you've been brandishing your athame). If you want to use a park or other public place for ritual, plan ahead. Get a permit if you need one, and talk to the local police precinct before you begin and before a frightened bystander calls them.

Sanctuary: Indoor vs. Outdoor Altars

Many witches prefer to work outdoors. What better way to honor the Goddess and God than to be among Nature? Despite this preference, many are not able to work outside because it is difficult to find a safe and private space outdoors. Even if you have a backyard or garden, you may not have sufficient privacy to practice ritual there. As a result, most witches do ritual inside. Besides ensuring privacy, there are other advantages to working indoors. If you work indoors, you can have a permanent altar that you leave up to honor the God and Goddess after your ritual is over. In addition, when you do an indoor ritual, you have all the comforts of your home, including the bathroom.

Permanent vs. Moveable Altars

In an ideal situation, you would have a permanent altar. That way, even when you are not home, your altar is there honoring the God and Goddess. It's also nice to come home after a long day and see your religious and magickal items all laid out and ready to use. And of course, having a permanent altar can save you time cleaning it up and putting it away. If, however, a permanent altar is not an option for you in your present living situation, don't worry. A temporary or moveable altar is just as good in the eyes of deity. And witches have probably used them for hundreds and hundreds of years.

WHAT GOES ON YOUR ALTAR?

Here's a list of basic tools for your altar:

- One or two illuminator candles
- One red candle for Fire
- A silver candle to represent the Goddess
- A gold candle to represent the God
- A pentagram
- A censer
- Water and salt in bowls
- An athame
- A chalice
- A bell
- A wand

When you place your tools on your altar, you'll want to pay attention to the four directions and the Elements. Because the censer and incense are associated with Air and the East, place your censer in the Eastern quadrant of your altar. The athame is associated with Fire and the South, so place it in the South along with the Fire candle. The chalice is associated with Water and the West, so it goes in the West along with the bowl of water. Your bowl of salt represents Earth, which is associated with the North, so it goes in the North. Your illuminator candles are placed at the top next to a statue of the Goddess and

God if you have them on the altar. A pentagram is placed in the middle of the altar, with the bell on the left. If you have a cauldron, it can go in the North.

You should also keep a lighter nearby to light your illuminator candles. Some people keep one under their altar or in a nearby drawer, so they always have one when they need it. It's a good idea to keep a large bottle of water under your altar, too. You might get thirsty during ritual, or you might have to douse some flames! You also might want to consider investing in a small fire extinguisher to keep near your altar. Candles can fall over or suddenly flare up. And wouldn't it be better to be prepared for such an occurrence? As Denise says, "There's nothing in the world worse than a witch in flames."

You can keep your wand on your altar if you want. Your wand also should be placed in the South. There are all kinds of other things you can put on your altar—a representation of your totem animal, crystals, herbs you plan to use, or images or statuettes of the deities you are working with. In Native American tradition, a totem animal is an animal that represents a clan or a family. The word *totem* comes from an Ojibwa word that means "my family mark." Some witches and some covens have totem animals, or power animals, that help them in their magickal work. Such an animal does not have to be a pet. Neither does it have to be a real live physical entity. Rather, the spirit or the power of the animal is called upon.

If you don't have a censer, you can use a small cauldron, which is also great for burning other objects and for Fire magick. If you can't afford to buy that beautiful pewter pentagram that you saw in your metaphysical store last week, don't worry. Draw a pentagram on a piece of paper, and while you are saving your pennies, use it on your altar instead of the fancy one. Your paper pentagram will serve the purpose just as well.

Here's another tip: the country of Morocco uses the pentagram as its symbol. A pentagram appears on the Moroccan flag and on some Moroccan currency. If you can get a Moroccan coin, you've got a pentagram for your altar or to carry with you!

If you choose to work with the Goddess alone, you can honor her in her three phases—Maiden, Mother, and Crone—with three separate candles—white, red, and black. If you can't find a silver candle to represent the Goddess, you can use three candles to represent the three phases on your altar instead. If you choose to work with just the God, you can honor him in his three phases—Prince, King, and Elder. His candles are black, gold, and white.

PORTA-PAGAN: CARRYING YOUR ALTAR WITH YOU

Some witches carry a small altar with them all the time, either in a little bag on their persons or in a box in their cars. This way they are able to do ritual anywhere, which is great if they run into friends. For example, a witch might stop by to see a friend who is under the weather and use toning to infuse essential oils with magickal healing powers to help him feel better.

When you add tools to your altar, fixed or portable, say this prayer:

> *As above so below*
> *As the Universe so the Soul*
> *What I place upon this space (in this bag/on this ground)*
> *Grow in power and be blessed*
> *This my altar, this my Soul, this the Universe*
> *Herein contained for my magick.*
> *So mote it be.*

CHAPTER 10

CAST A MAGICK CIRCLE

Magick circles are a major component of Wiccan ritual. Witches use circles to do magick. Are you ready to practice solitaire? Have you celebrated the Sabbats with Wiccan friends? Did you celebrate the Goddess in a ceremony to Draw Down the Moon? Maybe you've dedicated yourself already and taken a magickal name. Then you're ready to cast a circle and do magick.

Whenever you are going to do magick, as a solitaire or in a group, you should create a magick circle. One of the reasons you do this is to contain any undirected energy that gets stirred up within the circle. The magick circle also protects you from any outside—and uninvited—magickal beings. Inside your circle you are safe; only beings, entities, and things you invite inside can enter. Within your circle you should feel comfortable and relaxed so you can meditate, visualize, and build up your energy into a cone of power.

WHAT IS A MAGICK CIRCLE?

A magick circle is a protective area of energy you create to work in. Some people like to think of it as a magick bubble. They believe the idea of a bubble better represents the three-dimensional nature of this protected area. A magick circle or bubble is not just a line on the floor. It goes through the floor and surrounds you on all sides. When you pull up a magick circle, you want to think of yourself as being inside a sphere of protective energy. In addition to protecting you, a magick circle serves to hold and concentrate your energies.

When to Cast a Circle, and When Not To

Whenever you want to do magick, you need to cast a circle. The circle will protect you from any outside influences or little creatures from a different plane that want to meddle with you or your magick.

If you are sick or exhausted, you should not cast a magick circle. You should plan to do magick only when you are feeling well. You also should not cast a circle when you are unprepared. Remember that you need to plan your magick and be focused on your intent. Finally, never cast a circle when you are angry. The circle is supposed to be full of your positive energy, not your annoyance or wrath.

Round vs. Square

Because a circle has round edges, not corners and straight edges, it's hard to break into one. (Circles denote continuous strength; corners are weak joints.) A circle also has no beginning and no end; it goes around and around and is both the beginning and the end. If, when you are casting a circle, you walk the perimeter of a square room, the circle will pass through the walls so that it holds the entire room inside. Or you can cast a smaller circle inside the room. Either way you end up with your room sealed inside a protective bubble, or you have a protective bubble inside your room.

CAST THE CIRCLE

You've planned your ritual. You've made sure you have all your tools. You've taken your ritual bath. You're dressed in your robes and magickal jewelry. Now you are ready to cast your circle.

First Cleanse and Consecrate the Sacred Space

Your first step is to cleanse your sacred space, the area in which you plan to do ritual, by sweeping out all the negativity. With your magick broom, sweep out the negative energy, and don't forget to sweep the corners!

While you sweep, say this little rhyme:

> *Sweep, sweep with this broom*
> *All that is bad out of this room.*
> *Sweep, sweep all the good in*
> *Bad never to return again.*

Once you have swept out all the negative energy, you need to consecrate the area. To do this, walk around the room in a circle three times. Each time, carry a representation of an Element—first Air and Fire together, then Water, then Earth—from your altar.

First, take your incense and walk deosil (clockwise) around the circle. (Burning incense represents the Elements of Air and Fire.) As you walk, say:

> *I walk the circle once around*
> *To cleanse and consecrate this ground.*

Then pick up your bowl of water. (The water represents the Element of Water.) As you walk deosil around the circle, say:

> *I walk the circle once again.*
> *Between the worlds all time can bend.*

When you are finished with your second tour around the circle, pick up your salt (salt represents the Element of Earth) and sprinkle it as you walk deosil around the circle for the third and final time. While you do this, say:

> *I walk the circle thrice this time*
> *For the protection of the Lord and Lady are mine.*

Now that your sacred space is cleansed and consecrated you are ready to get to work on your circle.

Define the Circle

When doing ritual outdoors in an open area, especially when working with a group of people who are not adept at feeling the raised energy of a cast circle, witches sometimes make an actual mark on the ground in chalk or lay down a length of rope to define the edge of their circle. Placing something that you can see at the edge of your circle is a good idea when you are working outdoors in a large circle. Otherwise, you might forget where the boundaries of your circle are, or you may not be able to see the boundaries easily. Working indoors, you probably don't need to use actual physical markers, because you will have limited space. After a while, you should be able to feel the energy wall as you approach the edge of your circle.

Once you have walked the circle three times with your Elements, take your athame, wand, sword, or staff and trace the edge of the circle with it as you walk deosil around again. Walk slowly, but with purpose. In your mind, see yourself pulling up a circle.

Pull Up the Circle

To pull up the magick circle, you need to concentrate and use your powers of creative visualization. Some people, as they walk around the edges of the circle, imagine a white light flowing through them, through their athame or wand, and out. They see it pouring out in the form of white fibers that spin out until the whole circle is cocooned. Some people see the circle as a bubble that grows up from the floor, curving overhead until it meets on top. Some people visualize plates of armor surrounding them, and others see the circle as made up of the scales of a dragon. You can even imagine the circle as a magick web that grows so it is all around you. It doesn't matter what image you pick, just be sure it works for you.

Are you having trouble visualizing your magick circle? You'll probably need to use the same image for a while before you can tell if it works. Remember, practice does make perfect. A classic bubble visual appears in the film *The Wizard of Oz* in the scene after Dorothy's house falls. That's when Glinda the Good Witch floats down inside a shimmering pink bubble—and that is one super-magick bubble! Watch the scene a few times. Change the color of the bubble. Visualize a similar bubble floating onto your sacred space. Know that you may call the Goddess to appear within and bless your circle.

Where's the Altar?

You can place your altar in the North part of your circle, in the East, or in the center of the circle. Your decision about placement will depend on what ritual you're planning to do. If you want to sit in the center of the circle and drum, you should place the altar to one side.

MAGICKAL HELP

There are many different entities that you can ask to help you with your magick. Some kinds of magickal help include dragons, fairies, winds, deities, angels, ancestors, and familiars. We'll talk about the Elements and Elementals here, and tell you more about magickal help and how to summon, stir, or call it in Chapter 14.

The Elements

Each of the four Elements—Air, Fire, Water, and Earth—has either a masculine or feminine quality, a color, and a direction. The masculine or feminine quality of an Element is not an assignment of gender. Rather it is a recognition that the energies that flow from each Element are either masculine or feminine.

Because the Elements are all around us and in that sense never leave us, if you want to work with them, you can summon them to your circle. It is absolutely imperative, when dealing with any of the Elements, that you understand you are dealing not only with the physical but the spiritual realm of that particular Element. You must not only demonstrate but also feel the respect each Element commands.

Remember also that your altar is set up to resemble a miniature circle. Each quadrant of your altar relates to one of the four directions and, hence, is associated with a different Element. Your tools also represent different Elements. If you place your tools within the appropriate quadrant on the altar, then the energy contained within the altar will flow in a more harmonious way.

◆ **Air is a masculine Element, cool and dry; its color is yellow and its direction is East.** Air is associated with all forms of communication, education, intellect, wind, and sound. Air is also linked to creativity, meditation, divination, and awareness—in short, anything that flows through the air and any energy that passes quickly. The way that you communicate to deity and the way deity communicates to you is tied up with the Element of Air. It's also important to understand that Air is the breath of life. Without Air we would die. Air is not a force to be taken lightly, for just as Air gives life, it can also take it away. Air has the ability to destroy whatever gets in its path.

◆ **Fire is also a masculine Element, hot and dry; its color is red and its direction is South.** Fire represents the passion and desire burning inside all of us. As sexuality, Fire is the most physical and the most spiritual of Elements. Fire is also linked to courage and transformation. It is the Element of change and the spark of spirit within us all. Fire is probably one of the most beloved and yet the most difficult Element to work with. Fire is swift and unpredictable, yet it captivates us with a deep primal fascination. It is both tangible and intangible. You can feel its warmth, see its flames. It will burn you if you get too close; you feel its power, but you cannot hold or touch it. Fire can burn both fast and furious or smolder until just the right moment. You will be able to connect easily with Fire's magick. Be careful and don't get burned.

♦ **Water is a feminine Element, warm and wet; its color is blue and its direction is West.** Water is associated with psychic energy, emotion, intuition, the subconscious, and cleansing. We all have Water within us and are subject to its ebb and flow. Contemplation of the Element of Water also reminds us that we all have heights and depths of emotion. It is also the Element of reason. Both Water and the West are associated with death. The West is the place of endings, the opposite of the East, which is the place of beginnings. Water is usually a soft and predictable energy. This Element deals with emotions such as love and joy, but Water can also be associated with emotions of pain and sorrow.

♦ **Earth is also a feminine Element, cold and moist; its color is green and its direction is North.** Earth is associated with beauty, growth, nurturing, abundance, stability, healing, and the bounty of our planet. Earth also represents prosperity and wisdom. It is a place of darkness, the womb of the Goddess, and from the womb you emerge into the light. This is a very stable energy that builds slowly with its fibers tightly woven together. Even though its energy is steady, Earth has its unpredictable moments. Without warning, the earth itself can erupt in an earthquake and release its mighty power.

When summoning the Elements, hold pictures in your mind of both the positive and the negative aspects of each Element you are invoking. Conjure up the following sequences of images:

For Air: Start with a scene of no movement, then build to imagining a light breeze. Then see a brisk wind. See the wind grow stronger and stronger until it has gained the force of a tornado. Then imagine the power pulling back to a strong wind until it diminishes back to a scene of calm.

For Fire: Start by imagining the flame of a match. Then move on to a small campfire. Let the fire grow into a house-warming hearth fire. Then let the fire burn hotter and hotter until you can see the flowing magma of a volcano, and move back down the scale of intensity until you are back again with the flame of a match.

For Water: Start by imagining a gentle flow pouring from a fountain into a bowl of still, clear water. Then see a flowing stream; move on to a rushing river, then to the oceans' waves. Imagine the huge transformative power of a tsunami, then move back through your sequence of images until you are back with the image of a calming fountain.

For Earth: Start by imagining a deep cavern. Then see a flat plain, undulating hills, and then mountain peaks. Imagine the enormous force of an earthquake. Then move from mountain back down to cavern and feel the grounding energy of the Earth.

Practicing these visualizations will help you understand just what powerful energies you are summoning when you ask the Elements to guard, protect, or witness a rite, or when you engage them in your magick.

The Elementals

The Elementals are personifications of the four Elements. The Elemental associated with Fire is the salamander. Undines, or water nymphs, are associated with Water, while sylphs are associated with the Element of Air, and gnomes are associated with the Element of Earth. If you want to work with the Elementals, you can summon them.

MOVING AROUND WITHIN A MAGICK CIRCLE

When working magick, stay within the circle that has been cast. The circle is there to protect you and your magick. The circle also helps to hold your personal power and all the energies raised until you are ready to send them out into the universe to manifest your magick. Think of the circle as your magickal office. That's the place you receive and make magickal calls, the place where you aren't subject to interruptions from friends and family. It is the place for you to focus and do your work.

You'll want to keep in mind when working in your circle that you always want to move deosil (clockwise). You should only walk widdershins (counterclockwise) when it is time to take the circle down. So, say you are standing in the East and want to move toward your altar, which is located in the North. It is proper to move three quarters of the way around the circle, passing through South and West to reach North and your altar. If you moved from your position in the East to the North via the shortest route, you'd be moving widdershins and thus weakening the energy flow of the circle.

Entering and Exiting a Magick Circle

We talked about leaving a magick circle in an earlier chapter, but we'll give you a little recap here. If you need to leave, you must cut a door in the energy that makes up the circle, or have someone else cut a door for you. You can't just walk through the circle. Doing so would break the circle and allow whatever energy is in the circle to get out. It would also allow any magickal beings in the vicinity to get in. The person who cuts the door in the magick circle must stand guard at the door and then seal the door when you return. If you are working alone, leave your broom to guard the door, and when you come back, remember to seal the door yourself.

If you are joining a circle that has been cast, you also need someone to cut a door for you so you can enter. Don't just wander into circle! (And don't be late for ritual!)

Conversation Within the Circle

When working with other people, you will probably engage in conversation inside the circle about a variety of topics. You might turn to the feelings that ritual left you with, or someone in the circle might give the leaders of ritual a bit of constructive criticism or point out a mistake that someone made during ritual. One thing you usually do not talk about is what you want to have happen as a result of your magick. In most cases, that is a subject you discuss only with deity and sometimes with coven elders. Keeping silent about your magick is an important part of the Witches' Pyramid—a kind of magickal checklist— that you will read about in Chapter 18.

Conversation within the circle can get very personal, and often people will discuss difficulties they are having in their lives. Whatever comes up in the circle remains in the circle. You must keep anything you hear in the strictest confidence and never gossip about it. If you gossip, that is a sure way to get thrown out of the circle and banished. If you are performing an open circle (with public participation), make sure that you discuss topics that will include everyone so your guests can also enjoy the energies and feelings of closeness that come from the circle's group mind.

If you practice ritual on your own, you can talk with deity while you enjoy your cakes and wine or spend time recording your ritual in your Book of Shadows. This is also a great time to meditate on an issue that is bothering you or communicate with your familiar (an animal, plant, or created being with which you can communicate telepathically), if you have one.

Take Down the Circle

First you say farewell to the Goddess and God and thank them. Then respectfully say farewell to the quarters and thank them for providing the requested energies. Say with reverence to each quarter,

We bid you hail and farewell. Stay if you will, go if you must.

Finally say,

May all beings and Elementals attracted to this ritual be on their way, harming none.

Then start to take down the circle. With your athame, start in the East and walk widdershins around the circle's edge. Imagine the energy of the circle getting sucked into your athame. See the energy moving through the athame and traveling up your arm, through your body, then down your legs, out from the bottom of your feet, and into the earth. After sending the energy back into the ground, say,

The circle is down.

Stamp your foot to seal off the energy.

The Circle Is Open, but Never Broken

At the very end of ritual, after you have taken down the circle, join hands with the others in the circle. The High Priestess or whoever is leading says,

> *The circle is open, but never broken.*

This statement signifies that even though you are no longer in circle, you still have that connection to deity and the Elements, and as you entered the circle in "perfect love and perfect trust," you still have that bond with each of the other members in the circle.

The circle members respond by saying,

> *Merry ye meet, and merry ye part, and merry ye meet again.*

Then everyone exchanges hugs and kisses, and you wish everyone well until the next time you can be together in circle.

Recording and Housekeeping

Record what you did in circle using a Magickal Record form. If you are working with friends, you might want to relax with them some more after ritual. You might find that you're very hungry, so make sure you have some good things to eat. After you've recorded your ritual, put away your tools. Take the bowl of salted water from your altar and the libation bowl with cakes and wine in it outside, and give the contents of both bowls back to the Earth by emptying them on the ground. Do not pour the water and wine down the drain. These are gifts that you need to give to deity by placing them on the ground for the animals to eat. In this way, we—people, wild things, and even insects—all share in the Earth's abundance. Rinse the bowls out and place them back on your altar.

Magickal Record

Type Of Ritual: _____

Date & Time: _____ Approximate Length: _____

Phase of the Moon: _____

Planetary Positions

Sun in: _____ Moon in: _____

Mars in: _____ Mercury in: _____

Venus in: _____ Saturn in: _____

Jupiter in: _____ Uranus in: _____

Neptune in: _____ Blue Moon: Yes / No

Weather: _____

Location of Ritual: _____

_____

Purpose of Ritual: _____

_____

Physical Health: _____

Deities Invoked: _____

Ritual Tools Used: _____

_____

Chants/Music Used: _____

Oils/Herbs/Crystals Used: _____

_____

People taking part in Ritual:

_____ _____

_____ _____

Magick Performed/Spells etc:

_____ _____

Format: _____

_____

_____

_____

_____

Date of Manifestation: _____ Results: _____

_____

_____

After Ritual

You will probably feel great after ritual, full of zip and energy. You will feel spiritually nourished, and later you'll probably sleep wonderfully well. Often people sleep deeply and have prophetic dreams after doing magick. So keep your notebook or Book of Shadows handy in case you need to record dream messages. And remember this prayer:

May only good enter circle, may only good leave. Blessed be.

CHAPTER 11

THE WITCHES' SYMBOL

Wicca's symbol is the pentagram. Pentagrams have been around for thousands of years. They have long been used as a sign of protection against evil. Given the strong reaction that some people have to pentagrams, you'll want to think seriously about whether you want to wear a visible one as a symbol of your faith or whether you want to keep your faith and its symbol private. The information in this chapter should help you decide when and where the pentagram is right for you.

ALL ABOUT PENTAGRAMS

To some people the very word *pentagram* conjures up thoughts of evil. The association of pentagrams with devil worship is relatively recent. The pentagram has a long history and once was even used by the Catholic church. Today it is a symbol of the Wiccan faith.

Pentagrams vs. Pentacles

A pentagram is a five-pointed star. It's a lot like the star that you drew as a kid without picking your pencil up from the paper, but the sides are interwoven. Because the pentagram can be drawn with a single line, it has also been called the Endless Knot.

The pentagram: a symbol of the Wiccan faith.

A pentacle is a pentagram with a circle drawn around it. It can be made of wood, stone, metal, or clay. It is a powerful symbol of protection, and there is usually one on a witch's altar. Pentacles and pentagrams can take physical form or they can be completely abstract. If you draw a pentagram in the air over an object, the object is just as protected as if you placed a physical pentagram on or alongside that object. The pentacle and the pentagram have long been associated with mystery, magick, and protection against evil.

How Old Is the Pentagram?

Archeologists have found pentagrams on Mesopotamian potsherds that date back to 3500 B.C.E. Pentagrams also appear in ancient Egyptian, Greek, and Roman art. Pentagrams were even used by Christians in the early Middle Ages.

The pentacle.

In the twelfth century, because of the writings of Hildegard of Bingen, a Benedictine nun and abbess, the pentagram became the central symbol of the microcosmos, the reflection on Earth of the divine plan and the divine image.

What Does the Pentagram Stand For?

Hildegard of Bingen saw the pentagram as representing the human form because we have five senses—sight, smell, hearing, taste, and touch—and five "members"—two legs, two arms, and a head. And, because humankind was made in God's image, she also saw the pentagram as representing God.

Other Christians saw the pentagram as representing the five wounds of Christ. As such, it was considered a potent protection against evil. Earlier Hebrew tradition associated the pentagram with the Pentateuch, the first five books of the Bible. It was also seen, at that time, to represent truth.

During the Inquisition, the pentagram first became associated with evil and the devil in the form of Baphomet, a goatlike creature thought to be a demon or representation of the devil. In the popular imagination of the time, the pentagram was thought to represent the head of this goat, the devil, or a witch's foot.

Today, the pentagram and the pentacle are symbols of the Wiccan faith and of neo-paganism. Many witches wear one on a daily basis for protection. Some display their pentacle jewelry to show pride in their religion. Others wear one, but keep it to themselves. Some witches get a pentacle tattoo where it will not be visible to others. One discrete pentacle comes in the form of the Egyptian cat goddess Bastet (or Bast). She has a tiny pentagram drawn on her chest. To the casual observer, it will look like you are just displaying your love for our feline friends.

THE PATH OF THE PENTAGRAM

The five points of the pentagram and pentacle represent *Akasha*, the Sanskrit word for Spirit, and the four Elements, substances that are crucial to all life. In some pentagrams, each point is the color associated with that Element's point. Some witches also view the five points as representing the three aspects of the Goddess—Maiden, Mother, and Crone—and the two aspects of the God—dark and light.

To truly understand the pentagram, many witches will follow the path of the pentagram. To do this, you start with a given point—Water, Fire, Earth, or Air—and use it as your focus of study. You usually don't start with Spirit as this is the most difficult to truly understand.

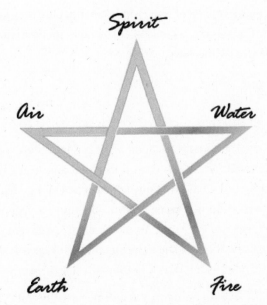

Pentagram points represent Akasha (the Spirit) and the Elements (Water, Fire, Earth, and Air).

Point by Point

The following list explains what each point represents and lists the most common color associated with it. To find the correct point, face the pentagram as you read this list:

- **Water.** The point representing the Element of Water is on the top right. The color associated with Water and this point is blue.

- **Fire.** The point on the right that slants down represents the Element of Fire. If the pentagram is multicolored, the color of this point is red.

- **Earth.** The point on the left that slants down represents the Element of Earth. Because the color associated with Earth is green, this point is green.

- **Air.** The point representing the Element of Air is on the top left. The color associated with this Element is yellow.

- **Akasha.** The top point of the pentagram represents Spirit. If the pentagram is multicolored, this point will be white or purple. Akasha is often described as space or ether—the background upon which reality is perceived.

In some traditions, the points represent the four Elements plus Magickal Will. Spirit is seen to inhabit the central pentagon, which touches and empowers each of the points, just as it empowers the Elements themselves.

Walk the Path

Many witches walk the path of the pentagram by starting with Earth, moving to Water, then Air, then Fire, and finally Spirit. Decide at what point you are going to start, learn everything about that Element, and work with it in ritual and in magick. Meditate with the Element that you have chosen. Learn all about its aspects, colors, Elementals, and power. This is not something you can do in a week. It can take up to a year to fully understand each Element. When you feel you are ready to move on to a different Element, move along the pentagram to the next one. Follow the same agenda with each Element until you reach Spirit. Remember that the practice of Wicca is the path of a lifework.

Spirit will be the most difficult. As humans, we will never fully understand the power and unconditional love Spirit has to offer. Just remember that as long as you continue to work to understand the energy of Spirit, then you yourself will continue to grow in the spiritual dimension.

PENTAGRAMS IN THE AIR

The pentagram drawn in the air can be an important part of consecrating objects that you want to make holy. You make banishing pentagrams to remove all the negativity from your object. Then you can make an invoking pentagram to draw in positive energy.

At the beginning of ritual when you call in the quarters, you can make the appropriate invoking pentagram in the air for each quarter. For example, when you call in the East, or Air, make an invoking Air pentagram. When you call in the North, or Earth, make an invoking Earth pentagram. When you bid the quarters farewell, make the banishing pentagram for each one.

If you see other witches making banishing or invoking pentagrams differently from the way you've learned, don't worry. There is some variation from tradition to tradition in the way that they are drawn. Similarly, if you are practicing ritual on your own and you make a mistake, never fear. If your intention was to make a banishing Earth pentagram but what you drew was closer to a banishing Fire pentagram, you have still made a banishing Earth pentagram. Spirit, unlike a computer, always knows your intentions.

You can also use invoking pentagrams to help with your magick. If you are working a spell to help you study or learn something new, you might want to draw an invoking Air pentagram to pull in the positive mental energies of Air. In addition, you might want to invoke Water to help you use intuition in your learning process.

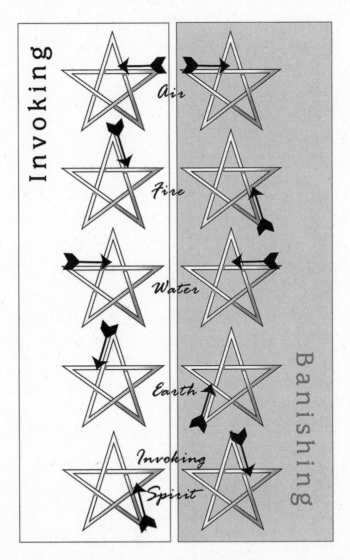

Invoking pentagrams and banishing pentagrams for Akasha (Spirit), plus each of the Elements.

Banishing Pentagram Spells

Here are two examples of spells that use banishing pentagrams to take away negative energies. Try them if they feel right for you. Or use them as models to create your own spells. As always, ground yourself, feeling the earth firm beneath you, before you begin working a spell.

Electronic Message Glitches Be Gone

When plagued by computer or electronic mail or message problems, face your computer or device and with a stick of lit incense trace the banishing pentagram of Air in front of the screen. While you do this, say these words:

> *Messages sent and messages received*
> *In cyberspace and on my screen*
> *Of error, bug, and glitch be clean.*
> *Communication be retrieved!*

Say this chant a total of three times. Trace the banishing pentagram of Air each time. If you don't have any incense handy, use a feather, which also represents Air, instead.

Brighter Tomorrow

To ease sadness after a loss, face the West and hold before you a chalice of water into which you have put a pinch of sea salt. Slowly and carefully trace the banishing pentagram of Water in the air saying:

> *Pentagram of Water, wash away*
> *Some of the pain I have felt today.*
> *Lift from me some weight of sorrow,*
> *Help me find a brighter tomorrow.*

As with the other spell, say these words and draw your pentagram three times. Then, either leave the water in the chalice and place it on your altar, or pour the water just outside your door so you will cross over it each time you enter or leave your home.

Understand that we all have painful emotions for a reason. Before doing magick to ease your discomfort, spend some time really experiencing your emotions. Think hard on the lessons to be learned. All humans grieve sometimes, even Wiccans. This spell is not designed to keep you free of sorrow, but rather to lighten your pain and ease your heart so you are able to move on when the time is right.

Invoking Pentagram Spells

You can try these invoking spells to call Elemental energies to come to your aid.

Free Speech

To invoke the ability and composure you need to make a speech in front of a group of people, call on the Element of Air. Face the East, the direction associated with Air, and light a stick of incense. Using the incense, trace an invoking Air pentagram in front of you. As you do this, say these words:

> *Power of the East and of the Air,*
> *Let my speech flow free and be clear.*
> *Away with the stumble, the mutter, the block,*
> *Brave is my manner and composed is my talk.*

Repeat the words and draw your pentagram a total of three times. Then, place your incense in a censer or other fireproof container and let it burn until it goes out by itself.

Perfect Home

For success in finding a new home, use the invoking pentagram of Earth. To do this, find a smooth, brown stone. Hold it firmly in your right hand as you draw the invoking pentagram of Earth in the air. While you do this say these words:

> *Pentagram of Earth, drawn in the air,*
> *Lead me to a secure lair.*
> *By rock and tree, by leaf and loam,*
> *I seek to find my perfect home.*

Repeat this chant for a total of three times, each time drawing the invoking Earth penta-gram. While you do this, try to envision everything you want in a new home. Then, place the stone on your altar. Once you have moved into your new home, take the stone out into your yard or to another outdoor spot near your new home. Thank the stone for its help and return it to the earth by leaving it on the ground.

PICK YOUR PENTACLE

Pentacles made from various substances carry specific significance. Silver is used to represent the Goddess energy, while gold is used to represent the God's energy. Copper is for drawing energy. A pentacle inset with an amethyst represents healing or Spirit. Onyx is for protection. Hematite is for grounding. Moonstone represents lunar Goddess energy. You can also focus on a special energy by placing it at the center of a pentacle for emphasis.

What About Inverted Pentagrams?

Typically, a pentagram has one point at the top and two points at the bottom. The single point on top represents the idea that the Spirit rules over matter. An inverted pentagram has two points on top and one on the bottom. The inverted pentagram suggests that Spirit is subservient to matter. Satanists use the inverted pentagram to express their belief that their immediate, physical needs are more important than any spiritual or moral value.

In the Gardnerian tradition of witchcraft (discussed in Chapter 2), the inverted pentagram has been used as a symbol of Second Degree Initiation. This symbol is used to remind the witch that he or she will have to learn to face his or her own internal darkness before attaining Third Degree Initiation. Because of its associations with Satanism, some Gardnerian witches have abandoned the use of the inverted pentagram.

Wear the Blue Star

Remember the couplet from "The Rede of the Wiccae"?

> *When misfortune is enow,*
> *Wear the blue star on thy brow.*

You can visualize the blue star, or a pentagram, on your forehead or draw it with holy water or oil. When doing this, imagine that a white light surrounds you. The pentagram you visualize will be just as potent a protection as one that you can actually see. Many witches believe you are blessed if you wear the pentagram and twice blessed if you wear it privately.

PART 3

WORKING MAGICK

The Wiccan holidays can be great times to work magick. During Esbats—the monthly celebration of the Goddess—you can draw on her energy for your magickal workings by Drawing Down the Moon. During the eight annual Sabbats, you celebrate the God and his life cycle, the Wheel of the Year. You'll further your understanding of magick and learn how other beings can aid you. Whether you are calling the Goddess, stirring the Ancestors, summoning a spirit animal or a fairy, or simply inviting your familiar, your magick is enhanced by your work with these entities.

You'll also be introduced to a huge array of techniques, such as toning or building a cone of power, and natural materials that will help make your magick even more effective—from magickal alphabets to channeling chakras, and from crystals and stones to herbs and botanicals. You're working magick!

CHAPTER 12

ESBATS CELEBRATE MOON MAGICK

Wicca has both religious and magickal elements, and an Esbat is a Moon ritual in which these two aspects are represented. Esbats are times of celebration of the Goddess and her energy; they are also great times for many types of magickal workings. Many witches prefer to work with the full Moon, but you can work with any phase of the Moon. As a solitaire, you can plan your ritual and magick for any day of the month. If you are working with a coven, you will meet with the group at a prearranged time. You can also hold more than one Esbat a month, either on your own or with others.

At least once a month, witches honor the Goddess by celebrating an *Esbat*. During an Esbat, which is celebrated at night, you pay homage to the Goddess and you draw on her energy to do magick. You can celebrate the different phases of the Moon, depending on what kind of energy you want to draw on. Many witches prefer to honor the Goddess on the full Moon. (Remember the words from Denise's "The Charge of the Goddess" in Chapter 3? "Assemble in a place of secret, better it be when the Moon is full and give praise to the spirit of me.") Some witches will do their magick on the phase of the Moon best suited to the magickal task at hand, and then formally honor the Goddess when the Moon is full.

WORKING WITH LUNAR ENERGY

The energy of the Moon changes depending upon the phase the Moon is in. You've probably noticed that the energy of the full Moon is quite strong. On full Moon nights, police departments and hospital emergency rooms often have their busiest times. In Wicca, each phase of the Moon is noted, because different kinds of Moon energy are used for different kinds of magick.

Some witches celebrate Diana's Bow—the first sliver of Moon visible in the sky. This usually occurs about three days after the Moon has gone dark and is a great time for new projects that would benefit from a gradual increase in energy.

Waxing Moon—Initiation and Growth

When the first silver thread of moonlight shows itself, the time is right for starting new projects and making new plans. Say you decide to go back to school to study something totally different from what you've done before. Do magick to bless that endeavor. Or maybe you want a makeover of your wardrobe or your lifestyle. Apply your magickal energies to that end. Bring new things into your home: plants, pets, or decorations for a harmonious blending of energy.

Full Moon—Seek Your Heart's Desire

Remember the ninth couplet from "The Rede of the Wiccae"? In case you haven't got the Rede memorized yet, here it is:

> *When the Moon rides at her peak,*
> *then your heart's desire seek.*

The energy of the full Moon is about going for the gusto. The time of the full Moon is good for calling in what you really want, be it money, love, peace, or what have you. Full Moon energy enhances your own magickal flow. Spells you do under the full Moon's glow are especially powerful. Seek visions and wisdom through divination, scrying, or just being open to the voice of the Goddess as you meditate. Full Moon energy is available three days before the actual full Moon and three days after.

Just because the full Moon is a good time for magickal workings doesn't mean you have to do magick at every full Moon. Resist the temptation to use this lunar energy for everything. During your Esbat, you can just choose to honor the Goddess and feel close to her, and that can be a superpower experience!

Waning Moon—Remove What You Don't Need

When the Moon is on the wane, it is the best time for banishing magick. Use spells to remove things like bad habits or negative energy. Say you moved into a new home where the previous occupants were quarrelsome and angry and you want to clear the house of those energies. At the waning Moon, place a large onion in a bowl of salt in each room of the house to absorb any leftover hostile feelings. Leave them there for a full lunar cycle, until the Moon is waning again a month later. Then gather the onions into a dark-colored bag and carry them away from your home. Toss them in a moving body of water or leave them to decompose in a wooded area where you don't ordinarily go. Dispose of the bag before returning to your home. This is waning Moon magick.

Dark Moon—Take a Break

Many witches believe you should not practice magick at all during the three days a month when the Moon is dark and is not visible in the night sky. This is the time of the month when the Goddess is thought to have descended into the underworld. She is in mourning, and her energy is at its lowest point. During the Dark of the Moon, Hecate, the Goddess in her aspect as queen of the underworld, rules. Meditation and relaxation are best now under cover of dark Moon nights with their sprinkling of starlight.

DRAWING DOWN THE MOON

Many witches Draw Down the Moon during Esbats. When you Draw Down the Moon during a full-Moon ritual, you pull the energy of the Goddess into yourself. In terms of ritual structure, you Draw Down the Moon after you have cleansed and consecrated your space, cast the magick circle, and called the quarters and the Goddess and God.

To Draw Down the Moon

Picture yourself standing in a meadow while above you the full Moon is glowing brightly. (Or go out and actually stand in the light of the full Moon.) Gaze at the Moon and stand with your feet apart and planted firmly on the ground. Raise your arms until they are over your head, but keep your elbows slightly bent. Picture white light streaming from the Moon down through the night sky and into you. This light is the energy of the Goddess. Fill yourself with her energy and let it totally join and become one with you.

The first time Denise Drew Down the Moon she felt a strong tingling in her hands and feet and around her mouth. The sensation spread up her limbs and it intensified to the point where she became frightened. She took a little gasp of air, and in an instant, the feeling vanished. For six months after that, every time Denise tried to Draw Down the Moon she was unsuccessful. She figures she just wasn't psychologically ready to feel that kind of intense energy. Now Denise still feels the Moon energy as an intense tingling, but she doesn't find it scary anymore. Instead, she feels intense connection to deity and a great spiritual high.

Other witches describe Drawing Down the Moon differently. Some feel it as an intense heat spreading through their limbs and body. Some get the tingling sensation Denise experiences accompanied by the feeling of a cool breeze. Most people get quite emotional, and some cry. Whatever the feelings you encounter, stand there with them and let the Goddess fill you up.

After you have Drawn Down the Moon and are filled with the Goddess's energy, you can do magick, or you can just enjoy the deep connection you feel with deity. You probably won't need to Draw Down the Moon every month. If you've been doing a lot of magick, helping people and healing them, you'll probably want to Draw Down the Moon and allow the energy of the Goddess, the endless source of the All, to recharge and replenish your spiritual batteries. Afterward, you will feel cleansed and replenished.

To Draw Down the Moon, raise your arms during a full Moon to prepare to pull the Goddess energy into your being.

In a coven, the High Priestess Draws Down the Moon. When she has done that, she is seen to have become the Goddess. (When you do this on your own, you, too, will be the Goddess incarnate.) Some High Priestesses will share the Goddess's energy with the other coven members. In some traditions, only the High Priestess, and not the High Priest, can Draw Down the Moon. And Drawing Down the Sun is reserved for the High Priest. As a solitaire, there is no reason that you can't pull down either one. If you are male, you have just as much right to pull down the energy of the Goddess as a woman does. And if you are female, you can pull down the energy of the God as well.

To Draw Down the Sun

When you Draw Down the Sun, you are calling the energy of the God into you. To do this, assume the God position. Stand with your feet together and your arms crossed over your chest with your hands up by your collarbones. In the same way that you did with Drawing Down the Moon, imagine the energy of the Sun pouring into you and filling you up.

SEASONAL MOONS OF THE LUNAR CALENDAR

Each full Moon of the month has its own name and its own qualities. Because Wicca draws from a number of folkloric traditions, you will probably see different names assigned to different months. Here we'll use some of the most common terms.

January: Wolf Moon

The Wolf Moon, also known as the Cold, Snow, or Winter Moon, is a time of protection and strength. While it is the first full Moon of the calendar year, in terms of nature, it occurs in the middle of the cold winter season, a season of death and desolation. The Wolf Moon can be seen as a time of both beginnings and endings. You can do magick so that as the spring approaches, your magickal goal will grow closer and closer to fruition.

February: Storm Moon

The Storm Moon, also known as the Death or Quickening Moon, is a time to do magick for fertility and strength. For most people in the Northern Hemisphere, February is a time of storms and bleak, short days. This is a good time to do magick to help you face life's challenges. This is also a time of cleansing, both internally and externally. Gather and donate physical things you don't need and release any mental or emotional baggage you might be hauling around with you, too.

March: Chaste Moon

Also known as the Seed or Worm Moon, the Chaste Moon is a time to plant mental seeds—thoughts of success and hope. This is also a time of purity and newness. It's the time to bless the magickal herbs and plants in your garden and to start preparing the soil for the seeds that you will plant. Mentally prepare yourself for new experiences: a new job, a new class, a pregnancy, taking a trip, or bringing a new animal into your home.

April: Seed Moon

The Seed Moon signals a time of fertility, growth, and wisdom. This Moon is also known as the Egg, Grass, or Wind Moon. Sow the seeds of magick. If you are planting a magickal garden, you want to get out there now and put things into the earth. Empower seeds for Earth magick. Move from the planning phase into action. If you want to get pregnant, go for it. Fertility is in the air.

May: Hare Moon

The Hare Moon, also known as the Flower or Planting Moon, is a time of health, love, romance, and wisdom. Plant the seeds that you have empowered in April. As the seeds begin to grow, the energy you have filled them with will start to manifest in your life. Rekindle the romantic spark and passion in a relationship. Use divination magick to make decisions for your career.

June: Lover's Moon

Also known as the Strawberry or Rose Moon, the Lover's Moon brings with it energy for love, marriage, and success. Nurture your garden and marvel at its beauty and abundance. If you have a new career start, or you've begun a new course of study at school, make sure you have everything going smoothly. In romance, delete that dating app from your phone and focus on strengthening your relationship with your partner.

July: Mead Moon

The Mead Moon, also known as the Blessing, Lightning, or Thunder Moon, is a time of enchantment, health, rebirth, success, and strength. This is the time of the first harvests, when you begin to enjoy the fruits of your labors. This is also a time of celebration and magick. Remember that mead is the nectar of the Gods. Gather your magickal herbs and do prosperity magick so you get that response to your new website, podcast, or social media profile.

August: Wyrt Moon

The Wyrt Moon, also known as the Wort, Barley, Corn, or Red Moon, is a time of abundance, agriculture, and marriage. (*Wyrt* is the Old English word for "plant" or "herb." So, a Wyrt Moon is also a Plant or Herb Moon.) Collect your magickal herbs and store them for the winter. Remember to give an offering back to the Goddess. Celebrate the Festival of Diana on August 17. Broaden your fan base. Post information that promotes health and well-being among your followers on social media. If you are pregnant, concentrate your energies on a healthy pregnancy.

September: Harvest Moon

Also known as the Barley or Hunter's Moon, the Harvest Moon is a time of protection, prosperity, and abundance. If you have had a long illness, this is the time to finally come back to full health again. Celebrate the start of a new cycle of studies at school, to deepen your understanding and commitment to knowledge. Be generous with your magickal powers. Remember the Rule of Three: Positive or negative energies you send out will return to you threefold.

October: Blood Moon

The Blood Moon is sometimes called the Falling Leaf or Hunter's Moon. It is a Moon of new goals, protection, resolution, and spirituality. The night of the Blood Moon is a great time for divination. At this time of year, all of Nature is making ready for the winter. Reflect on what you did during the year and evaluate your accomplishments. Read back through your Book of Shadows and meditate on your magickal doings. Think about how you'd like to grow in your Wiccan practice.

November: Snow Moon

The Snow Moon is also known as the Beaver, Mourning, or Tree Moon. Work with abundance, prosperity, and the bonds of family and friendship. Use divination to get an idea of what is up ahead. Remind yourself that although winter is coming, it will not last forever. Reduce your stress and strengthen your bonds with family and friends. Consider volunteering at your local food bank. Be aware of Wiccan friends and loved ones who need your help and assistance as winter months approach.

December: Oak Moon

Also known as the Cold or Long Night Moon, the Oak Moon is a time for hope and healing. This time of year the Moon has reign over the Earth, because there are more hours of night than day. Our thoughts turn to the rebirth of the light and the longer days that are promised after the winter solstice. Finish something you have worked hard on and make sure the task is truly completed, all the details dealt with. Let go of old patterns or problems and start anew. Let go of the negative and let the light of longer days shine inside you.

SPECIAL MOONS

Nature contains many phenomena and witches can use special happenings to enhance their magickal workings. Special magick happens on special Moons!

ONCE IN A BLUE MOON

You've probably heard the expression "once in a blue moon." But what does it really mean? A *Blue Moon* is the second full Moon that occurs during one calendar month. Because the Moon's cycle has 29½ days and January, March, May, July, August, October, and December have 31 days, sometimes you will see two full Moons in these months. This doesn't happen very often. In fact, it occurs every 2.72 years. So using the expression "once in a blue moon" to mean "rarely" makes sense. During the year 2018, two Blue Moons appeared in the night sky.

The Blue Moon is a special magickal Moon. You might want to save any really special magick you are planning for the night of the Blue Moon. Some witches use the Blue Moon as a time to set goals. You can also use the Blue Moon for doing magick for something you have never done before.

BLOOD OF THE MOON

Many female witches celebrate and welcome the Blood of the Moon—their own bleeding phase in their monthly menstrual cycles. Many female witches believe their cycles are connected to lunar energy. Some regard the days that they have their periods as Days of Power.

Have you ever noticed that a woman's menstrual cycle is about the same length as the Moon's 29½-day cycle? Many female witches pay close attention to the relationship between their own personal cycles and the phases of the Moon. Some witches have been known to use magick to sync their menstrual cycle to the Moon's cycle so that they will bleed on the full or the new Moon. You can do very powerful magick if you have your period on those nights.

Many witches feel that a woman's intuition is at its peak at the time of menstruation. Others feel that the days leading up to menses, the premenstrual phase, is one of supersensitivity and powerful intuition. They feel they have prophetic dreams and can better channel energy during those few days of the month than at any other time.

LUNAR ECLIPSE

What effect do you think a lunar eclipse might have upon your magickal workings? Yep, that's right. A lunar eclipse will amplify and intensify magickal potency. During a lunar eclipse, the Moon moves completely into the Earth's shadow; to the viewer, the Moon appears to be a bright red color. Many witches believe that a lunar eclipse gathers the magickal energy of all the Moon phases. This is a good time to do complicated magickal work that includes multiple steps. Remember the threefold law and consider performing magick that enhances positive energy during a lunar eclipse.

GODDESS MOON MAGICK ANY TIME

To Drawn Down the Moon anytime, find a reflective silver plate or bowl, or just use a round mirror that's been cleansed and consecrated. Envision opening up to Goddess energies while holding the reflective surface up to the Moon and looking into it for a long moment, holding your magickal intent in your mind. Lift the bowl or mirror over your head and pour out its Moonlight over yourself, feeling the Goddess light flow over your eyes and face. Acknowledge the presence of the Goddess as it fills your being, called to your soul.

CHAPTER 13

SABBATS CELEBRATE THE WHEEL OF THE YEAR

The Sun represents the God, the male spirit of the All. Like the Sun's energy, his is bright, vibrant, powerful, and protecting. He allows the plants to grow, warms the earth, and provides the Earth and all her creatures with light and crucial nutrients. Sabbats, the Wiccan holidays, are truly a time when you tune in to the Earth and the changes she undergoes with the turning of the seasons.

WHAT ARE THE SABBATS?

The Sabbats are holidays on which Wiccans celebrate the male energy of the All. These are days of celebration of the God, just the way the Esbats (as discussed in the previous chapter) are celebrations of the Goddess. There are eight Sabbats. (The word comes from a Hebrew word that means "to rest.") Unlike human-made holidays (such as the Fourth of July) where the date of the holiday is determined to commemorate an event in human history, the Sabbats are events that occur in Nature. They mark the Equinoxes—the two days a year when daytime and nighttime are of equal duration. The Sabbats also include the longest day of the year, the longest night of the year—known as the Solstices—and the midpoints between these four occurrences.

As the Lord and Lady Travel the Wheel of the Year

In Wicca, the year is seen as a turning wheel. Once it has completed a rotation, the Wheel of the Year keeps going and spins around again and again. The Lord and Lady, as manifestations of the All, play a major part in this continuous cycle. Many Wiccans look at the year as the repeating story of the Lord and Lady.

Although Samhain is the Wiccan New Year, let's start with Yule. Here's a quick tour of the Wheel of the Year. When the Lord is born at Yule (December), he is the incarnation of the God of Light. From Yule onward, the daylight hours will be longer and longer while the Lord grows from boyhood at Imbolc (February) as the Lady recovers from her pregnancy, to youth at Ostara (March), to manhood at Beltane (April) when the Lord falls in love with the Lady. In midsummer, when the Sun is at its highest at the longest day of Summer Solstice (June), the Lord and Lady are at their highest powers. After the lush peak of Summer Solstice, as the days begin to grow shorter, the Lord begins to weaken at Lughnassad (August), while the Lady is already pregnant and her belly beginning to swell. At Mabon (September), he becomes the Dark God, his powers at maturity and winter approaching. At that point, the shortest of days when the Sun is lowest in the sky heralds the Lord's coming death in his Lady's arms at Samhain (October). On Yule (December) he is reborn once more of the Lady, and the Wheel of the Year turns again.

Quartering the Year: Greater and Lesser Sabbats

The Lesser or Minor Sabbats, which sometimes are also called Fire Festivals, occur at the quarters of the year. They include the Vernal or Spring Equinox, the Fall or Autumn Equinox, and the Summer and the Winter Solstices.

The Greater or Major Sabbats—Samhain, Imbolc, Beltane, and Lughnassad—occur at the cross quarters, the midpoints between Solstice and Equinox. They mark the turning of the seasons and are considered to be very powerful days in and of themselves. Midpoints are considered to be times of great power because most things in Nature reach the peak of their strength when they are in the middle of their lives.

Sabbats: Quick Reference Guide

Date	Cycle of the Year	Holiday Name
October 31	Cross quarter	Samhain
December 21 (give or take a few days)	Quarter	Yule
February 2	Cross quarter	Imbolc
March 21 (give or take a few days)	Quarter	Ostara
April 30	Cross quarter	Beltane
June 21 (give or take a few days)	Quarter	Summer Solstice
August 2	Cross quarter	Lughnassad
September 21 (give or take a few days)	Quarter	Mabon

Because the Summer and Winter Solstices and the Autumn and Spring Equinoxes are actual astrological events, and because the yearly calendar that we follow was made up to approximate natural events in a standardized way, the dates of these events vary from year to year. To find the actual date of the Solstices or the Equinoxes for a given year, consult a witch's calendar or an almanac.

People have marked these events since megalithic times. The boulders of Stonehenge form alignments with both the Spring and Autumn Equinoxes and the Winter and Summer Solstices. People in ancient China, Egypt, and Peru also have left markers of these natural events.

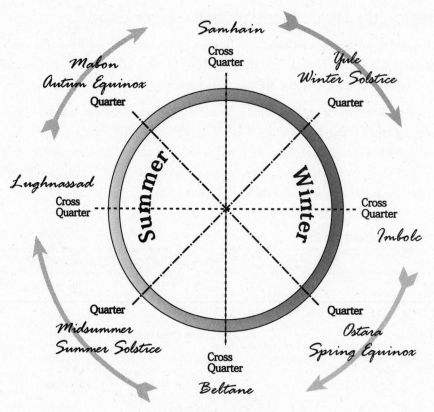

The Wheel of the Year.

CELEBRATE!

The Sabbats are holidays to celebrate deity. They are times for you to enjoy—with friends and family, if you like—but definitely with the Gods. Celebrating the Sabbats helps to keep you in tune with Nature and the cycles of the Earth's seasons. Living in cities, as many of us do, often leaves people feeling cut off from the cyclical nature of life. Observing the Sabbats can aid in realigning your rhythms and energies with the natural forces of the Earth.

Light the Balefire: When to Celebrate

Some of the Sabbats are best celebrated at night, and some are best enjoyed during the day. In olden times, many of these holidays were commemorated with *balefires*. A bale-fire is a bonfire or a smaller fire that is lit for magickal purposes. Some witches say that the balefire is traditional at Yule, Beltane, and Midsummer. Others list Beltane, Summer Solstice, Lughnassad, and Mabon. And of course, the Yule log is traditionally burnt at Yule. Samhain, the Witches' New Year, the night when the Lord dies, is typically celebrated at night. Yule and the other cool-weather holidays also usually are celebrated in the evening.

The spring and summer Sabbats are often celebrated during the day and outdoors. This way you can enjoy the Sun and all of Nature while you celebrate the holiday. Some witches try to celebrate each Sabbat on the actual day of the Sabbat. At times, this can be difficult because these holidays can fall on a week day. In case a Sabbat does fall in the middle of the week, you can celebrate on the Saturday or Sunday before or after the actual date. Even if you celebrate on a different date, you can still give reverence and recognize the holiday on the day or night of the Sabbat. Because the Sabbats are naturally occurring events, they will happen with you or without you.

As a Solitaire, or in a Group

You may want to celebrate the Sabbats one-on-one with the Lord and the Lady. You could write your own ritual and have a private experience, or you could ask a friend or two to come celebrate with you. Sabbats are just as meaningful celebrated alone with deity as they are in a large group.

In a coven, the High Priest and High Priestess either select a ritual they have written or use one from a Book of Shadows that has been handed down to them. Sometimes the coven will put on a Sabbat play that explains the story behind the given holiday. Each coven member takes a part, so everyone is involved.

WICCA'S WHEEL OF THE YEAR

The Wheel of the Year is the cycle of the seasons that turns from birth to death to rebirth again. A plant grows, dies, and leaves behind its seeds that in turn give life again. In Wicca, people look at their own lives in the same way. Many Wiccans believe that each time you are incarnated you have a lesson to learn. You live with that issue of spiritual growth, and you learn. After you die, you come back again, and you learn more until your spirit has reached enlightenment and becomes one with the All. Others see that Nature's cycles reflect the ups, downs, and normal variations of the life they are leading in the here and now.

Giving yourself a goal is a great way to celebrate the Sabbats. One way to do this is to relate the Lord's growth to your own. At Imbolc, set your mind on your goal. Think about how to implement it. At Ostara, start to implement it. At Beltane, act on it, and you'll see some initial results. In June, at the Summer Solstice, your goal, like the Lord, will be at its peak, and when fall approaches, it will come to fruition. At the end of the year, review your progress. If you have not achieved your goal, keep at it for another turn of the wheel.

Samhain (October 31): Halloween, Witches' New Year

Samhain (pronounced *SOW-wen* or *sah-VEEN*), one of the Greater Sabbats, is probably the witches' greatest holiday. And it is certainly the one the public always associates with witches! For witches, this holiday has a rather different tone than it does for the population at large. Samhain is a profound spiritual event. It marks the death of the Lord and also the start of Wicca's New Year. On Samhain, witches hold celebrations to honor the dead. Witches celebrate this holiday at night. Some witches have a silent supper during which they relive moments of life with a friend or loved one who has passed on. Some witches simply set a place at the table for loved ones who have died. Although the witches' New Year is a sedate holiday, witches also attend Halloween parties, but not on the night of October 31. That night is reserved for more solemn pursuits.

Yule (December 21): Winter Solstice

Yule (pronounced *YOOL*), one of the Lesser Sabbats, marks the Winter Solstice, the longest night of the year. It is also seen as the time when the God is reborn and light begins to return to the Earth. Wiccans celebrate by exchanging gifts, decorating a tree, hanging holly and mistletoe, singing, feasting, and by burning a Yule log. The exchange of gifts symbolizes hope for the future and the gift that the Lady has bestowed upon the Earth by giving birth to the Lord, who is also the Sun. The Yule log is burned in the evening in a fireplace or a cauldron. It symbolizes the Lord reborn and the return of the Sun. Every year, some of the log is saved and is used the following year to light that year's Yule log. In this way, the fire of the Yule log is symbolically reborn as well.

Imbolc (February 2): Rebirth of the Sun

Imbolc (pronounced *IM-bolk*), which is also called Candlemas, is the time when Wiccans celebrate the renewing fertility of the Earth. This can also be the bleakest time of the year when we start to fear that spring will never arrive. Sometimes, even though it is still cold, you can see early buds on trees on Imbolc. This is another way that Nature reminds us to hang on; life is getting ready to burst forth. Imbolc, a Greater Sabbat, is a time to celebrate with seeds, or with a newly germinating idea. Some covens like to initiate new members now. Imbolc is a holiday of purification. It's a great time for some early spring cleaning, too.

Ostara (March 21): The Spring Equinox

Many of the symbols of Ostara (pronounced *oh-STAR-ah*) are also common to Easter. Eggs have been a symbol of renewed life and fertility since the time of the ancient Egyptians and Persians. In the Wiccan tradition, the Goddess and God are seen as young and innocent now. The hours of light and dark are balanced, spring blooms in the air, and the Goddess and God, as do all the creatures of Nature, begin to wonder about one another. A Wiccan celebration of Ostara, a Lesser Sabbat, includes boiled and decorated eggs. Some Wiccans even do egg hunts and eat chocolate bunnies. In ritual, witches might bless seeds for future planting. I suggest you buy a new ritual broom for sweeping out negative energies.

Beltane (April 30): Handfasting of the Lord and Lady

At Beltane (pronounced *BEL-tayne*), one of the Greater Sabbats, the Lord has reached manhood, and he and the Lady unite in a handfasting. A handfasting is a Wiccan marriage ceremony in which a couple (a man and a woman, two men, or two women) is joined together for as long as their love shall last. If they decide that they no longer love each other, they can part. In this act they help the Earth to burst forth with life and new growth. To celebrate Beltane, Wiccans dance around the maypole, which is a phallic symbol that represents the Lord. Some Wiccans focus on the cauldron, the symbol of the Lady who becomes pregnant at Beltane. Celebrants wear flowers in their hair or wreaths of green foliage. It's a great day for spring cleaning and for bringing flowers into the house so all feels bright and fresh.

Summer Solstice (June 21): A Midsummer Dream

The Summer Solstice, a Lesser Sabbat (also known as Litha, pronounced *LEE-tha*), marks the longest day of the year. The Lord and the Lady are strong, and all is green and growing. It's a time for love and healing magick, and for working with fairies and forest spirits. In the past, this Sabbat was celebrated with large bonfires. People were even said to jump over the fires to promote purification, fertility, and love within themselves. The fire, of course, also represents the Sun at the height of his powers. Be aware that bonfires are illegal in many localities, and they certainly are potentially dangerous—to property and to all life. Avoid accidents involving fire. Even if people have done it throughout history, it is not a good idea to jump over a fire. When working with fire, make sure your clothing is not highly flammable. (Synthetic materials burn very fast.) Have a bucket of water and some sand on hand in case you need to douse the flames in a hurry. In short, be careful and don't become a burning witch!

Lughnassad (August 2): The Early Harvest

Lughnassad (pronounced *LOO-nus-uh*) is one of the Greater Sabbats and marks the beginning of the fall harvest, the day on which the first grain is cut. Lughnassad gets its name from the multitalented Celtic God Lugh, who, in addition to being king of the Gods, is associated with the Sun, magick, art, strength, courage, and music. Some witches in the Reclaiming tradition celebrate this Sabbat on the beach and build a sand sculpture of the moribund God to honor and mourn him. As the hours of sunlight begin to shrink, the God loses his strength. But the Goddess is already pregnant with the God, who will be reborn again at Yule. Lughnassad is also called the Feast of Bread or Lammas. Wiccans bake and hold feasts on this holiday to celebrate this time of plenty. Decorate with a wreath and place fruits and vegetables on your altar.

Mabon (September 21): Harvest Festival

Mabon (pronounced *MAY-bon*), one of the Lesser Sabbats, is the second harvest festival and is held on the Autumn Equinox to celebrate the last fruits of the year. Some people call this holiday Harvest Home. Night and day are of equal duration on this date, and you can feel the approach of winter and darkness. The Lord is preparing for his death at Samhain, and the Lady is beginning to mourn his loss. Rituals to honor this Sabbat include late-season vegetables such as squash, nuts, sheaves of late wheat, and ears of corn. Place a cornucopia, a symbol of prosperity and plenty, on your altar. Some witches hold feasts or do food magick on Mabon.

The Wheel Turns

Here is a blessing for the Wiccan Wheel of the Year. Use it to help you observe the Sabbats and honor their celebration. Memorize this blessing and you'll keep all the Sabbats to mind!

Approach the Wheel of the Witches' Year
With spirit bright and burning
Each celebration remember though
The Wheel is always turning

On Samhain when the veil is thin
We call the spirits near
Inviting Ancestors of our kin
We greet them without fear

The Sun returns at time of Yule
We welcome back the light

With candles, friends and burning logs
We keep our spirits bright

Imbolc marks the start of things
The core of life and birth
The seed that has not sprouted yet
But swells beneath the earth

Ostara when we hunt for eggs
Is equal night and day
We strive for balance in our lives
And sweep the dust away

The Lord and Lady handfast be
When spring is blooming bright
With flowers, Maypoles, food and dance
We celebrate their rite

Summer Solstice is the time
To walk between two flames
Rededicate and purify
Your thoughts, your words, your aims

Lughnassad we celebrate
With berries, and with bread
Sending prayers to the god of grain
His blessings keep us fed

When Mabon time comes nigh again
With harvest nearly done
We celebrate in gratitude
For all our victories won.

CHAPTER 14

SUMMON, STIR, AND CALL

We've talked about the various pantheons of Gods and Goddesses you can work with in the Wiccan religion. You can also work with other entities. Some of them you've probably heard of. Others will be less familiar (that's a Wiccan pun!), and still others you will be meeting for the first time.

When you work with these entities and with deity, it's important to treat them as honored guests. These beings are very old and very wise, but their intelligence is quite different from human intelligence. So don't expect them to act the way a person does. You must be very specific and clear about what you ask these entities to do, and you must do your asking with the proper respect.

SUMMON, STIR, CALL, INVITE, OR REQUEST?

In Chapter 6, we discussed ritual etiquette—how to behave toward fellow celebrants during a ritual. You also want to give the proper respect to the entities from other realms at your ritual. One way to show that respect is in how you ask them to attend. Summon, stir, call, invite, and request all mean close to the same thing, but these are not all the same in magick. You summon certain entities, such as the Elements or fairies. You stir more powerful entities because they are sleeping and need to be awakened for ritual. Calling denotes proper respect. When you invite entities to your ritual, you ask them to be present, but not to join you inside the circle. You can *request* the presence of any of the four winds and of your spirit guides. Tell the entities you have asked to ritual what you want them to do. You can ask them to protect, observe, or help you carry out your magick. Here is one of Denise's invocations.

Summon, Stir, and Call In the Quarters

I call to the Lord and Lady fair
I summon to us the Element of Air
I stir the Ancients with knowledge of old
Be here this night our spirits you hold.

Lord and Lady protect us, keep us from harm
Air empower us with communication and charm
Ancient Ones give us knowledge that lasts
Provide us this in the circle that's cast.

I call the Lord and Lady with loving desire
I summon to me the Element of Fire
I stir the Ancients, the old ones, the wise
To comfort our fears, our yearning, our cries.

Lord and Lady protect us with your strength of healing
Fire empower us with passionate feeling

Ancient Ones give us understandings that last
Provide us this in the circle that's cast.

I call the Lord and Lady to hear your sons and daughters
I summon to me the Element of Water
I stir the Ancients with truth from the past
Be here this night, be here at last.

Lord and Lady protect us, keep us close to your side
Water empower us with emotions of pride
Ancient Ones give us patience that lasts
Be here this night in the circle that's cast.

I call the Lord and Lady who gave us birth
I summon to me the Element of Earth
I stir the Ancients to be here this night
Travel upon their spiritual light.

Lord and Lady protect us, surround us with love
Earth empower us as below so above
Ancient Ones give us wisdom that lasts
Provide us this in the circle that's cast.

This invocation calls the Goddess and God, summons the Elements, and stirs the Ancients, or Ancestors. Plus, it spells out what each entity should do.

Summon the Elements: Air, Fire, Water, and Earth

Names: Air, Fire, Water, and Earth

From the Elemental Realm, you can summon the Elements to attend your ritual. Many witches summon them when they call in the quarters. Ask the Elements to stand outside your magick circle and guard it, or just have them witness your ritual and any magick that you do. Depending on the magick you are doing, you might want to summon one particular Element. For example, if you were working magick to help you communicate or refine your ideas, you'd want to summon Air to your ritual and draw on Air's mental and intellectual energy. If your ritual stirs the Ancestors, you might begin by calling in the quarters to the West, where the Water Element flows deep into the Underworld.

Stir Dragons Gently

Types: Air Dragon, Fire Dragon, Water Dragon, Earth Dragon, and Spirit Dragon

From the Elemental Realm, there is some disagreement among witches about the nature and characteristics of Dragons. Some see them as noble beasts. Other witches, Denise included, see them as the awesome powers of the Elements. Never make a Dragon angry.

Air Dragon is the Dragon of the Element of the East. The Dragon of the Air commands forces equal to the jet stream and those of a devastating tornado, while the Fire Dragon represents lava and the molten core of the Earth. Fire Dragon is the Dragon of the Element of the South. Water Dragon is the Dragon of the Element of the West. It wields all the power of the ocean—a tsunami that could sweep away a city in an instant. Earth Dragon is the Dragon of the Element of the North. It possesses all the strength of Earth itself. If provoked to anger, Earth Dragon will cause quakes and geological plate shifts. Spirit Dragon is the essence of the Goddess and God, the spirituality of the Akasha, the All.

For special occasions such as a Wiccaning (when a child is born), a handfasting (a wedding), or an initiation, you would stir the Dragons. You also might invite them to attend ritual if your group, community, or coven were facing a major issue that affected everyone. You probably should invite the Dragons only under unusual circumstances. They are very powerful and are not for everyday situations. Whatever you do, treat Dragons with tremendous respect. Dragons have minds of their own and can be unpredictable. If you have any doubt about your own ability to focus your magickal energy or intent, then we would not recommend you deal with Dragon energy. Better to wait until you become more adept.

Stir the Guardians of the Watchtowers Gently

Names: Guardian of the Watchtower of Air, Guardian of the Watchtower of Fire, Guardian of the Watchtower of Water, Guardian of the Watchtower of Earth

From the Elemental Realm, the Guardians of the Watchtowers are the guardians of the Elemental forces of each direction. Because they guard entities of such enormous force, they themselves possess tremendous power. Some witches are afraid of them and won't use them in ritual. They are to be invited only when what you are doing is important. You can have them observe, guard, or protect you during ritual.

You may ask them to watch and protect your circle during an initiation. Or you may ask them to witness the rite of an initiation ceremony. Having the Watchtowers witness an initiation can be a distinct advantage for the initiate. If they have witnessed your initiation, then they'll recognize your magickal name, protect and watch over you, and be aware of who you are if you ever need them to guard your circle. You also might invite the Watchtowers to a Wiccaning (childbirth) or handfasting (wedding), or if strife or some major conflict is occurring in your community. You could ask them to deliver your magick in matters of life or death.

Watchtower Invocation

> *I gently stir the North's Watchtower,*
> *Encompass us with nurturing power,*
> *Guard this circle with strength untold,*
> *Protect us from harm with courage of bold.*

> *I gently stir the East's Watchtower,*
> *Whose message is clear and filled with power.*
> *Guard this circle with strength untold,*
> *Protect us from harm with courage of bold.*

> *I gently stir the South's Watchtower,*
> *Stretching across us with flames of power,*
> *Guard this circle with strength untold,*
> *Protect us from harm with courage of bold*

> *I gently stir the West's Watchtower,*
> *To direct the Water of emotional power.*
> *Guard this circle with strength untold,*
> *Protect us from harm with courage of bold.*

When stirring the Watchtowers, most witches start with the North and work deosil (clockwise) around the circle. Some witches and many high priestesses begin in the East and move deosil from there.

Request the Presence of Winds Politely

Names: East Wind, Wind of the East, or Eurus; South Wind, Wind of the South, or Notus; West Wind, Wind of the West, or Zephyrus; North Wind, Wind of the North, or Boreas

From the Elemental Realm, the winds are great for taking your magick and delivering it quickly and forcefully. When you ask the winds to carry your magick for you, you are doing Air magick. Each wind has its own Elemental correspondence. The South Wind is associated with the Element of Fire. So, if you were sending out a love spell, the South Wind would be a good choice for its delivery. You would call upon the North Wind for its Earthy aspects, upon the West Wind for its Watery qualities, and upon the East Wind for its Air associations.

A LITTLE HELP FROM YOUR FRIENDS

You can have friends in the Realm of Fairy, but you need to be careful. Be sure you want fairies in your life before you ask them to help you.

Summon Fairies and Tree Spirits

Names: Flower fairies, mermaids and mermen, little people, sprites, and pixies.

You may picture the Realm of Fairy filled with cute little creatures. Well, fairies come in all shapes, sizes, and forms. They can appear as miniature humans, or they can appear as elves. Fairies can change their shapes to match their environment. You can summon fairies to ritual, but as a novice it's not a good idea to bring them into your magick circle. If you do, they might cause mischief with the energy you have raised. The best times to contact fairies are at dawn, dusk, noon, and midnight, and on the Equinoxes and Solstices. Fairies have arrived when the flames of your candles start to dance and your skin tingles. Know that fairies do not like to be constantly thanked; they expect payment. Leave out a bowl of sweetened milk or give them silver coins and shiny trinkets, and save your pretty words.

Fairies are skilled in the healing arts, metalworking, and all artistic pursuits. Fairies will guard your home and make sure nothing goes wrong. But be forewarned; fairies are extremely mischievous. They will borrow and hide your earrings. Or they will make your keys disappear. Once you bring fairies into your house, they're really hard to get rid of. They may stay and mess with your stuff for a long, long time. To discourage fairies, hang iron pots around the house. Iron renders fairies powerless and incapable of magick. They will flee from this metal and leave you in peace.

Fairies love tree spirits, and often hide in trees. Work with the spirit of a willow tree to learn to become more bending, forgiving, and adaptable. Go to an oak for strength, wisdom, and steadfastness. Summon a redwood to help you with longevity, wisdom, and issues of aging. Japanese tree spirits, Kodama, are said to inhabit very old trees and to share their beings with the trees they live in.

Summon the Elementals

Names: Sylphs, salamanders, undines, and gnomes

From the Realm of the Fairy, Elementals can be summoned to your ritual, but don't bring them into your magick circle. You can have them guard your circle, observe, or carry your magick to the place it needs to go. Some people believe we each have a sylph, salamander, undine, and gnome assigned to watch over us from birth. Elementals have a very basic mentality and are not compassionate creatures. Like fairies, they don't care to be thanked and will get irritated if you do so. Leave them gifts of milk, honey, coins, or small shiny objects.

Sylphs are forces of Air, from gentle breezes to gusts of wind to tornadoes, and they help to make Air. Associated with our thoughts and mental development, sylphs help human beings to breathe. The sylph king is Paralda. Summon him, or his subjects, to give you inspiration, heighten your intuition, or digest a lot of information. Sylphs can spur and activate your imagination and also can carry a message to another sylph.

Salamanders inhabit any place where there is Fire—from Earth's molten core to a candle to the Sun. Summon to work with issues of sexuality or love, to build up your passion, vitality, enthusiasm, and spirituality. Their king is Djinn, and salamanders influence our emotions, metabolism, and idealism. Their energy is transformative; they destroy and rebuild. They help to heal and detoxify the human body. Salamanders' energy can be difficult to control.

Undines exist where there is Water—from the depths of the oceans to rivers to drops of rain. Associated with our watery, or emotional, aspects, summon them if you are dealing with healing, purification, creativity, artistic performance, or issues of deep feeling. Taking a female form, their queen is Niksa. Undines influence our dreams. They awaken our empathy, imagination, and intuition. Undines help regulate water balance in the human body.

Gnomes are of the Earth and maintain geological structures. Associated with our Earthy nature—sensations and fertility, summon gnomes to work with issues involving growth, nurturing, abundance, or prosperity. Gnomes and their king, Ghob, guard the treasures of the Earth and can even help you to find such treasures. They give each rock and crystal its own unique energy and are skilled crafts-gnomes. Gnomes lend humans endurance and persistence.

IN THE COMPANY OF ...

The Goddess and the God are all around us all the time. So, too, are all the many varieties of angels. The Ancestors ... well, they dwell in the Realm of Spirit, too, but they sleep.

Calling All Deities

Names: The Lady and Lord, the Goddess and God, the All, and many others

Dwelling in the Realm of Spirit, deities, as we discussed in Chapter 3, are many, many different names and aspects of the All to call upon. Think of the All as the Lady and Lord, the Goddess and God, Hera and Zeus, Kali and Shiva, or Thor and Freyja. Call the Lord and Lady to ritual and ask them to protect, guide, or support you. Draw Down the Moon to call Goddess energy. Deities help you carry out your magick, if it is positive. They will also heal, nurture, and love you all the Wheel of the Year.

Call Angels from the Spirit Realm

Names: Seraphim, Dominions, Principalities

In the Realm of Spirit, there three different levels of angels manifest:

♦ **Level 1.** Seraphim—angels of pure love and thought; cherubim—spirits of harmony and the wisdom of the All; thrones—spirits of will and justice

♦ **Level 2.** Dominions—angels of wisdom and intuition; virtues—angels of choice and movement; powers—angels of form and space

♦ **Level 3.** Principalities—angels of personality and time; archangels—Michael, Gabriel, Uriel, and Raphael; angel messengers; guardian angels

Angels of the highest level are very intense and can be frightening. Guardian angels and the archangels are more accessible. Ask angels to help or enhance your magick, or to carry it to deity. Angels can help your magick reach its goal. Angels heal you from physical and psychological pain, and nurture health. You might call them if you've been hurt in a love relationship or if your child has suffered. Angels protect you any time you need them to. But don't call on them for day-to-day matters. Angels prefer to dwell on the spiritual plane.

Stir Ancestors Thoughtfully

Names: Merlin, Socrates, Pythagoras, Lilith, …

From the Realm of Spirit, the Ancestors are figures from the past who held great wisdom and knowledge. Many witches consider historical figures who were well versed in the magickal arts to be Ancestors. If your own relatives were particularly wise, you could look to them as your magickal Ancestors. You might want to do some research into your family's ancestry. Who knows, you could be related to a famous witch! If you have a deceased grandmother or other relative who has passed on who possessed unusual knowledge, insight, and the wisdom of an old reincarnated soul, and whose decisions you respected, you could consider her an Ancestor. But remember, just because someone is dead does not automatically make that person wise. You can stir the Ancestors and ask them to attend your ritual to aid your creativity and give you wisdom for making good decisions.

TAPPING INTO THE POWER OF ...

We are still in the Realm of Spirit. Now you are going to meet some more allies who can help you—spirit guides, spirit animals, and familiars. These entities can be all your own.

Request the Presence of Spirit Guides

Names: Varies from individual to individual

Like guardian angels, spirit guides, from the Realm of Spirit, are assigned to us at birth, and we can have as many as seven. Sometimes a spirit guide is a soul who doesn't need to incarnate again. Your spirit guides help you to learn your spiritual lessons. They also watch over you and often will quite literally guide you on your life-path, sometimes appearing in dreams. Your spirit guides will help you evolve spiritually. When you do ritual, request your spirit guides to come into circle. Actually, you probably won't need to—they will already be there with you. Consult spirit guides for the same kind of help you would ask from deity—to help carry out your magick and to protect, guide, and support you. The more you work with spirit guides, the more aware you will become of their presence. Some people can feel them. Others smell them. If you meditate, you may start to see them. Spirit guides usually present themselves in a form comfortable for you.

Summon Your Spirit Animals

Names: Various species of animals on Earth

From the Realm of Spirit, a spirit animal represents the spirit of a particular species, not of an individual animal, such as your beloved family dog who passed on when you were a child. Spirit animals possess all the knowledge and habits of their species. Many people have one particular spirit animal—a wolf, raven, otter, or bear, for instance. They feel this spirit animal represents them, and will ask the animal for help. Even if you are not in touch with your own spirit animal, you can ask one to help you. You can ask spirit animals to carry messages or magick to their destinations. When you ask a spirit animal to take something somewhere for you, keep in mind that it will perform this action in the manner of its species. For this reason, do not choose a spirit animal lightly; give serious thought to your choice and to the intent of your magick.

Many indigenous cultural traditions, such as those of the First Nations peoples of Canada and the United States, are imbued with spirit animals and mythic stories of Nature and humanity. These stories are epic, beautiful, and saturated with meaning. A close study of their art may reveal spirit animals who speak to you and to your magickal purpose.

If You Want Your Message Delivered with …	Pick This Spirit Animal
Artistry, Creativity	Sea Lion, Spider
Bravery	Elk, Lion
Caution, Protection, or Defensive Energy	Armadillo, Porcupine, Skunk, Squirrel
Docility, Family	Cow, Duck
Faithfulness, Loyalty	Dog, Horse
Fertility	Bumblebee, Rabbit
Friendship, Transformation	Butterfly, Peacock
Grace	Gazelle, Seahorse, Swan
Helpful Energy, Patience	Donkey, Ladybug, Squirrel
Humor, Optimism	Chickadee, Dolphin, Elephant, Panda
Independence, Magick	Cat, Hawk
Insight, Intelligence	Fox, Owl, Pig
Joy, Welcome	Hummingbird
Patience	Ant, Vulture
Resourcefulness	Beaver, Caterpillar, Squirrel, Woodpecker
Strength	Bear, Horse, Whale
Teacher, Wisdom	Eagle, Whale

Invite Familiars (Before They Invite Themselves!)

Names: Various

Familiars are individual animals (not whole species) inhabited by spirit. Familiars work with witches to help with their magick. Typically, a familiar seeks you out, and not the other way around. Familiars have more dignity than regular pets because they communicate with you telepathically, and tend to be drawn to ritual, so you usually don't have to invite them to attend. Familiars can enter and exit your magick circle at will. You don't need to cut a door in the circle for them to go in or out. While you are doing ritual, your familiar will give you confidence. It will warn you if you have made a mistake or if you are about to have an accident with a candle. The presence of a familiar will also enhance your magick. If you are practicing as a new solitaire, be on the lookout for your familiar to show up. A familiar may come to you as an unexpected gift, often at the time when its companionship is most needed. True to form, a familiar has no trouble inviting itself into your life, and your magick!

CHAPTER 15

WHY DO MAGICK?

Magick is something that people have done for thousands of years. But in modern times, most of us have suppressed our magickal abilities. Adding the element of magick to your life can make you feel whole and complete. Doing magick can help raise your consciousness and bring you good experiences. Magick is empowering, and it's also fun and interesting. It can help you heal or can smooth out a bumpy life path. It can help you control bad habits, build your self-esteem, give you peace of mind, and help you achieve your goals. Why *not* do magick?

WHAT IS MAGICK?

Magick is the direction and application of energy using psychic forces to create change for a specific, desired outcome. Magick is also a system of symbols, which are programmed in your mind, that help you achieve your magickal goals. As such, it is a form of mental training through which you can alter a situation by using your will. Magick can also take the form of change and growth within yourself. You change how you look at things or how you feel about a given situation. Magick can be a wonderful force in your life. Or you can manipulate magickal energy to negative, destructive ends. It's your choice.

Magick, Magic, and Prayer

Magick with a *k* is what witches do. Witches use the Elements—Water, Fire, Earth, and Air—and other forces of Nature, along with their will and their good intentions. This magick can be slow, but sometimes you see results begin in a day or two.

Magic without a *k* is what stage performers do. A magic act is a theatrical production of illusions. You see something that does not really exist. The magicians trick you. Because this type of magic does not create real change and is only illusion, its effects are immediate and fleeting.

If you ask for something in prayer, it is not the same as doing magick. Prayer is a form of communication with deity. During prayer, you get closer to deity, feel the love the Goddess and God have to offer, and connect in your spirit. In prayer you can ask for something, but that is not magick. In magick, you put forth effort by using your energy to get what you need. Doing magick, you work along with deity instead of just asking from them.

Where Magick Starts

Magick starts within you. Because your own energies and the outside energies you pull in are what you use to do your magick, you want to learn to focus. Once you begin to focus your magickal potential, things will start happening for you. Magick allows you to open up to new ideas and new understandings of spirituality. It can help you to know yourself, and to relate better to other people and situations.

How Magick Works

Here are four basic laws of magick. Spending time thinking about each one will help you become aware that there is magick all around you and that you are connected to that magick:

1. **The universe abounds with energy.** As you may remember from your high school physics class, everything is energy. Objects that appear to be solid are actually mostly empty space. They consist of tiny subatomic particles bound by pure energy. According to the brilliant theoretical physicist Albert Einstein, even the particles themselves can be seen as energy. A rock is energy. Water is energy. Wood is energy. The various tissues of your body are energy. Energy is all around us all the time. Everything has an energetic signature. You can use this universal energy.

2. **Everything is connected to everything else.** Remember the metaphor of throwing a stone into a pond and watching the ripples move away from the spot where the stone has splashed down? The ripples move out in concentric rings, just as the repercussions of your actions do. You see these ripples form because all the water molecules in the pool are connected. If you move one, or in this case a few, you move them all. In esoteric teachings, you're taught to see the universe as a network of fine threads called Indra's Web. The web connects us all to one another and connects each individual to all things. Besides connecting us to physical, material things, the web also connects us to the higher realm, to spirit. As the witches say, "As above, so below." A movement in the heavens will cause a corresponding movement down here on Earth.

3. **There are an infinite number of possibilities.** Have you ever looked at the stars on a clear night and seen them go on and on? (Go out and look!) Just as there are an infinite number of stars, there are an infinite number of events that might occur. Possibilities really *are* limitless.

4. **The path is within you.** To do magick, you have to tap into your subconscious mind. With your conscious mind, you decide what kind of magick you are going to do and what you need to do it. Once you have begun the actual act of magick, you communicate your purpose to your subconscious. Your subconscious increases the energy that you raise and sends it to your higher self, your superconscious, and to spirit. At that point, the energy is ready to create the desired result.

When doing an act of magick, you use the connectedness of all things plus part of the huge supply of naturally occurring energy to turn possibility into reality by following the path within.

Witches: Highs and Lows

Sometimes High Priestesses and Priests will do high magick, even conjuring up other entities to work their magick for them. Witches don't usually do this; they tend to direct their own energy toward their goals. Because it is formal, high magick can take many years to learn. Though it may seem cumbersome, there is a lot of power in ceremonial magick. If you are really interested in magick, you may want to do some research on high magick. You can learn a lot about magickal energy by reading about the rituals and ceremonies of the New Reformed Orthodox Order of the Golden Dawn, the Egyptian, and Druid traditions—just three examples of viable high magick practices.

Low magick consists of taking your raw energy and emotion and channeling them toward a goal. While engaged in an act of magick, a witch chants, sings, dances, says spells, and plays drums to build up internal energy. Once the energy has been built up, the witch releases the energy to affect change. Low magick is a fairly simple type of magick, but it is extremely effective. Even though most witches practice low magick, some witches work high magick.

Low magick is more accessible than high magick. Most of us probably do low magick on a daily basis without even realizing it! With the proper training, anyone can practice either form of magick. Although many witches are Wiccan, you don't have to be of any particular religion to do magick.

MAGICKAL ETHICS

Remember the Law of Threefold Return? Whatever you do will come back to you three times. Keep this law in mind when you are contemplating doing magick, and do no harm. If you do, you will get three times as much harm coming back at you. Ouch!

When the mundane way of handling an issue fails, then magick may be the answer. Witches should never attack, but they can use their magick to defend themselves. There is nothing wrong with sending all the negativity being thrown your way back at the person from whom it came. That energy will work like a karmic wake-up smack. Always place a shield of protection around yourself if you choose to do this. Then, if the person doesn't learn from his or her mistakes, the negative energy will continue to bounce off you and go right back to him or her.

If you want to do magick for someone else, stop and get that person's permission first. Even if the magick is completely for that person's benefit, get that person's permission before you act. Why? Because your magick will affect change in someone else's life. If you act without a person's permission, you could be impinging on that person's free will. Maybe deep down your friend, who always gripes she can't keep her desktop organized, really likes having this insoluble problem to complain about! If she asks for your help, go for it; but without her permission, any magick for her benefit is a no-go.

You also have to use some common sense. If you know someone is ill and you know he or she doesn't want to be, then by all means use your magick to help encourage healing for that person. You would certainly pray for the person to get better, and as magick, like prayer, is directed energy, why not use it to promote health and well-being?

What about love spells? (We knew you were going to ask about that!) Again, any magick that involves another person must not in any way manipulate that person's free will. So you can't make the amazingly cute guy (or girl) you see in the coffee shop every day fall in love with you. But here is what you *can* do—you can do a love spell to increase your own powers of attraction. You can also do a spell to attract the person who is right for you without focusing on any particular individual. Who knows? That spell might just cause you to attract the attention of your object of affection. Or you might attract someone even better!

Parents, in their roles as caretakers, can do spells for their young children. But once children are old enough to make their own decisions, parents should ask their children if it is okay first. You want to do a spell for your sister's baby who is in the hospital? Ask your sister first! If she does not agree for whatever reasons, don't do it.

WORKING WITH MAGICKAL ENERGY

Magickal energy is real, and it is powerful. You need to respect it. Before you do magick, try to resolve whatever the problem is by mundane means. If all else has failed, only then should you turn to magick. Also, know your intent—are you 100 percent clear on what you want? Are you sure that you want it? Is getting what you want going to hurt anyone?

Working with magickal energy requires time, patience, and planning. No witch just wiggles his or her nose and achieves a goal. Because magick works with natural energies, you want to select a good time to do the particular type of magick you are planning. You want to be sure that the Moon is in a phase conducive to your plans. You may also want to check an almanac or witch's calendar for any significant planetary movements. (See Chapter 19 for more about the planets and planning your magick.) Be aware of the advantages of working magick at different times of the day or night. (For more information, see Chapter 20.) Of course, in an emergency a witch has to do what a witch has to do. So cast that spell! Denise has found when the need is great, some of her best magick has been created on the spur of the moment.

You shouldn't do magick when you aren't feeling well. Remember, magick comes from within you. It is your energies that are going to be put out there. So don't wipe yourself out! Wait till you're over that icky cold before you cast your great new spell.

Resist the temptation to do magick when you are angry. After you have calmed down, you may feel differently. If you've already done some magick, you can't take it back without a lot of work, and maybe even then your spell will cause the change you'd asked for anyhow. Spells, unlike computers, don't come with "undo" edit keys. And remember, what you send out comes back to you three times.

The Magick Circle Revisited

As you learned in Chapter 10, you work in a magick circle when you are doing magick. You can think of it as your magickal office or workshop. Inside your circle, you are protected from any negative energy. May only good enter, may only good leave. The circle will also keep any outside entities from changing your magick. The circle holds the energy that you have raised until you are ready to release it.

Your magick circle is not just a two-dimensional area described by a line on the floor. Your circle goes through the floor. Using creative visualization, you will create a sphere or bubble around yourself. Imagine that you are in the center of this bubble.

Building a Cone of Power

Once you are safe inside your magick circle with all your tools, begin to build up your energy. The energy raised by you while you are doing magick takes the form of a cone. That's where the term *cone of power* comes from. In your mind's eye, visualize the cone of power, which is made of your energy, so that its peak points toward your desired goal.

After grounding yourself and preparing your work area and magickal objects, start out with your magickal intent—what do you want to have happen? Concentrate on that positive outcome. See it happening in your mind. Build your energy by chanting, swaying, or drumming. Put your intent into your activities and increase their volume, pace, and intensity.

Directing a Cone of Power

When you feel the heat from all the energy you have built up, you are ready to direct your cone of power into a magickal tool or another object. If you are using a candle, grab the candle and channel all that energy into the wax. When you light the candle, the stored energy will be sent out to do your work. Or if you are working with Air magic, you can direct your cone of power out into the Air. In either case, focus on your intent, visualize the magick happening, and know that it will happen.

Toning

Like raising a cone of power, toning is a fast and lovely way to call up magickal energies such as when blessing an amulet or magickal tools. Toning is the combining of sound with other people. If you ever have sung in a choir you probably have experienced a thrill at finding a perfect harmonic connection with others. It feels good in our bodies and uplifts our spirits. Toning is similar to this, but witches do not use a melody, just sound.

Magickal toning can be done with as few as two people. You may be able to do it alone, but it won't be as strong a feeling and may not boost your magick much. To tone in a group, you stand in a circle with everyone knowing the purpose of the magick to be done. One witch begins to make a low, sustained tone. Usually singing the word "Oh" is the best way to start. All others match the tone or try to harmonize with it. When it feels like a powerful harmony is reached, the tone gets higher pitched.

The group focuses on the magickal energy being channeled in the sound, visualizing it flowing through their bodies and upward as the pitch gets higher. All should feel a buzzing with energy. The witch leading the toning will know when the time has come to aim the musical energy and send it forth. Everyone lifts their arms up, as if throwing the toning energy out to the universe. It's very important for all to ground afterwards because powerful magickal work has been done.

Protect Yourself

The best protection when doing magick is to stay positive yourself. If you don't mess with negative stuff, it won't come bothering you. You want to call upon positive forces to protect you and help get your magickal work done. And when working magick, stay inside your protective magick circle. That's what it's there for.

Magick is like electricity. It is neither good nor bad. It just is. For a number of reasons, many modern witches avoid using the terms black magick and white magick. Thinking of black things as bad and white things as good is relying on an inaccurate and possibly racist stereotype. Furthermore, all things in life exist along a continuum. They are neither totally good nor totally bad, but lie somewhere between these two polarities. You may hear witches speak of ethical magick or unethical magick, positive or negative magick. What matters when doing magick is your intent. If you intend to harm, you are doing negative magick. If you intend the greatest good for all, then you are working positive magick.

WHAT MAGICK CAN DO FOR YOU

Magick is a wonderful healing tool. It can help you psychologically, physically, and spiritually. You become strong and confident in your body. It can also help you to break bad habits. Do you tend to come home and binge on junk food? Do you feel worse every time you do it? The period in which the Moon is waning, or appearing to get smaller in the sky, is great for ridding yourself of things you don't want—bad habits, addictions, or illnesses.

It's interesting to note that many of the herbs and spices that we use to flavor our food have magickal and healing properties. Basil, that staple of summer pasta dishes, will help you attract money. Allspice is also good for drawing money to you, and it can be used to improve your luck and for healing.

From High Ritual to Everyday Magick

The magick that you do can involve a lot of formalized ritual, or it can be casual. Some covens use high ritual, meaning they follow a very detailed plan in casting the circle and in building and directing the cone of power. High rituals, because they are so detailed, can take a lot of time. Often, they feel kind of solemn and serious. (Wiccans also use high ritual for religious ceremonies that are distinct from magickal work.)

But magick can be as simple as making a bowl of soup or throwing a handful of dirt over your shoulder and mumbling a spell. As a solitary witch, the amount of ritual you use depends on what feels comfortable and what works for you. For some people, the more ritual they use, the more effective their spells. Others don't like ritual and avoid it. As a solitaire, you can do whatever you want. Try using a complex ritual or two out of a book. Or write your own. Do what works for you.

All Kinds of Magick

There are many kinds of low magick. All of them are accessible to you, so you have lots of magickal choices! The type of magick you decide to work with will depend on your magickal intent, your personal preferences, and what kind of tools you have at hand.

- Binding magick
- Candle magick
- Crystal magick
- Dream magick
- Elemental magick
- Fairy magick
- Flower magick
- Gem magick
- Glamour magick
- Healing magick
- Herbal magick
- Incense magick
- Kitchen magick
- Knot magick
- Mirror magick
- Paper magick
- Poppet magick
- Potion magick
- Powder magick
- Protection magick
- Scrying
- Sex magick
- Weather magick

Sex magick! Yup, there is some sex in witchcraft. When doing sex magick, you raise your cone of power, either alone or with a partner, by stimulating your sexual energy. All the while, you must concentrate on the magick and not think about the sex. Actually, it is really difficult to do. But fun to try, right?

CHAPTER 16

ENHANCING YOUR MAGICK POWER

Witches use many different means to enhance their magick. Some are as simple as selecting the color of the object you will work with or getting dressed in special clothes for ritual. Others involve a little more knowledge and understanding of magickal correspondences. When you first start using magick, you'll want to begin with one or two simple enhancements so you don't get frustrated. As you gain more practice with your magick, you can add more. How elaborately you design your spells and how many magickal objects you use is up to you. The important point with magick (and with so many other disciplines) is to practice, practice, practice!

WORKING WITH MAGICKAL COLORS

Because our ability to perceive colors is dependent upon the light waves that bounce off objects, colors really do have their own energies. The energy of each color, or its light-wave vibration, has an effect on the human body. Colors have been scientifically proven to affect our moods and to aid in healing. In magick, colors help you fine-tune your intent, focus your energy, and help your magick work. To use the energy of colors in your magick, select magickal objects—candles, powders, fabric, or string, for example—of a color appropriate to the work you plan to do.

Colors have many associations. Some of your associations with a given color will be personal. Maybe you dislike green because, as a child, you were forced to wear an itchy, green shirt that you hated. Even so, if you listed all the thoughts and images that occur to you about green, you would probably write down "money." Here is a list of colors and their magickal associations.

Colors and Their Magickal Associations

Color	Magickal Association
Black	Divination, banishing, absorbing negative energy, protection, binding
Blue	Truth, tranquility, protection, hope, honor, change, psychic ability, the color of the Element of Water
Brown	Stability, integrity, justice, sensuality, endurance, animals, concentration, grounding
Gold	The God, vitality, strength, success, action, courage, confidence
Gray	Vision, neutrality, absorbing negativity
Green	Abundance, growth, healing, prosperity, fertility, employment, luck, jealousy, the color of the Element of Earth
Indigo	Insight, vision, change, flexibility, psychic abilities
Magenta	Intuition, change, spiritual healing, vitality
Orange	Courage, pride, ambition, enthusiasm, energy, friendship, communication, success, opportunities
Pink	Compassion, tenderness, harmony, affection, love, romance, spiritual healing

Color	Magickal Association
Purple	Growth, self-esteem, psychic ability, insight, inspiration, spirituality, success in business
Red	Sexual love, lust, passion, fire, willpower, courage, energy, strength, anger, the color of the Element of Fire
Silver	The Goddess, spiritual truth, intuition, receptivity, psychic ability, stability, balance
Turquoise	Creativity, discipline, self-knowledge, honor, idealism
Violet	Success, intuition, self-improvement, spiritual awareness
White	Cleansing, peace, protection, healing, truth, divination, tranquility; white also can be used in place of any other color
Yellow	Joy, vitality, intelligence, study, persuasion, charm, creativity, communication, the color of the Element of Air

If your loathing of green is so strong that it does not suggest abundance, growth, and prosperity to you, then don't use it for those purposes. Say you are working a spell with candle magick to get the money you need to pay off your student loans, and you hate green. You could use a violet candle for success and self-improvement, an orange candle for success and opportunities, or a white candle for cleansing, and which can substitute for any other color. Or you could pick the color of your candle based on your own preferences and any personal associations that suggest the right energies to you. The point is to do what works for you.

MAGICKAL SIGNS AND SYMBOLS

In addition to the pentacle and the pentagram, Wiccans use many other symbols. There are even magickal alphabets that you can use for writing anything magickal—from spells to your Craft name.

Magickal Alphabets

In Chapter 7, we introduced you to Theban Script. There are several other alphabets you can use, too. Using a magickal alphabet can help tell your subconscious that it is time to get to work to do magick. Because the magickal alphabet you choose is not something that you encounter every day, it can make your magickal workings feel more special. Its unfamiliarity can also help you to focus because, when writing in a magickal alphabet, you'll have to pay attention to the formation of every letter, instead of dashing something off the way you could if you wrote normally. An added benefit to writing your spells in a special alphabet: no one else will be able to read them! Some witches use ancient languages such as Latin or Greek for their spells. Others like the way spells sound in German, French, or Italian.

Magickal alphabets.

Magickal Symbols

You can put magickal symbols on any of the tools that you use for magick. You can even wear magickal symbols on your clothing. Like a magickal alphabet, magickal symbols speak to your unconscious. You can use symbols to make a statement. For example, a Goddess symbol on your wand could stand for your dedication to the Lady and your commitment to use magick for the good of all.

You can also use symbols to further define your magickal intention—carve them on a candle for candle magick, sew them on a poppet, or draw them on paper and place them inside your poppet. You can even use magickal symbols when writing in your Book of Shadows. If you don't feel like writing the word *cauldron*, you can draw the symbol instead.

Many witches use the magickal symbols listed here. Others use runes, and some use a combination of both.

Runes

A rune is a character in an ancient Germanic alphabet. There are several different types of runes—Anglo-Saxon, Danish, and Swedish-Norwegian, for example. The word rune comes from a Middle English word that means "secret writing." Runes are also used as tools in divination and magick. Each letter in the runic alphabet has symbolic and magickal significance. According to legend, after the God Odin hung upside down from a tree for nine days he became the only true rune master. Only he completely understands the magickal significance of each rune. Many witches see the Hanged Man in the Tarot deck as Odin, hanging upside down reading the runes.

Each rune is usually written or inscribed on its own piece of wood or small clay tablet. You can pull on the energy of a rune when doing your magick. When doing this, you might want to inscribe the rune on one of your magickal tools. For example, if you were doing candle magick to help make yourself more attractive to a potential new mate and pulling on the energy of Wynn, you might want to draw Wynn on your candle. As a tool of divination, you can use runes in some of the same ways you use Tarot cards. You also can meditate on one rune and its meaning. Or you can use runes as guides in helping you decide how to handle a given situation. Are you having difficulty making a decision about an issue in your life? Try this: hold the issue in your mind and draw three runes from a bag. What do they say about your situation?

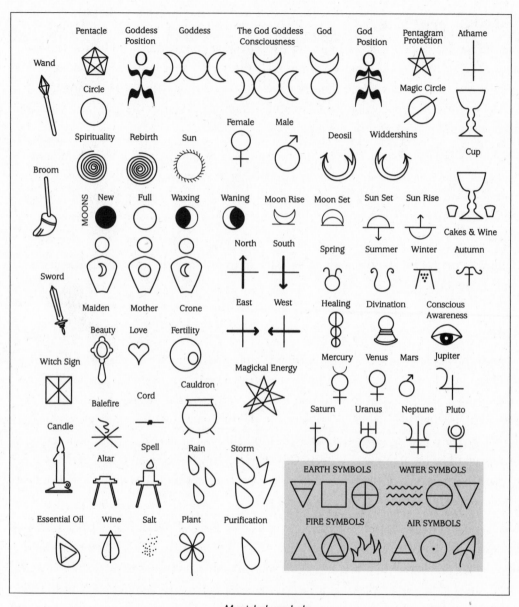

Magickal symbols.

Feoh or Fehu
Energy, power, wealth, good fortune, sexual passion

 Ur or Uruz
Quick change, strength, determination, good health

Thorn or Thurisaz
Fate, protection, overcoming, obstacles, unfortunate events

 Ansur or Ansuz
Communication, wisdom, learning, social magnetism, divine inspiration

 Rad or Raido
Travel, discovering inner wisdom, change

 Ken or Kano or Kenaz
Creative energy, music, protection, movement, change

 Geofu or Gebo
Giving and receiving gifts, generosity

Wynn or Wunjo
Happiness, especially in love, success, control, celebration

Hagall or Hagalaz
Change due to outside forces, frustration, disruption, destruction

Nied or Nauthiz
Need, obstructions, success in the future, overcoming difficulties

 Is or Isa
Wait, take a break, stand still

Jara or Jera
Cyclical return, harvesting, success in legal actions, birth, new beginnings, gradual change, fulfillments

Yr or Eihwaz
Remover of obstacles, protection, access to spirit world, endurance

 Peorth or Perth
Success in gambling or investments, finding the lost or hidden, mysteries soon revealed, magick

 Eolh or Algiz
Protection, friendship, success, luck

 Sigel or Sowolu
The life force, health, vitality, luck, success

Tir or Teiwaz
Facing difficulties, victory, bravery, return to health, honorable conduct

Beorc or Berkana
Women, Mother Earth, protection, nurturing, fertility, new beginnings

Eoh or Ehwaz
Change, adjustment, improvement, partnership, psychic ability

Mann or Mannaz
Relationships, cooperation, learning, communication, personal potential

 Lagu or Laguz
Creativity, intuition, imagination, psychic awareness, sensitivity

Ing or Inguz
Power, fertility, happy conclusion, success, limitless possibilities

 Daeg or Dagaz
Security, truth revealed, matters brought into the light, change for the better, enlightenment

Othel or Othila
Family, grounding, money, tradition, care of the elderly, property, home

Wyrd
Some people believe that this rune is a new addition to the ancient symbols and will not use it. Others see it to mean mystery, acceptance of what is to come, fate.

Magickal Inscriptions

Another way to enhance your magick is by carving inscriptions on your magickal tools. For example, you could use an inscription to dedicate your tools, or you could simply inscribe them with your magickal name. Some witches create a sigil for themselves or make magickal monograms out of their names. A sigil is a magickal sign, seal, or image. The word comes from a Latin word that means "little distinctive mark," "small seal," or "signal." You can use sigils for just about anything—from inscribing your tools to letter writing to empowering a poppet. When you make a magickal inscription, concentrate on the intent of the words or symbols you are forming. Your concentration will help to empower the object with your energy and good intentions.

Try creating a magickal sigil or symbol for yourself. Play around with your initials or the letters of your magickal name either in our regular Roman alphabet or in another alphabet, or use a combination of letters, magickal symbols, and runes. Once you've come up with your sigil, you can use it on your tools. You can even use it as a seal on your magickal correspondence.

INTENT, ENERGY, AND ATTITUDE

When you do magick, you focus your intent and your energy on your desired goal. Obviously, to do this you must be able to concentrate and focus. Because the quality of your energy can affect your magick, you want your energy to be as clear and strong as it can be. And your attitude toward your goal, your magick, and yourself will also affect your energy and the outcome of your magick.

Channeling Chakras

The seven chakras are energy centers in the body that lie along your spine. Each chakra picks up and sends out a specific type of energy. Imagine them as wheels of spinning energy.

- The root or base chakra is all about survival and our basic physical needs.

- The second chakra is the center of sensuality and emotions.

- The third chakra is the seat of the will.

- The fourth chakra concerns giving and receiving love.

- The fifth chakra deals with our communication, both mundane and spiritual.

- The sixth chakra is the seat of psychic visions and clairvoyance.

- The seventh chakra, the crown chakra, is our spiritual door, our connection to spiritual wisdom and the All.

If you have energy blockages in any of your chakras, they will negatively affect your magick by making it difficult for you to send or receive certain types of energy. A blockage in a chakra usually has physical manifestations. For example, if you have chronic problems with receiving or giving love, you may have a problem in your fourth, or heart, chakra.

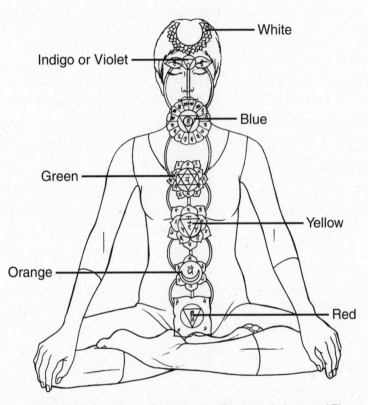

Each of the seven chakras has a color associated with it. The root chakra is red. The second chakra is orange, and the third is yellow. The heart chakra's color is green. The color of the fifth chakra is blue, while the sixth is indigo or violet. The seventh chakra, the crown chakra, is white.

(Drawing by Wendy Frost)

Magickal Attitude

Because your magick comes from you and is a product of your energies, keeping the right attitude is crucial. You must be absolutely clear on your magickal intent. You must know that you have tried all the mundane means at your disposal to get what you want. You also must know that your magick will not harm any other living thing. And you must have thought out how your magick is going to affect everyone involved, including you!

When you send out your energy to do magick, you must be able to see the desired result happening. Envision yourself reaching your goal. Give the image in your mind as many concrete details as you can. Imagine the smells, tastes, sounds, and physical sensations associated with the reaching of your goal as well. Feel that your magick is going to happen, and *know* that your magick is going to happen. Just hoping it will come true is not enough.

By the same token, you don't want to start taking your magick for granted or using it for fun. What you do with magick is work. That's why we use the phrase "magickal workings." Keep the proper respect for your powers and the powers of other entities that you draw on, and magick will serve you well. Yes, the energy of your magick comes from you, but you are only a tiny little part of the universe. Without the aid of other larger entities, your magickal work would not manifest. You may be the catalyst for the changes that you affect through magick, but you are not the sole operator. Respect and give thanks to all the entities, beings, and energies that aid the manifestations of your magickal work, and your magick should continue to work for you throughout your lifetime.

TALISMANS, AMULETS, AND CHARMS

Wearing or carrying talismans, amulets, or charms can enhance your magick and protect you from negative energy. All talismans, amulets, and charms need to be charged and blessed before you put them on. Sometimes talismans look like the thing that you want to draw to you. For example, a money-drawing talisman might be round like a coin. Alternatively, your money-drawing talisman might be square but have symbols or runes for money or prosperity inscribed on it. A horseshoe that brings good luck or protection is another type of talisman. Some witches define talismans as human-made objects that have been imbued with power, and amulets as naturally occurring objects that have been so charged.

You wear or carry the charged amulet or talisman until the magick that you have charged it for is done. For example, say you were going into the hospital, you could make a healing talisman for yourself. You might want to use a piece of rose quartz, a stone that has healing energy of its own, to do this. During ritual, build up a cone of power, then focus it and all your healing energy into the piece of rose quartz. After you have done this, the quartz will be a healing talisman. Amulets are worn for protection. Alligator teeth are considered to be amulets that will protect you against danger.

Charms are usually personal possessions that are not designed as magickal objects, but with which you have a special relationship. This relationship imbues the object with power. Say you were wearing a particular pair of striped socks the day that your soccer team won a game for the first time. After that win, you might feel that wearing those socks will bring you either luck or protection. You may then wear the socks whenever you play sports.

Hospitals are required by law to respect your religious beliefs. So, if you want to bring healing charms, talismans, or crystals into the operating room with you, the hospital will let you. The staff at many hospitals now understands that the spirit plays an important role in healing. They no longer just tolerate your ideas, but they respect your beliefs and may even encourage you to use alternative methods to help you heal.

MAGICKAL RECIPES

You can turn your favorite dish into a magickal dish by empowering one or more of the ingredients with magick. Remember in Chapter 15 how we talked about building a cone of power and directing the energy into a magickal tool such as a candle? Well, you can do the same thing with food. You can turn your favorite almond cookies into special cookies used for ritual, sometimes known as Sabbat cookies, by directing concentrated energy into the almond, vanilla, and other ingredients. In magick, vanilla and almond are both ingredients associated with wisdom and promoting mental energy.

Once you have baked these empowered vanilla almond cookies, you want to treat them properly. Keep them in a special tin. You can make the tin special by cleansing and consecrating it and then marking it with magickal symbols. Make sure to store it in a special place, too.

Eat these magickally empowered cookies, along with a special ritual tea, while preparing yourself for ritual or during ritual when you do the cakes and wine. Whether you eat the cookies as a part of your preparation for ritual or have them during ritual will all depend on what magickal intent you put into the cookies. While you eat your magickal cookies, meditate on the magick that you intend to do and give thanks for all that the Goddess has provided. Or reflect on the magick you have just done. With each bite, see the magick coming to pass, with wisdom and focused intent.

Magickal Ingredients

Another way to prepare magickal recipes is to use herbs and spices with the appropriate magickal properties. You might drink mugwort tea before ritual to help open up your psychic awareness. Peppermint tea will also help increase your psychic abilities. Or you might want to add some cinnamon to a recipe to draw money or success to you.

Use caution when working with herbs. Never ingest herbs that you are unfamiliar with. Before adding an herb to a recipe or making a tea from it, double-check that the herb is indeed edible. Many magickal herbs can be toxic, and some can be harmful if you are pregnant or nursing. Get all the facts before you partake. It's better to be safe than sorry! We'll talk more about magickal herbs in Chapter 17.

A Blessing for Cakes and Wine

As you enjoy ritual cakes and wine (or tea), always give thanks to the Goddess.

> *May this food and may this drink*
> *Honor the bounty of the Goddess*
> *And for this blessing we are grateful*
> *We give thanks for our companions*
> *We give thanks for the magick of this circle cast*
> *And the fellowship we share. Blessed Be.*

MAGICK POWERS OF CRYSTALS, HERBS, AND ESSENTIAL OILS

Flowers open in the spring, and plants grow toward the Sun. Nature has its own magick. You can harness some of that energy when you do your magick. Witches honor and respect Nature. Doing so is part of the Wiccan religion. To truly give Nature her due, you have to understand her awesome power. Witches cultivate their knowledge of all aspects of Nature's energy and work in concert with that endless supply to pay homage to deity and to heal themselves, their loved ones, and Earth herself.

Crystals and stones, plants, and oils all have their own individual vibrational frequency. In that respect, you might say they are very similar to humans. When you first start working with these materials, you may find that you migrate toward a particular crystal or stone, herb or botanical, or essential oil, just as you migrate toward certain people. Call it the coming together of two minds.

WORKING MAGICK WITH CRYSTALS AND STONES

You can use a crystal's or stone's energy to enhance your magick. Rose quartz, for instance, has a healing and loving energy. You could wear a piece of rose quartz to help heal a broken heart. Or you could build a cone of power and use toning to put your specific intent into a piece of rose quartz. Probably you would want to use a crystal or stone with an energy that "goes with" your intent and amplifies it. So it would make sense to put a loving or healing intent into rose quartz, while you might want to use malachite or bloodstone if your intent were to build wealth and a successful business.

When you first get a stone, cleanse it and energize it. You can do this by washing it in saltwater, seawater, or holy water. Then take it out into the light of the full Moon. The Moon will both cleanse and energize the stone. You might say it wakes it up. You can also awaken it by tapping it gently on sand after washing it, or giving it a gentle slap with your fingers. This action gets the stone's attention.

Magickal Properties of Crystals and Stones

Which crystal or stone you use for which magickal purpose will depend on your own feelings and intuitions. If you are drawn to a particular stone, try it. It may be just what you need. The following crystals and stones are generally considered to have the properties listed.

Crystal or Stone	Magickal Properties
Agate	Courage, strength, love, protection
Alexandrite	Luck, love, spiritual transformation, joy
Amazonite	Success, joy, self-expression; awakens heart and throat chakras
Amber	Changes negative energy into positive energy; protection
Amethyst	Courage, psychic energy, dreams, healing addictions, peace, happiness, love; opens crown chakra
Apache's tear	Protection, luck

Crystal or Stone	Magickal Properties
Aquamarine	Courage, purification, peace, psychic awareness, self-expression; balances all chakras
Aventurine	Money, luck, mental agility, visual acuity, peace, healing; opens the heart chakra
Azurite	Psychic energy, dreams, divination (the art of looking into the future), healing, concentration, transformation
Beryl	Energy, love, healing, psychic awareness, protection (from the weather and water)
Bloodstone	Courage, strength, victory, wealth, self-confidence, success in business and legal affairs; stops bleeding; helps regulate the first four chakras
Calcite	Centering, grounding, calming, purification, money, peace
Carnelian	Courage, sexual energy, verbal skill, peace; alleviates rage, jealousy, apathy, and fear
Celestite	Verbal skills, healing, compassion, calm; aids growth
Chrysocolla	Wisdom, peace, love, communication, vitality
Chrysoprase	Prosperity, luck, happiness, friendship, protection, healing
Citrine	Psychic powers, protection, creativity, sexual energy; deflects nightmares
Clear quartz	Intensifies energy (both positive and negative)
Coral	Protection from evil; resolves conflict
Diamond	Courage, strength, healing, protection, spirituality, mental and sexual abilities
Dolomite	Relieves sorrow
Emerald	Prosperity, mental and psychic abilities, dreams, meditation, visual acuity, love, peace, balance; opens the heart chakra
Fluorite	Balances and stabilizes relationships
Garnet	Strength, physical energy, healing, protection, purification, compassion; opens the root and crown chakras

(continues)

(continued)

Crystal or Stone	Magickal Properties
Geode	Fertility, childbirth, meditation, freedom, psychic ability, dreams, astral travel
Hematite	Grounding, calming, healing, divination, intuition, physical strength; aids restful sleep
Herkimer diamond	Enhances psychic abilities and clairvoyance
Infinite	Works with angels and your past, present, and future
Iolite	Establishes accurate visions
Jade	Healing, protection, wisdom, prosperity, love, long life, fertility, courage, peace
Jasper	Healing, protection, health, beauty, energy
Jet	Protection, hex breaking; dispels fear
Kunzite	Creativity, communication, peace, grounding, relaxation
Kyanite	Balances energies and aids in meditation
Lapis lazuli	Courage, joy, love, fidelity, psychic abilities, protection, healing, beauty, prosperity
Lepidolite	Peace, spirituality, physical strength, luck, protection, psychic ability, emotional balance; deflects nightmares
Lodestone	Cleanses crystals and aligns their energies, balances the chakras, removes obstacles
Malachite	Power, energy, protection, love, peace, business, vision quests, gardening
Marble	Protection, dream recall, meditation
Meteorite	Enhances work with spiritual and celestial beings
Moldavite	Psychic abilities, mental and emotional balance
Moonstone	Grounding, love, divination, sleep, gardening, protection, youth, harmony, magick, travel

Crystal or Stone	Magickal Properties
Obsidian	Grounding, divination, protection; deflects negativity
Onyx	Emotional balance, self-control, binding, protection (especially against someone else's magick), strength
Opal	Beauty, prosperity, luck, power, psychic abilities, vision, emotional balance
Pearl	Manifests truth, peace, and serenity
Peridot	Protection, prosperity, sleep, health, emotional balance, intuition
Rhodochrosite	Energy, peace, calm, love, mental activity, emotional balance; balances root chakra
Rhodonite	Peace, mental clarity, memory, confidence; opens crown chakra
Rose quartz	Love, peace, happiness, healing (especially of the emotions)
Ruby	Prosperity, power, courage, integrity, joy; deflects nightmares
Rutilated quartz	Intensifies any quartz energy, enhances communication
Sapphire	Psychic abilities, inspiration, love, meditation, healing, power, prosperity, protection
Smokey quartz	Healing, directing and absorbing energy, altered states; dissolves negativity
Sodalite	Healing, meditation, wisdom, calm, grounding, stress reducer
Sugilite	Eliminates negative energies, creates love and harmony
Sunstone	Protection, energy, health, passion, sexuality
Tektites	Enhances any energy field; enlightenment
Tiger's eye	Courage, prosperity, protection, energy, luck, common sense, honesty, divination; eases depression
Topaz	Protection, healing, dieting, prosperity, love, emotional balance, creativity

(continues)

(continued)

Crystal or Stone	Magickal Properties
Tourmaline	Love, friendship, prosperity, business, peace, sleep, energy, courage, protection, inspiration; opens the third-eye center, or the sixth chakra
Turquoise	Courage, protection, prosperity, luck, friendship, healing, communication, emotional balance, astral travel; strengthens all chakras
Unakite	Enhances personal power, changes negative energy into positive energy
Zebra stone	Promotes physical energy
Zircon	Protection (especially from theft), beauty, love, peace, sexual energy, healing, mental alertness, emotional balance

Finding, Buying, and Storing Crystals and Stones

Experts say you do not find a crystal or stone; it finds you. Most crystals and stones find their people in stores, although sometimes they hook up in quarries, riverbeds, forests, or beaches. If you are interested in crystals and stones, you probably should begin by reading as much as you can about them. You may also want to attend a rock and mineral show and investigate displays at metaphysical and mineral shops.

When looking for a crystal or stone, examine a lot of them. Pick up the stones and see how they feel. Pay close attention to which ones attract you most strongly. The crystal or stone that pulls your attention may not be the prettiest one in the bunch. If you are attracted to an ungainly stone, just know that it is the stone you are meant to have.

Some witches make crystal tinctures by soaking their stones in oil or distilled water. After a few days, they remove the stones and use a few drops of the liquid in tea or as anointing oil. Of course, they always check to make sure that their crystals are completely nontoxic and clean before they ingest any such tincture.

If you find a stone with a natural hole through it, hang on to it. Such holey stones, or holy stones, are rare. It's said that if you look through the hole, you'll be able to see into the Realm of Faery.

Unless you intend to use a crystal for scrying, you don't have to seek out the clearest, most translucent one. Crystals that have cloudy "ghosts," inclusions of other minerals, and other crystals inside of them carry a lot of energy. You may not need the stone or crystal right at the moment, but you will need it in the future. Sometimes a stone to which you are attracted will turn out to be something that a person you know needs. When this happens, you'll usually be able to tell because you'll have the urge to give that stone to the person in question.

You can also learn a lot from the stones themselves. To do this, you need to develop a relationship with your crystal. Try meditating with it and keep an open mind. Crystals communicate in subtle ways. Because they have been around for hundreds of years, their energy can seem very slow. After some time, you may start to receive messages from your crystal in the form of intuitions.

Stones and crystals are best stored in a cool, dark place. You can keep all your stones and crystals together in one bag and store it in your magickal tool chest. You'll need to cleanse your stones of energy periodically, especially if other people have been handling them. Because stones and crystals are so sensitive to energy, the people who touch them will have an effect on them, and you don't want someone else's negative vibe hanging around your stones. So cleanse your stones regularly with sunlight, moonlight, saltwater, or holy water.

WORKING MAGICK WITH HERBS AND BOTANICALS

You can use herbs and botanicals in many ways. If, for instance, you are working with abundance, you can choose an herb or botanical associated with abundance and sew it into a poppet or a dream pillow. Or you can place it in a small bag and wear it around your neck, or hang some of the herb in your bedroom. Some herbs can be burned, and others can be added to the water of your ritual bath. If you suffer from allergies, be aware that even in dried form herbs can be powerful allergens. You might want to try using herbal extracts instead.

Magickal Herbs and Botanicals

Here are a few herbs (plants used for seasoning or medicinal purposes) and botanicals (other plants) commonly used in magick.

A word of caution—many magickal herbs and botanicals can be toxic. Never ingest an herb unless you have checked it out with an herbalist first. You should know both the magickal and the medicinal properties of an herb. You should also be aware of any interactions an herb could have with another herb, with any medication that you are taking, or any possible allergic reactions it could cause. If you are thinking of making your own herbal tea, stop by your local herb shop first. Read to someone on staff a list of your ingredients to make sure what you are planning is safe. There are also many excellent books that can tell you whether an herb is edible or not.

Herb or Botanical	Magick Properties
Angelica	Protection, healing, visions; removes hexes
Balm of Gilead	Love, manifestations, protection, healing
Burdock	Protection, healing, happy home
Carnation	Protection, strength, healing, vitality
Celery seeds	Lust, mental and psychic powers
Dandelion	Divination, calling spirits, favorable winds
Dill	Money, love, lust, protection (especially of children)
Echinacea	Strengthens spells
Elderberries	Prosperity, protection, sleep, banishing of negative entities
Fenugreek	Money, mental powers
Frankincense	Spirituality, protection, banishing of negative entities, consecration
Gardenia	Love, peace, healing; enhances spiritual connections
Ginger	Power, success, money
Ginseng	Love, lust, vitality, wishes, healing, beauty, protection
Horehound	Protection, mental powers, banishing of negative entities
Hyssop	Purification, protection, prosperity

Herb or Botanical	Magick Properties
Irish moss	Money, luck, safe travel
Jasmine	Love, money, sleep, dreams
Juniper	Protection (especially from thieves), love, health, banishing of negative entities
Mugwort	Divination, clairvoyance, psychic powers, dreams, protection, strength, astral projection
Mustard	Fertility, money, protection, mental acuity
Nettle	Protection, healing, lust, banishing negative entities
Orris	Long-lasting love, divination, protection
Parsley	Purification, protection, lust, fertility
Passion flower	Peace, friendship, popularity, sleep
Pennyroyal	Protection, peace, strength (especially during travel), antiseasickness
Peppermint	Healing, purification, sleep
Pine	Healing, protection, fertility, money, banishing negative entities
Poppy	Fertility, love, money, luck, sleep
Raspberry	Love, protection of the home; alleviates labor pains
Rose	Love, beauty, luck, psychic powers, protection
Rosemary	Protection, purification; chases away nightmares
Rue	Mental powers, healing, love, curse-breaker
Sage	Wisdom, prosperity, healing, longevity, money
Slippery elm	Stops gossip, aids verbal development
Star anise	Psychic and spiritual powers, luck
Valerian	Love, sleep, purification, protection, peace
Vetivert	Love, luck, money, protection against theft
Violet	Spiritual protection, luck, love, lust, wishes, peace, sleep, healing

(continues)

(continued)

Herb or Botanical	Magick Properties
Willow	Love, divination, protection, healing
Witch hazel	Protection, chastity, healing of broken hearts
Wormwood	Psychic powers, protection, safe car travel, love, calling spirits

Finding, Buying, and Storing Herbs and Botanicals

You can grow your own magickal herbs and botanicals, or you can buy them at a metaphysical or herb shop. Some of them may even be available at a local farmers' market. If you grow your own, you can consult an almanac to find good planting and harvesting times. You should also read up on the best methods and necessary precautions for drying your herbs. Some herbs, especially toxic ones, can give off a noxious vapor while drying. There are many books available about growing and preparing plants for magickal purposes. If herbs are new to you, you may be more comfortable buying what you need. As you gain experience, you can begin to forage for herbs or cultivate your own magickal garden.

You'll want to store your dried herbs in a cool, dry place and keep them out of the light. Sunlight will bleach your herbs and pull the energy out of them. You should also make sure that insects or mice don't get into them. If you find that your herbs have become infested, don't use them. They should keep for a long time, but once they do begin to deteriorate, dispose of them and get new. When you need to throw herbs away take them outside and give them back to the earth.

Because plastic can start to break down, it is best to keep your herbs in glass jars. Use big labels so you can clearly mark each container. In addition to the herb's name, put the date of purchase on each label. It's also a good idea to note on the label if the herb is toxic. (And if so, keep the jar in a safe place out of reach from children, pets, and inquisitive adults!)

It's also a good idea to take a class on the medicinal uses of herbs. Many metaphysical shops offer such classes, as do herb shops, and farmers' co-ops. If your local herb store does not have classes, you should at least be able to ask questions of the herbalist on staff.

Many herbs, such as the hallucinogens that were used in flying ointment—a toxic preparation that, when rubbed on the body, caused witches in the historical past to feel as if they were flying—are readily absorbed through the skin. So, when preparing fresh herbs for drying, it's a good idea to wear gloves to protect yourself from any toxins and safeguard your skin in case you turn out to be allergic to any of the plants you are using.

WORKING WITH ESSENTIAL OILS

You can use essential oils for healing, cleansing, blessing, banishing, empowering, anointing, and consecrating. And, of course, you can enjoy them for their great scents! When working with pure essential oils, wear gloves; the oils are very potent and can burn your skin. Because they are so strong, essential oils are usually cut with carrier oil, such as grapeseed, apricot, jojoba, almond, or vegetable oil. This way they won't damage or burn your skin. In addition, carrier oils help to stretch your dollar. When you're dealing with an essential oil that can cost as much as $90 a dram (the equivalent of 0.0625 of an ounce), you'll want to stretch it as much as you can!

After they are mixed with the carrier oil, essential oils are blended together according to your magickal purpose. When designing a mixture, you'll also want to pay attention to how well the different scents combine and your own preferences and associations. You can also mix in the energy of plants and stones by adding herbs or crystals to your oils.

When blending oils, you should concentrate on putting energy and your magickal intent into the mixture. You can do this by saying a chant or incantation, such as …

> *With this magick oil I mix,*
> *Another magickal spell I'll fix.*
> *Water, Fire, Earth, and Air,*
> *To know, to will, be silent, and dare.*
> *As this magick is sent out to thee,*
> *Let it grow and set it free and three.*
> *This is my will, so mote it be!*

Or you can mix your oil and then charge it during ritual by raising a cone of power and directing the energy into the oil. One easy way to do this is to stand before one of the Elements in your magick circle. If you were working with love, passion, or sexuality, you would face Fire in the South. Repeat over and over the name of the Element that represents your intent, in this case Fire. Start out softly and slowly and increase the speed, volume, and intensity until you feel ready to burst with all the energy. Grab your vial of oil and send the energy into the oil. Once you've done that, your oil is charged with the power of the Element and ready to use. Many witches like to dress candles for candle magick with essential oils. You can also use it to anoint your body, your magickal tools, or other objects.

Another great way to use essential oils is to put a few drops of them in an oil burner. The oils don't actually burn, but are heated to the point of evaporation, and their scent fills the air. The scent will affect you psychically and physically. You can use certain oils to stimulate a meditative state during ritual or use them as part of your routine to prepare for ritual. Either way, you can't go wrong. And your nose, surrounded by great, natural smells, will be happy, too!

All About Essential Oils

Consult the following list of essential oils and their magickal correspondences before making a blend. Pick your oils based on your magickal purpose and your sense of smell. But however delicious they may seem, never, never ever take essential oils internally! Be aware that camphor oil can cause toxic reactions in some people, even at a dilution of 4 percent essential oil to a base of carrier oil. For safety's sake, don't use camphor oil on the skin, even in a blend.

Essential Oil	Magickal Properties
Basil	Money, harmony; promotes sympathy, happiness, peace
Benison	Peace; increases power, awakes the conscious mind
Bergamot	Money, protection
Black pepper	Protection, courage, banishing; spices up a romance
Camphor	Purification, healing (particularly of respiratory problems), chastity
Cardamom	Love, lust, sexual energy

Essential Oil	Magickal Properties
Cedar	Balance, spirituality, courage, dreams
Chamomile	Meditation, peace, dreams
Cinnamon	Money, psychic awareness, lust, purification
Clove	Courage, protection, sexual attractiveness, lust; adds spice to any situation
Coriander	Love, health, and healing
Cypress	Consecration, protection, healing (especially of psychological pain), longevity
Eucalyptus	Health, healing (especially of respiratory problems), purification
Geranium	Protection, happiness, love
Ginger	Sexuality, love, courage, money, prosperity
Grapefruit	Purification; banishes a sour disposition
Jasmine	Love, psychic awareness, dreams, peace, sex
Juniper	Protection, meditation, purification, healing, communication
Lavender	Health, peace, relaxation, sleep, purification, love
Lemon	Energy, mental clarity, wit, cleansing
Lemongrass	Psychic awareness, purification, lust
Lemon verbena	Love, purification
Lime	Purification, cleansing, protection, fertility, love
Lotus	Healing, luck, opening to spirit
Magnolia	Meditation, psychic awareness, love, fidelity
Myrrh	Spirituality, meditation, healing, blessing
Neroli	Happiness, protection, purification
Oak moss	Money, prosperity, fertility
Orange	Purification, heightened awareness, luck
Palmarosa	Love, healing, protection

(continues)

(continued)

Essential Oil	Magickal Properties
Patchouli	Money, physical energy, attraction, protection, sex
Peppermint	Purification, mental energy, psychic powers
Petitgrain	Protection, removing evil or negativity
Pine	Purification, money, healing, cleansing
Rose	Love, peace, sexual desire, beauty, maternal love
Rosemary	Love, healing, energy; breaks hexes
Sandalwood	Spirituality, meditation, sex, healing, psychic awareness
Sweet pea	New friends, love, happiness
Tangerine	Strength, power, vitality
Tuberose	Calm, peace, love, happiness, psychic powers
Vetivert	Money, prosperity, attractiveness; breaks hexes
Yarrow	Courage, love, psychic awareness; banishes negative entities
Ylang-ylang	Love, peace, sex, healing

Finding, Buying, and Storing Essential Oils

When you first start using essential oils, you'll probably want to buy prepared blends. For example, it is often cheaper to buy a small bottle of house blessing oil (which can include basil, angelica, hyssops, and lavender oils, among others) than it is to acquire all the ingredients to make the blend. Whether you're buying blends or pure essentials, you should make sure that what you're getting really are essential oils and not fragrance oils. Fragrance oils, synthetics that are designed to smell like the real thing, often trigger asthma attacks in people who are susceptible. Although many witches don't like to use fragrance oils, sometimes a substitution is necessary. If you do decide to get some oils, buy only the few you need the most. There's no sense in buying a bottle of each kind of oil if you're not going to use them. And buy in small quantities as oil will go bad.

Keep your oils and oil blends in a dark place, preferably in a dark glass bottle. Light and heat will cause your oils to go rancid. Most blended oils will keep for about six months. Remember to label and date all your oils before you put them away. And smell them before you use them—you don't want to work magick with rancid oil.

BONUS: WORKING WITH FLOWER MAGICK

We already talked about herbs and botanicals. But did you know that many common garden flowers have magickal properties? You can use them the same way you use herbs. But please don't eat them. Many flowers are poisonous, and others can be very irritating to the skin and the digestive tract.

If someone you love brings you flowers (especially roses), dry them after you are done enjoying them. Flowers that have been given as gifts hold lots of great energy you can use in your magick. You can dry them by tying them together and hanging them upside down in such a way that air can circulate around and through them. The dried petals will hold the loving energy of the giver. Use the petals in any magick having to do with love, and your energies will be amplified by the love that is already in the flowers.

Flower	Magickal Properties
Blue Bell	Constancy, strength, luck, truth
Buttercup	Prosperity, happiness
Camellia	Gratitude, prosperity
Daffodil	Love, luck
Foxglove	Protection (poisonous plant!)
Geranium	Fertility, health, protection, love
Honeysuckle	Money, psychic and mental powers
Hyacinth	Love, protection, happiness
Lavender	Happiness, healing, peace, sleep, purification
Lilac	Protection, beauty, love
Lily	Protection, purity, breaking love spells
Lily of the Valley	Happiness, mental powers (poisonous plant!)
Marigold	Protection, dreams, psychic powers, business
Mullein	Courage, love, divination, protection
Periwinkle	Love, lust, money, protection
Primrose	Love, protection

(continues)

(continued)

Flower	Magickal Properties
Rose	Love, healing, divination, fertility
Rhododendron	Peace, strength (poisonous plant!)
Snapdragon	Protection, friendship
Sunflower	Wishes, wisdom, health, fertility
Tulip	Love, happiness, dreams
Yarrow	Courage, protection, love, psychic powers
Zinnia	Love, lust, strength

To use flowers in your magick, dry the petals and grind them with your mortar and pestle. You can mix them with herbs or essential oils. Or you can add flowers to a vial of oil. Flower petals also make nice additions to dream pillows, the water of your ritual bath, or potpourri.

PART 4

MAGICKAL TIMING— WITCHES' BREW

As long as you are prepared—in mind, body, and spirit—you can do magick at any time. You can also select the best time of the day, week, month, or year for the particular type of magickal work you are planning to do. You'll find out how to time Elemental energies and harness the points of the pentagram.

In addition, we'll also look at your level of preparedness. Are you ready to live the Witches' Pyramid—*to Know, to Dare, to Will, and to Keep Silent?* We'll also look to the heavens, and you'll learn how the stars and a basic knowledge of astrology can enhance your magickal workings. Do you want to learn even more about magick? In this part, you'll find hints, tips, and guidelines for how you can start writing and doing your own spells. We've written some spells for you to try to get you started. We've also designed a year-and-a-day-long seasonal calendar for you to follow as you enter into your new practice of Wicca and witchcraft.

Dedicating yourself to a religious path is a profound choice to make. To help you grow with your Wicca practice, we've shown you how to create magickal gardens, both possible indoors or out. As your garden takes root below and reaches up and outward above, so will your life as a witch ground itself in the Earth while you reach to the Goddess.

CHAPTER 18

TO KNOW, TO DARE, TO WILL, TO KEEP SILENT

When looking at the larger picture, the macrocosm, the Witches' Pyramid can represent the entire concept of the Wiccan lifestyle. This is perhaps the toughest challenge of all. But without a firm base of strong convictions, a witch cannot progress. The stronger and richer the soil of your conviction, the stronger and better witch you will grow to be.

BEFORE THE MAGICK

The Witches' Pyramid is a kind of magickal checklist that some witches use before they do magick. It describes a few conditions you may want to meet prior to performing magick. You must be ready to …

1. **Know** who you are and what you are. You have to *know* the rules. You must *know* what magickal rites you are going to be doing. And you must *know* your intention.

2. **Dare** to do what you are planning. Do you *dare* to follow through?

3. **Will** the magick to happen. Do you have the ability and the *will* to follow through? Can you *will* your energy to make it happen?

4. **Keep silent** and not brag or boast about what you have done. You don't take your magick for granted, but you sit back quietly, watch, and know that you are growing.

The idea of the Witches' Pyramid—to know, to dare, to will, to keep silent—is used by many witches as a way to direct, assess, and redirect their magickal practice. It's a handy tool you can use to check your development. By reviewing the four steps of the Witches' Pyramid, you can see if you are following its good advice. You can also see how well you are meeting your magickal goals.

TO KNOW …

To know is the first building block of the Witches' Pyramid. Before witches do magick they must know what they are going to do, what magickal tools they will need, what their intent is, and what the karmic repercussions of their actions will be. And finally, they must know that their magick is going to happen.

… If Wicca Is Right for You

Most people who come to the Craft have always marched to the tune of a different drummer. Or as Denise puts it, they've felt like round pegs in square holes and have not found the right answer in other religions. Maybe as a kid you hugged a tree and felt there was life and something really precious inside it. Or maybe you have always had a special feeling for animals. Many Wiccans were plagued by a sense of dissatisfaction when they practiced religions that don't take into account the central role of Nature and our planet Earth. If God created both humankind and Nature, how is it possible, they ask, that he cares only about humans? Isn't Nature equally his creation? Doesn't he care about it, too? And where is the Goddess energy? How can she be ignored when considering the life-giving nurturance of Nature?

Most Wiccans don't like to be told what to do or to hear stock answers. They find their truths for themselves and define their own inner spirituality. Many have found great joy and fulfillment in working one-on-one with deity. Wiccans are also open to new ideas, to the existence of other realms, and are seekers on the unconventional path of the spirit.

... Where to Start

You have to start within yourself. After you have determined that you want to try Wicca, you need to start listening and gathering information. Open your ears and pay attention to what people are talking about in metaphysical shops. Visit libraries and bookstores. Surf the internet, and read everything you can get your hands on about the Craft. The more you read, the more it all starts to make sense and form comprehensible patterns. The ideas that you have heard and sort of believed will fall into place. But you have to be hungry for it because it does involve working, searching, and studying on your part. You also should start by trying simple rituals.

... How to Advance Yourself in the Craft

Before you start to practice magick, it is really important that you take the time to learn the basics. Learn all you can about deity, the Elements, and ritual. Only when you really understand what magick is should you try to work with it. You need to know a lot before you commit yourself to the Wiccan path.

... What to Do with the Responsibility

The responsibility of being a witch is not a burden. It is part of what it means to be empowered. When you shoulder your responsibilities instead of avoiding them, you become empowered. The more you are willing to take on, the stronger you will become. And the more empowered you are, the more able you will be to empower others and to change the world. In helping to change the world, you want to make sure that you do not force your beliefs on anyone. You may believe fervently in the Wiccan path, but you cannot try to convert your friends and relatives. You have to maintain respect for their beliefs. If you live with other people, you may have to be discreet and not discuss your personal beliefs.

TO DARE ...

We've reached the second level of the Witches' Pyramid. When it comes to magick, you have to determine if you have the desire to cause real change to happen. Do you dare, in your life at the present time, to make the life changes to become a witch?

... To Take the Challenge

Becoming a witch is an immense challenge. It could require that you change your entire lifestyle and will probably spur you to look at the world and yourself differently. For one thing, you'll have to confront yourself. A lot of us would rather not examine the truth about ourselves. Neither do we wish to contemplate what we have done and are doing with our lives. But we need to confront these issues squarely and change the aspects we don't like.

You may face the challenge of outgrowing friendships as you begin to change. If you're a woman and are part of a family in which the women are very dependent, you will seriously disturb the family dynamics when you begin to stand on your own two feet, as all witches must do.

Choosing to walk the Wiccan path is also a challenge in terms of your stamina. To be a witch, you need the mental stamina to study for years. No one will hand you the answers. You must seek out your own truths.

... to Accept Responsibility

There are many responsibilities that come with being a witch. One of the major responsibilities is to understand what you are doing. If you practice magick without a firm base of knowledge and an understanding of your own actions, you can make your life miserable. And you can make the lives of other people miserable as well. When you become a witch, you literally take on responsibility for the care of the Earth. Sharing what you have is part of the bond you have made with the Goddess. In keeping with your promise, you'll want to put food out for the local birds, squirrels, raccoons, and other animals that live nearby.

As a witch, you also have to take responsibility for yourself and your own power. That may mean looking at different ways to handle situations in your life. Witches don't whine and yell about situations they don't like. They consider, and act. As a witch you can no longer blame things on other people. You have to accept the responsibility for what occurs in your life. So, instead of blaming your financial problems on others, you will take control and fix them. Witches don't expect to be taken care of. Once you become a witch, you will probably find that rather than having people come to your rescue, you'll dare to do the rescuing yourself.

... To Confront the Issues of the Day

As a witch, and as an informed citizen, you need to read the newspaper and listen to the news. Keep abreast of politics on the local, national, and worldwide levels because the decisions made by political leaders affect what happens to our planet. The people in office may facilitate the destruction of wetlands, the building of pipelines, the pollution of our oceans, the devastation of global warming, or they may help to protect ecologically sensitive areas. You need to pay attention to what is going on, get out and vote, and get your friends to vote, too. If you keep your head in a box of sand, many acres of land and many species of animals could be lost. We all have the responsibility of care to Mother Earth. You also need stamina to get involved in what is going on around you, in this realm and in other realms. During our lifetimes, advances in technology, genetics, and healthcare, for example, will bring radical and profound changes. Are you ready?

... To Get Involved in Your Community

Many Wiccans put their energies into political, social, or environmental action. The important thing is that you reach out to the world beyond you. Add your voice to the Pagan voices calling and working for social and political change. Keep up with the political issues of the day. Or check out your local community service center and see what's happening in your community.

TO WILL . . .

"To will" is the third level of the Witches' Pyramid. When working magick, this is seen as gathering the will to form a cone of power and focusing the will so that you can see the magick happen as you send the energy out. Can you muster sufficient willpower to become a witch? We can see it happening, but can you?

... To Follow Through

Most people start their study of witchcraft with all the good intentions in the world. They run out and buy all these wonderful new tools—athames, cauldrons, pentacles, and candles—but then don't know what to do with them. They sit down with a book, discover how much work is involved, and put everything in the box with the old knitting. If you want to be a witch, you've got to have willpower on several fronts. You'll need the willpower to get up and go to class, network, and meet people. If you want to be a witch, you need to go out and take that class on magick or Tarot or essential oils. Focus your energies and muster the willpower to make yourself do it. Lots of people want to do it, but wanting isn't enough. You have to act on that want.

And willpower comes into play with your ritual as well. You will need willpower to make sure you say a devotion to the God and Goddess each night before you go to bed. You'll also need to exert your will to keep ritual special. Your Wiccan practice involves dedication so you may grow in the faith. Resist the temptation to give up without having really tried. Yes, being a witch is a challenge, but challenges have their own rewards. And the more accustomed you become to facing and meeting challenges, the more you will feel able to do so. Remember, real magick takes time.

... To Make a Change in the World

Witches are strong-willed leaders who keep at it. As a leader in your community, you will inspire your neighbors to care for the Earth and take on community projects, as well. Sometimes it takes a witch to grab the broom by the handle and get things started.

... To Stand Firm in Your Beliefs

Some people, when they find out you are a witch, will try to save your soul. They could very well talk about you behind your back, ridicule you, and even fear you. Some of these people may be individuals you had counted on as your friends. It can be very difficult when people are questioning your beliefs all the time. What makes matters worse, many of your questioners will be angry with you because they don't understand what you are doing, or what you believe.

People may challenge you by quoting from their religious texts. When they do this, you need to exercise your will to stay calm and firm in your beliefs. Don't let others deter you from your path. But you also don't want to lose your temper. Be kind and gentle; be respectful, but stick to your beliefs. (If you find yourself getting angry, look inward at the source of your feelings. You may want to spend some time journaling or meditating on the issues that come up for you.) Be patient with those who doubt you, and be patient with yourself.

TO KEEP SILENT ...

We have reached the fourth and final level of the Witches' Pyramid. When practicing magick, witches keep mum about what they have done. You should never brag about how effective your magickal workings have been. Many witches find this the hardest part. While becoming a witch, silence is still golden.

... And Do Good Works

Do your good works in the public realm, but don't brag about what you have done. Your good actions will serve as an example to others who then may decide to do good works or even investigate the Wiccan path for themselves.

... To Listen and Learn

You should discuss the Craft and what you know only when you are working with your teacher or when you yourself are teaching. You can also talk about your knowledge if someone asks you a question. You should speak in a gentle and nurturing manner, and remember that yours is not the only answer. Within the tenets of Wicca there is only one hard-and-fast rule, "An it harm none, do what ye will." There are many ways to honor the Wiccan Rede. There is no one right answer. Each individual must find his or her own truth.

THE MICROCOSM—YOUR MAGICK

We've talked about the larger applications of the Witches' Pyramid. Now, we'll look at how you can use this idea when preparing to do a spell. By now you probably get that before you cast your spell, you'll want to make sure you fulfill all the conditions of the Witches' Pyramid. You can also use the pyramid as a way to help organize all the parts of your spell and record them in your Book of Shadows. In the example here, you can use some, just a few, or all of the ingredients and factors listed. And, when casting your spell, feel free to speak some of the words written here, or write your own chant or incantation.

Protection Spell Using the Witches' Pyramid

I know ... correspondences for protection:

♦ Flower: Carnation

♦ Herb: Comfrey

♦ Incense: Dragon's Blood

♦ Stone: Onyx

♦ Phase of the Moon: Waning or Full

♦ Sign Moon is in: Leo (or other Fire sign)

♦ Time of day: Noon

I will ... the existence of a protective bubble of energy around me.

You can say the preceding words, and then envision the bubble. See it surround you. Visualize your bubble deflecting negative energy that may come toward you.

I dare ... to incorporate all my knowledge to create this spell of protection.

You can say the preceding words while you gather all your ingredients together. Place them in a small bag to form a power bundle. Then hang the bundle on your door. Each time you pass by your protective power bundle, remind yourself that you dare—you dare to go forth into the world with your magick.

I keep silent ... and I don't brag about or advertise my magickal workings.

Spells, like flower bulbs or newly planted seeds, do their early growing in the dark, deep under the rich Earth's soil. Let them start their work in silence.

CHAPTER 19

MAGICK'S ASTROLOGICAL CORRESPONDENCES

Remember that phrase "As above, so below"? So let's look at the sky and get an idea of what is going on up there. You may know a little about astrology. You probably know your Sun sign. Maybe you check your horoscope in the paper on a regular basis. But there is more to astrology than the 12 signs of the zodiac. As a witch, you'll want to familiarize yourself with astrology, and you'll probably want to have your chart drawn up by a professional astrologer. Astrology will help you to understand yourself—your potentials and challenges—and the people and energies that surround you.

A WITCH'S CALENDAR

Because the Wiccan holidays occur on days of actual astronomical events—the full Moon, the solstices, and the equinoxes, for example—most witches pay attention to the stars. Commercially available witches' calendars track these important events. They also record the movement of the planets through the 12 signs of the zodiac. You probably know that the Sun's position in the sky at the time you were born determines your Sun or zodiac sign. But did you know that there is also an Element associated with your date of birth? Find your birth date, your Sun sign, and the Element associated with your sign on the following chart.

Date	Sign	Element
March 21–April 20	Aries ♈	Fire
April 20–May 21	Taurus ♉	Earth
May 21–June 22	Gemini ♊	Air
June 22–July 23	Cancer ♋	Water
July 23–August 22	Leo ♌	Fire
August 22–September 22	Virgo ♍	Earth
September 22–October 23	Libra ♎	Air
October 23–November 22	Scorpio ♏	Water
November 22–December 22	Sagittarius ♐	Fire
December 22–January 21	Capricorn ♑	Earth
January 21–February 19	Aquarius ♒	Air
February 19–March 21	Pisces ♓	Water

The Element of your sign can help you understand your sign better. And, of course, you can learn more about the energy of a given period of time by considering the prevailing sign and its Element.

Planets, Their Symbols, and Energies

The planets, in which group we will include the Sun and the Moon, represent various energies. In your birth chart, the planets describe your desires, soul, will, vitality, and your mental and emotional nature. They also represent the people in your life. Here are the planets with their symbols and energies.

The Planets and Their Symbols	Energies
Sun ☉	Self, creativity, life spirit, willpower
Moon ☽	Emotions, subconscious, instinct, memories
Mercury ☿	Communication, mental activity, intelligence
Venus ♀	Love, beauty, art, sociability, harmony, money, resources
Mars ♂	Action, desire, courage, physical energy, ego
Jupiter ♃	Abundance, luck, wisdom, learning, philosophy, exploration, growth
Saturn ♄	Responsibilities, limitations, perseverance, discipline, structure
Uranus ♅	Change, originality, radicalism, liberation, the unexpected, intuition
Neptune ♆	Idealism, spirituality, intuition, clairvoyance, subconscious
Pluto ♀	Regeneration, destruction, rebirth, transformation, power

When preparing to do magick, you may decide you want to pull on the energy of a certain planet. The planet might be one that has special significance in your chart, or it might represent the particular energies you'd like to have help you on a given day. Before you call on a planet, be sure you know all you can about that planet's energy. You also should know where in the sky the planet will be located on the day you plan to do ritual.

Zodiac Signs and Their Planetary Rulers

Each sign of the zodiac is ruled by a planet (or two). One way to determine which planets have significance for you or the spell you want to cast is to look at the planetary rulers. Here are the signs and their planetary rulers.

Zodiac Sign	Planetary Ruler(s)
Aries ♈	Mars and Pluto ♂ and ♀
Taurus ♉	Venus ♀
Gemini ♊	Mercury ☿
Cancer ♋	Moon ☽
Leo ♌	Sun ☉
Virgo ♍	Mercury ☿
Libra ♎	Venus ♀
Scorpio ♏	Pluto and Mars ♂ and ♀
Sagittarius ♐	Jupiter ♃
Capricorn ♑	Saturn ♄
Aquarius ♒	Uranus and Saturn ♅ and ♄
Pisces ♓	Neptune and Jupiter ♆ and ♃

A sign shares certain characteristics with its ruler. For instance, Libras are usually concerned with harmony and balance and so, too, is Venus, the planetary ruler of Libra. As we noted earlier, Libra is an Air sign. While Libra shares some traits with Taurus, which is also ruled by Venus, Libra embraces these traits in an Airy way—through ideas, communication, and mental abilities—while Taurus, as an Earth sign, remains more physical and grounded. Some signs have more than one planetary ruler. Both Pluto and Mars, for instance, rule Scorpio. People born under the sign of Scorpio tend to exhibit characteristics of Pluto—the planet of power, destruction, and regeneration—and of Mars—the planet of physical energy, boldness, and warrior ways.

LUNAR CORRESPONDENCES FOR WICCAN RITUALS

When planning ritual, in addition to paying attention to the phase of the Moon (waxing, waning, new, or full), you also want to look at what sign the Moon is in. Because the Moon travels around the earth quite fast, the Moon usually passes through all the signs of the zodiac in one month. That means that in a given month, the Moon spends a day or so in each sign. Each sign the Moon passes through has a different vibe, and that energy will affect your ritual. If you know the Moon's sign, you can plan your ritual so that lunar energy aids you in your endeavors. (For more about the energies associated with each sign of the zodiac, see Chapter 20.)

♦ **Moon in Aries** ♈ Energy and ideas abound under this Fire sign. A great time to start new things. Also great for leadership, willpower, and spiritual conversions.

♦ **Moon in Taurus** ♉ A dependable, steady energy emanates from this Earth sign. A great time for dealing with issues of love, money, abundance, and material goods.

♦ **Moon in Gemini** ♊ A quickly moving force describes the energy of this Air sign. Super for communication, writing, and travel.

♦ **Moon in Cancer** ♋ This Water sign has a nurturing energy. A great time for looking at issues centering on your home, domestic life, and emotional support network.

♦ **Moon in Leo** ♌ Courage and power are what this Fire sign is all about. An excellent time for working on acting, self-presentation, and fertility. Also, a good time to increase your own power and courage.

♦ **Moon in Virgo** ♍ A focused energy prevails under this Earth sign. A great time to start self-improvement projects. Work on issues related to the intellect, employment, health, and anything involving details.

♦ **Moon in Libra** ♎ The energy of this Air sign is one of balance. The best time for issues of emotional balance, artistic expression, karmic justice, and spiritual work.

- ◆ **Moon in Scorpio** ♏ This Water sign holds the energy of desire and transformation. A good time for change, sex and sexual fantasies, and psychic growth.

- ◆ **Moon in Sagittarius** ♐ The energy of this Fire sign is one of exploration. Great for ferreting out the truth, legal matters, and publishing enterprises.

- ◆ **Moon in Capricorn** ♑ This Earth sign carries an energy of achievement. Perfect for working on issues of your career, organization, political matters, and recognition.

- ◆ **Moon in Aquarius** ♒ This Air sign is all about revolution. A fabulous time for creativity, problem-solving, or any issue that involves freedom. Also good for cultivating psychic abilities and friendships.

- ◆ **Moon in Pisces** ♓ This Water sign is one of compassion. A great time for healing, working with dreams, clairvoyance, or telepathy. A good vibe for musical projects.

VOID OF COURSE MOON

As the Moon travels around the Earth through the signs of the zodiac, it "goes void" between each sign. The period between the times when the Moon leaves one sign and enters the next one is called the Void of Course Moon. During this time, it's as if the Moon were in a tunnel. Much the way you lose the station you were listening to on your car radio when you drive through a tunnel, the Moon's energies don't do what they usually do. The Void of Course Moon or Moon Void period is best for nonmaterial, passive activities—play, yoga, psychotherapy, prayer, meditation, and sleep. While you can do ritual at this time, this is not a good time to start on magickal workings. It's also not a good time to make decisions, start a business, or buy things.

PLANETARY POSITIONS FOR WICCAN RITUALS

Using the planets to figure out the best time for your ritual and magickal workings is a bit like doing word problems. Say you wanted to work some magick to improve communication between you and your lover. You decide you want to work with Mercury, the planet of communication. You might want to plan your ritual for a time when Mercury is in Taurus, a sign ruled by Venus, the planet of love. There are many different ways to work with the planets as they move through the signs of the zodiac. Make sure to keep records of ritual you do. Fill out a Magickal Record each time you work (see Appendix B), and you will start to see what works best for you.

♦ **The Sun** ☉ The energy of the Sun is the most powerful of all the "planets." Start new things when the Sun is in Aries, the first sign and the sign of fresh beginnings. Of course, you can start a project at other times, but spring is a great time for new work. Be aware of the energy found under each sign of the zodiac, and do what feels right for your magick.

♦ **The Moon** ☽ The second major influence on the energies that you feel here on Earth, which we discussed earlier in this chapter. Initially, you'll want to really focus on only the Moon and the Sun. Looking at lunar and solar energy combined can help you pinpoint the timing of your spells. For example, if the Sun is in Libra and the Moon is in Cancer, use magick to nurture your sense of balance or to balance your nurturing energies.

♦ **Mercury** ☿ The planet of communication, thinking, logic, reason, intelligence, and education. When Mercury is retrograde, which happens three times a year for periods of about three weeks each, communications go awry and travel plans meet with obstacles. Because much of magick is about communication, Mercury retrograde is a good time to take a break from spellcasting. Use this time to reflect, reconsider, and review your magickal workings.

A planet is retrograde when it appears to move backward in the sky. Of course, the planet does not move backward. It just looks that way as viewed from Earth. All the true planets have retrogrades. (The Sun and the Moon do not.) Because Mercury is fairly close to Earth, its retrograde period has a big impact. When a planet is retrograde, its energy is reversed, reconsidered, or turned inward.

♦ **Venus** ♀ The planet of love, harmony, and balance. Want to add some enthusiasm to your love life? Try working on that area when Venus is in Aries, the sign of new beginnings and fresh energy. The Venus retrograde period is a great time to reconsider your relationship and material needs.

- **Mars** ♂ The planet of action, desire, courage, physical energy, and ego. The Mars retrograde period is a good time to sit back, look at your motivations, and develop new strategies for dealing with your anger issues.

- **Jupiter** ♃ The planet of abundance, luck, wisdom, learning, philosophy, exploration, and growth. The Jupiter retrograde period is best used for internal growth and preparation. Concentrate on developing yourself to benefit from opportunities offered to you.

- **Saturn** ♄ The planet of responsibility, limits, control, discipline, and structure. During a Saturn retrograde, work to become aware of your own power and examine how you fit into society. Are you letting societal rules limit you and your potential?

- **Uranus** ♅ The planet of change, originality, radicalism, liberation, the unexpected, and intuition. The Uranus retrograde period is a time to look at the role you are playing in making the world a better place.

- **Neptune** ♆ The planet of idealism, spirituality, intuition, clairvoyance, and the subconscious. The retrograde period is best spent tuning in to the collective unconscious.

- **Pluto** ♀ The planet of regeneration, destruction, rebirth, transformation, and power. The retrograde period is a time to look at how you are contributing to the evolution of humankind and the Earth. Try to become more conscious of how you impact the Earth and all of her creatures.

PLANETARY RULERSHIP OF HOURS

Now you know about Sun signs, the impact of the Moon in the various signs, and the movement of the planets. There's even a way to determine what hour of the day is best for your magick. As you may know, different days of the week are associated with different planets. The ancients decided that there should be seven days in a week because that was how many planets they could see. Each day is named after one of these seven. Here are the days of the week and the planets that rule them. In some cases, if you look at the Spanish names for the days, it's easier to see which planet rules which day.

Day of the Week	Ruling Planet
Sunday	Sun ☉
Monday (*lunes* in Spanish, like lunar)	Moon ☽
Tuesday (*martes* in Spanish)	Mars ♂
Wednesday (*miércoles* in Spanish)	Mercury ☿
Thursday (*jueves* in Spanish)	Jupiter ♃
Friday (*viernes* in Spanish)	Venus ♀
Saturday	Saturn ♄

And on each day, every hour also has its own planetary rulership. The planet whose day it is rules the first hour of that day. In other words, the Sun, the planet of Sunday, rules the first hour after sunrise of Sunday; and the Moon, the planet of Monday, rules the first hour after sunrise of Monday, and so on. The remaining 23 hours in each day are ruled by different planets throughout the day. The following table details all of the hours of the week and the planets that rule them. Note that in this system there are 12 hours between sunrise and sunset. This means that each daylight "hour" is actually shorter than a real 60-minute hour. Each hour here is $^1/_{12}$ of the time between sunrise and sunset.

Planetary Rulership of the Hours

Hours	Sun.	Mon.	Tues.	Wed.	Thurs.	Fri.	Sat.
1 (sunrise)	Sun	Moon	Mars	Mercury	Jupiter	Venus	Saturn
2	Venus	Saturn	Sun	Moon	Mars	Mercury	Jupiter
3	Mercury	Jupiter	Venus	Saturn	Sun	Moon	Mars
4	Moon	Mars	Mercury	Jupiter	Venus	Saturn	Sun
5	Saturn	Sun	Moon	Mars	Mercury	Jupiter	Venus
6 (midday)	Jupiter	Venus	Saturn	Sun	Moon	Mars	Mercury
7	Mars	Mercury	Jupiter	Venus	Saturn	Sun	Moon
8	Sun	Moon	Mars	Mercury	Jupiter	Venus	Saturn

(continues)

Planetary Rulership of the Hours   (continued)

Hours	Sun.	Mon.	Tues.	Wed.	Thurs.	Fri.	Sat.
9	Venus	Saturn	Sun	Moon	Mars	Mercury	Jupiter
10	Mercury	Jupiter	Venus	Saturn	Sun	Moon	Mars
11	Moon	Mars	Mercury	Jupiter	Venus	Saturn	Sun
12	Saturn	Sun	Moon	Mars	Mercury	Jupiter	Venus
1 (sunset)	Jupiter	Venus	Saturn	Sun	Moon	Mars	Mercury
2	Mars	Mercury	Jupiter	Venus	Saturn	Sun	Moon
3	Sun	Moon	Mars	Mercury	Jupiter	Venus	Saturn
4	Venus	Saturn	Sun	Moon	Mars	Mercury	Jupiter
5	Mercury	Jupiter	Venus	Saturn	Sun	Moon	Mars
6 (midnight)	Moon	Mars	Mercury	Jupiter	Venus	Saturn	Sun
7	Saturn	Sun	Moon	Mars	Mercury	Jupiter	Venus
8	Jupiter	Venus	Saturn	Sun	Moon	Mars	Mercury
9	Mars	Mercury	Jupiter	Venus	Saturn	Sun	Moon
10	Sun	Moon	Mars	Mercury	Jupiter	Venus	Saturn
11	Venus	Saturn	Sun	Moon	Mars	Mercury	Jupiter
12	Mercury	Jupiter	Venus	Saturn	Sun	Moon	Mars

Say you were planning some candle magick to help you feel more attractive. You might want to light that candle on Friday, the day of Venus. Or you could light the candle at the hour of Venus on another day, or, to increase the Venus energy, you could light the candle at the hour of Venus on Friday. If you wanted to communicate your love better, you could light a candle on Wednesday, the day of Mercury (the planet of communication) at the hour of Venus. If you are fascinated by all this, you might enjoy *The Complete Idiot's Guide to Astrology, Fourth Edition*, by Madeline Gerwick-Brodeur and Lisa Lenard. It is chock-full of everything you need to know about the planets and their movements.

CHAPTER 20

THE RIGHT TIME FOR MAGICK

There is a right time for every action. After reading the last chapter, you know about the major astrological issues involved in choosing when to do ritual and magick. But there's more …

If you coordinate your magick with the optimum time of day, position of the planets, and season, you can make it stronger. Of course, you don't have to make elaborate plans. You can use magick at a moment's notice with little or no advance planning, and you'll probably still get results. When there is something important coming up in your life (and you have tried all the mundane solutions at your disposal), why not plan ahead and give your magick an energy boost? Make sure that you write down what you've done and the circumstances under which you've done it in your Book of Shadows so you can compare magick that has been planned to what happens when you don't plan.

MAGICK ALL DAY LONG

Different parts of the day have different energies, and you'll need to consider the inherent energy that surrounds us at these various times. Remember that you can do your magick any time you want. So, if you are not free to practice ritual at 2 A.M. on a Wednesday during the full Moon, when the time might be perfect for your new spell, don't worry. However, your magick will be even more effective if you do your workings at the time of day that is most conducive to the energies you are using. The great thing about working with daily magickal timing is that you'll always get another chance tomorrow.

Morning Magick: Sunrise

The Sun is up; the birds are singing. Doesn't this seem like a good time to start something? Well, it is! Even if you are a late sleeper, you are fresher in the morning when you first get up, and so is your energy. You can channel that extra energy into your magick and start something new with the new day.

This is also a great time to get rid of any negativity that might be hanging around you from the previous day. If you've had a fight the night before with a parent or partner, or have run into aggravating issues at work, chase away those bad feelings to start your day with a clean slate.

First thing in the morning is also a good time to work with addictive behaviors and bad habits. For example, if you overeat compulsively, you could do a spell in the morning to have a binge-free day. Most people start their diets in the morning. So, to help yourself reach your goals, why not do magick when you first get up, and have an empty stomach? Do this when the Moon is waning, and you'll have the willpower to get rid of the weight.

The start of the day is also good for magick having to do with business, school, or anything else that gears up in the morning. You might want to work with employment issues—getting a job, receiving that raise or promotion—early in the day. If you're looking for a job, magick at this time could help connect you with the people who have the right job for you.

Midday Magick: Sunshine

During the middle of the day the Sun is at its strongest. This is a good time to call on the strength of the God. You might want to work on overcoming a weakness that you have, or seeing a problem with greater clarity and focused intent. The energy of the God and the

Sun can help you to do just that. Most people take a break from working in the middle of the day. Reset yourself. Have some lunch and do some magick to help you see the project of the day through. Ask for guidance or inspiration to rethink something that needs to be started all over again. Do some magick for success at high noon.

Evening Magick: Crepuscular Light

The light of the Sun fades in the sky and evening is drawing nigh. You might get home feeling tired and cranky from your long day. Although lots of people come home and have a drink or raid the refrigerator, why not arrive home, take a hot shower, and do ritual instead? This is a great time to do magick to break up routines or banish bad habits. If you do ritual one night when you come home, it may stop you from eating that bag of chips. And the next night you'll be more likely to reach for a piece of fruit. Work magick to boost your willpower, to help you relax, and to give yourself calmness and serenity.

Nighttime Magick: Resonating in Tune

After the Sun has set, we are better able to feel the energy of the Moon and the Goddess. This is a great time for divination and working with psychic energies. You might also want to work with issues involving love or beauty. And of course, this is a good time to reflect on what has happened during the day. By the time you reach night, you may be pretty overwhelmed with your work, school, or family. Doing magick at this time can help you remember that things are not always the way they appear. Getting some perspective and sorting out the events of your day can help you banish any negativity around you. That way you can start the cycle again in the morning with a fresh outlook and renewed energy. You'll be able to see what you've already accomplished and plan for what still needs doing.

Try not to stay up very late doing divination when you need to get up early the next morning. Nighttime may be a great time for looking into the future and tapping into your psychic energy, but even witches need sleep. And remember—you can do your magick at any time. Dreamtime can be a great time to harness magickal energy. Many witches use lucid dreaming to gain insights into their psyches and foster self-knowledge by exploring the subconscious mind.

MAGICK ALL WEEK LONG

You can also look at the cycle of the week when planning your magick. Remember in the previous chapter we talked about each day of the week being named for a different planet? Well, the days of the week also have genders based on their planetary associations. You'll want to keep this in mind, too, when planning the optimum time for your magick.

Sunday (Sun ☉) Magick

The energy of Sunday, which is named for the Sun, is male. Sunday is the best day of the week to work with issues involving fathers and other authority figures. Sundays are great for working on questions of leadership, confidence, money, prosperity, and power. Focus on health, vitality, energy, and happiness. Sunday is a good day to call to God deities and work with their energy if you feel ready to do that.

Monday (Moon ☽) Magick

The energy of Monday is associated with the Moon and is female. Monday is the best day of the week to work with Moon energy, so you might want to do divination. Focus on issues involving mothers, nurturing, fertility, and growth. Monday is also a good time to work for clarity, beauty, or to help with women's issues. Monday is a good day to call to Goddess deities and work with their energy if you feel you are ready to do that.

Tuesday (Mars ♂) Magick

Tuesdays are full of the male energy of Mars. The name Tuesday comes from the Germanic God Tiu. Tiu, like the Roman God Mars and the planet Mars, is associated with war. This energy is one of courage, success, and attraction. It is a good time to give attention to issues dealing with violence, competition, or survival. The right use of power and sexuality can be explored today. Tuesdays are good for questions of money, endurance, and leadership.

Wednesday (Mercury ☿) Magick

Wednesday is named for Mercury, a planet with male energy. Wednesday comes from the Old English name "Woden's Day." This name was a direct translation of the Latin term mercurii dies, "day of (the God and planet) Mercury." When they translated the name, they also translated the God into one to which local people could relate. This is a great day for working with communications, thought, self-expression, wisdom, and the arts. Matters related to social media, the internet, and electronic devices are a focus today. The energy of Mercury will also aid magick with issues of addiction and psychology. Wednesdays are good days to do divination.

Thursday (Jupiter ♃) Magick

The male energy of Jupiter prevails on Thursdays. Thursday comes from the Old English and Old Norse word or name for "Thor's day," a translation of the Latin name that meant "Jupiter's day." This energy is conducive to growth and expansion, business, prosperity, abundance, success, and health. This is a day to focus on equality, equal pay for equal work, entrepreneurship, and goals. Thursdays are also great times to focus your magick on the big issues in your life. Magick for work/life balance is harmonious energetically today. Growth energy can mean getting out in Nature to nurture that work life balance.

Friday (Venus ♀) Magick

Friday is associated with Venus and has female energy. Friday comes from the Old English name Frigedaeg, which is derived from the name of the Norse Goddess Frigg, who, like both the planet and the Goddess Venus, is associated with love. Fridays are great days for workings having to do with love, beauty, and romance. The Venus energy of Fridays will also aid magick involving healing, protection, loyalty, fidelity, trustworthiness, and women's issues. Focus on partnerships and family harmony. Issues involving pets and animals can be considered.

Saturday (Saturn ♄) Magick

The Saturn energy of Saturday is female. Work with divination and psychic abilities. Saturn energies will aid magick concerning the elderly, illness, death, and end-of-life issues. Make connections to the deceased, both human loved ones and adored pets and animals that have passed over. Connect with Spirit guides and other entities. Saturday is also a good day to do binding spells (if you have the magickal experience and confidence to work with binding energies) and to deal with constrictions, limitations, or infidelity.

TIMING ELEMENTAL ENERGIES

You've read quite a bit about the Elements and are probably starting to get a good feel for their energies. In addition to being associated with a direction and a color, each Element is associated with three astrological signs (see Chapter 19).

Air Time

Gemini, Libra, and Aquarius are the Air signs of the Zodiac. When we are under an Air sign, you may want to do Air magick. One way to do this is to take a piece of paper in a color that corresponds with your magickal intent. Write your intent on the center of the paper, place 1 tablespoon of an appropriate incense in the center of the paper, bring up the corners, and tie them together with a piece of cord in an appropriate color. Then burn the packet of incense. Use a feather to fan the smoke and help send your intent through the Air and off to Spirit.

♦ **Gemini ♊: May 21–June 22** Symbolized by the Twins, Gemini has an amusing, witty quality. You might want to tap into that vibe and bring more humor into your life. Gemini energy is also concerned with communication, writing, knowledge, information, consistency, patience, focus, flexibility, motion, and travel. A great time to work magick to learn something new, facilitate communication, travel, and to change—especially your mind.

♦ **Libra ♎: September 22–October 23** Symbolized by the Scales, Libra is concerned with balance, harmony, and justice. This period is also a good time to work magick concerning charms, compassion, art, fairness, anger, dishonesty, indecisiveness, ambivalence, fickleness, diplomacy, culture, cooperation, and idealism. You might want to use your workings to establish cordial relations with someone from whom you have been estranged. This is also a great month for magick that has to do with mental energy, idealism, spirituality, love relationships, friendship, and popularity.

♦ **Aquarius ♒: January 21–February 19** The energy of Aquarius, which is symbolized by the Water Bearer, is inventive, creative, and original. This is a great time to do something different, maybe even something revolutionary. Aquarius energies will help you bring something to light so that it is obvious. You might want to use this renegade energy to make a statement or take a stand on an issue. This is also a great month for humanitarian projects. So maybe you'll use the psychic abilities this month fosters to come up with a revolutionary solution to the problems of homelessness and hunger in your community. Aquarius energy will help you with issues involving idealism, individuality, open-mindedness, originality, science, detachment, inflexibility, repression, logic, temperament, tolerance, and innovation.

Fire Time

Aries, Leo, and Sagittarius are the Fire signs. During these periods, you may want to use candle magick. Anoint the appropriate color candle with oil such as Aries, Leo, or Sagittarius oil, place your intent into the candle, and build your cone of power with a fiery chant for blazing magick!

- **Aries ♈: March 21–April 20** Symbolized by the Ram, Aries says, "Charge ahead and start that new project now!" Aries energy will help you do it. This is also a good time to work magick around issues of creativity, anger, independence, new beginnings, self-awareness, taking action, patience, intolerance, putting others before yourself, and following through projects to completion. You also may want to focus your magick on issues involving leadership, assertiveness, aggression, and enthusiasm.

- **Leo ♌: July 23–August 22** Symbolized by the Lion, Leo is all about courage, showmanship, creativity, fertility, and willpower. You might want to do magick to enhance your leadership skills or to become the leader of a group. Leo energy will also help you with issues involving fun, power, inspiration, influence, dignity, pride, arrogance, conceit, laziness, insecurities, self-indulgence, status, generosity, ambition, physical appearance, drama, and being in the spotlight. Yes, Leo, time for your close-up!

- **Sagittarius ♐: November 22–December 22** Symbolized by the Archer, Sagittarius energy is about enthusiasm, exploration, freedom, independence, and fun. This is a great time to work magick to free yourself of the things that bind you—addictions, bad habits, objects that you don't need. You could also look at questions involving truth, honesty, optimism, philosophy, legal matters, generosity, humor, intuition, inspiration, travel, visualization, temper, patience, procrastination, realism, responsibility, restlessness, and publishing. Do some magick to have a really good time.

Water Time

Cancer, Scorpio, and Pisces are the Water signs. During these time periods, you may want to perform Water magic. You could do this by taking a magickal bath and infusing yourself with the energies that you wish to obtain. Or you could use your magickal bath to wash away any energies that you wish to banish.

♦ **Cancer ♋: June 22–July 23** You can use the nurturing energies of Cancer, which is symbolized by the Crab, to work magick having to do with your home, warmth, family, and family relations. This is also a good time to look at issues involving feelings, sensitivity, memory, intuition, loyalty, protectiveness, sentimentality, sympathy, possessiveness, insecurities, manipulation, and giving of the self. Work magick to allow you to give of yourself more freely, or you could do magick for someone else (with that person's consent, of course). Bring your family together or build a strong team or support network.

♦ **Scorpio ♏: October 23–November 22** You can use the energy of Scorpio, symbolized by the Scorpion, to effect change in the areas of your life involving sexuality, desire, and power. This is another good time to work on issues of leadership. You also could look at the profound questions—life, death, birth, sex, and transformation. Scorpio energy is also conducive to developing psychic awareness, and issues involving emotions, passion, trust, regeneration, willpower, jealousy, secrecy, self-destructive behavior, and intolerance.

♦ **Pisces ♓: February 19–March 21** Because Pisces energy, which is symbolized by the Fish, is compassionate, this is a good time for healing work of any kind. This is also a great time to work magick to develop compassion or spirituality. You might want to work with issues concerning emotions, empathy, faith, forgiveness, dreams, intuition, clairvoyance, and telepathy. Pisces energy can also help with questions of illusion, laziness, sacrifice, sensitivity, loyalty, music, mysticism, understanding, pessimism, and self-indulgence. Get in touch with your higher power.

Earth Time

Taurus, Virgo, and Capricorn are the Earth signs. Under an Earth sign, you may want to perform Earth magick to engender slow, steady growth. To do this, empower some seeds with your magickal intent, then plant them in a pot. If you plant your seeds on the first day of the astrological month, you can empower them every day of the month. When the plants burst forth, so will your magick.

♦ **Taurus ♉: April 20–May 21** Taurus, which is symbolized by the Bull, is conducive to new beginnings. But the feeling is more stable and grounded than that of Aries. This is a great time to work magick concerning issues of prosperity, success, patience, beauty, friendliness, security, comfort, laziness, sensuality, greed, materialism, possessiveness, stubbornness, loyalty, comfort, peace, harmony, and dependability. You might want to do some work on your love life. You could also work magick on some volatile issues—if you have a lot of conflict at work, for instance—and the energy of the month would help to lend stability and steadiness to your task.

♦ **Virgo ♍: August 22–September 22** The vibe during the month of Virgo, which is symbolized by the Virgin, is one of service, organization, and self-improvement. This would be a good time to work magick to help you analyze and solve a problem that has been eating at you for a long time. This is also a good time to focus your magickal work on global problems and their solutions. Virgo energy will also aid you with issues of mental energy, efficiency, logic, methodology, dependability, judgment, obsessions, perfection, criticism, health, employment, responsibility, and details, details, details.

♦ **Capricorn ♑: December 22–January 21** Symbolized by the Goat, Capricorn is all about ambition, achievement, and self-control. So tap into that Capricorn vibe and reach your career goal. The energy of Capricorn is also concerned with efficiency, politics, structure, organization, responsibility, cautiousness, discipline, loyalty, commitment, reservation, responsibility, tradition, economics, domination, materialism, perfectionism, stubbornness, forgiveness, and helping others.

REAL MAGICK TAKES TIME

Avoid allowing feelings of being overwhelmed to stop you from doing your magick. Know that you don't always have to do everything at the best possible time. You can do magick at any time. Sometimes we do magick when we can, and sometimes we act when we have to. The type of magick that witches practice never yields immediate results on the material plane. Sorry, but that is the truth. What can happen quickly is the magickal change inside you—the feeling that you get when you practice ritual and know that your magick will happen. Often you can come away from your magickal workings with empowerment and a "spiritual high."

Real change—and that is what real magick effects—takes time. And magick will take its time. The goal you are working toward will manifest when it is supposed to. Sure, on rare occasions you will put your magick out there, and the next day the phone will ring and that ace assignment that you have been after will be yours. But know you have gotten it quickly because it was the time for the work to be yours. Usually you put your magick out there and then you wait a week or two, or a month, or more.

CHAPTER 21

MORE WAYS TO WORK MAGICK

We'll give you some specific spells to use. We'll also give you some ideas for how you can utilize still other materials in your magick. Remember, it is your magick, and your creativity is a part of it.

Magick is like a recipe; it's a pinch of this and a pinch of that, plus your intent. Magick works because you direct energy to make the desired result happen. As you know, you should always try the mundane solutions before you turn to magick. But remember, even if you do magick, you must still continue to act on the mundane plane. You'll still need to follow a healthy diet if you want to lose weight, and you'll need to take photographs as well as a few business and graphic design classes if you want to launch your own photography business.

Okay then, let's make magick.

POPPETS

Poppet magick—magick involving a specially empowered doll—is great to use for binding spells, healing, or losing weight. Some witches shy away from poppet magick because it reminds them of the stereotyped notion of voodoo dolls. (Many of us carry a negative impression of this Afro-Caribbean religion, but we shouldn't. Healing is at the heart of voodoo, which is often described as a mixture of African ancestor reverence, Native American Earth religion, and European Catholicism. And voodoo, like Wicca, gives all women a central and powerful role.) Others avoid poppet magick because they don't like to sew! But poppet magick is good, strong magick. Remember to keep any poppet you have made in a safe place. The doll you make represents the person for whom you have done the magick, so you wouldn't want anything unplanned to happen to that doll.

Let's say you want to do poppet magick to heal a sick friend. First, ask the friend if you have permission to do magick. If so, assemble the poppet while inside your magick circle, and put any herbs or other magickal ingredients that you want to use inside it. While you sew the poppet up, infuse it with your intent. Then give it to your friend. You can also make a poppet to safeguard the health of your pet. In such a case, you would make the poppet in the shape of your pet and keep it on your altar.

What You Need to Make Poppet Magick

To do poppet magick, you'll need some supplies:

♦ Fabric in a color that corresponds to your magickal intent. (For a list of colors and their magickal associations, see Chapter 16. Or use white, which substitutes for all colors.)

♦ A needle and thread

♦ Stuffing. (You can use scraps of cloth, cotton, wool, or fiberfill.)

Then you could add some of these:

♦ Herbs, flowers, fruits, or vegetables that correspond to your magickal intent

♦ Essential oils that correspond to your magickal intent

♦ Crystals or stones that correspond to your magickal intent (see Chapter 17)

- A piece of cloth, hair, or fingernail clippings that belong to the person for whom you are creating the poppet, or a photograph of that person

- Amulets or talismans

- Magickal messages or symbols. (You can write these on paper or fabric and sew them into your poppet, or you can attach them to the outside.)

If you want to incorporate the Elements into your magick, you could attach, sprinkle, or stuff your poppet with the following:

- Sand to represent the Element of Earth

- Feathers to represent the Element of Air

- Incense to represent the Elements of Air and Fire

- A magickal potion to represent the Element of Water

- Saltwater to represent the Elements of Water and Earth

- Holy water to represent Water and Spirit

After you are finished making the poppet, cleanse and consecrate it by passing it through each of the Elements. Use the smoke of your incense to represent Fire and Air and a sprinkling of salt water to represent Earth and Water.

How to Undo Poppet Magick

The biggest advantage to poppet magick is that it can be used for magick that is of temporary duration. If you want to stop the spell, take the poppet apart. If you have done a weight-loss poppet for yourself, once you have reached your goal, dismantle the poppet so you do not continue to shed pounds.

When you undo a poppet, you can use this chant to unravel the magick as you dismantle the poppet. Poppet magick is hard to contain, and so not as easily undone as performing a simple chant. This is just a start to help resolve the spell when the magick is done. Remember magick takes time to do, and time to undo as well.

With this spell that I've begun,
I now wish the magick to be done.

Be aware that the poppet represents a person (or animal) and should be treated gently and stored where it will be safe and secure. You never burn a poppet. If you want to work with the Element of Fire, you can try candle magick instead. In addition, you should make sure that the place you store your poppet is safe. The kids shouldn't play with it, and neither should the dog get his teeth into it. Put the poppet away until the magick manifests. Once the magick has come to pass, take the poppet apart and bury the pieces.

CANDLE MAGICK AND INCENSE MAGICK

You can use candle magick for just about any magickal purpose. You need to charge your candle with your magickal intent before you light it. This is the same when working with incense. Then, when you do light it, you're sending out your magick. See the magick rising toward the Gods. You can help send the magick upward by using a feather as a fan.

What You Need for Candle Magick

Candles come in lots of shapes, sizes, and colors. You can buy a candle in the form of a cat, angel, shell, skull, flower, or human. You can also get candles that have knobs, candles that burn for seven days, bicolored candles, multi-colored candles, multi-wick candles, floating candles, and ones that are one color on the inside and another color outside.

Here's what you'll need for your candle magick:

♦ A candle in a color that corresponds to your magickal intent

♦ A small pointed crystal or your bolline (magick knife used for cutting physical objects)

♦ An essential oil that corresponds to your magickal intent

♦ Herbs that correspond to your magickal intent

♦ A mortar and pestle

♦ A candle holder

To do a candle spell to bring yourself money, use your crystal or bolline to carve your desire on the candle. It's nice to use a crystal because the crystal itself will also pull in energy and infuse the candle with added magickal power. Be specific about what you write on the candle. And remember, be careful what you wish for because you just might get it.

Then dress the candle with a magickal oil. When doing candle magick to bring something to them, many witches use this candle-dressing method. Hold the candle so that one end faces you. Start applying oil to the candle from the middle and move your hand toward you. Then turn the candle around and coat the other half by moving your hand toward you. If you were doing magick to take something away, you would coat the candle with oil by moving your hand away from you. If you make your own magickal oils, you can empower the oil with herbs that also represent the intent of your spell.

You can also load a candle with magickal herbs. To do this, hollow out the bottom of your candle. Mix your herbs with some essential oil and fill the hole with the herb and oil mixture. (When you mix herbs and essential oils together, it's easiest to add the oil to the herbs, not the herbs to the oil. Drip oil on the herbs a little at a time and stir them together. If you try to add the herbs to the oil, they will just float.) Concentrate on your magickal intent while you work. Seal the hole up with wax, and your loaded candle is ready to use! When the candle burns down to your herb mixture, the herbs will ignite and blast your magick out to its destination. Be extra sure that you use this candle in an area where you won't start a fire, because the herbs can flare up quite a bit. It's usually a good idea to place your loaded candle in a deep candle cup or in the bathtub to finish burning.

A Candle Magick Spell

Here's an example of a candle magick spell, a blessing for a new or expectant mother. It's nice to do this spell at the baby shower or at a get-together to welcome the baby into your Wiccan community. The mother to be or the mother and new baby sit in the center of a circle of friends and family. Using a crystal, a bolline, or a needle, the people in the circle carve symbols of their blessings and good wishes for mother and child into a white candle. You can use tapers, which are traditional, or pillar candles, which are likely to get knocked over.

Anoint the candle with an essential oil of protection, love, and blessing. Myrrh, yarrow, or rosemary oils are all good choices. Light the candle and place it on a central altar next to the mother and child. Have all the participants chant, directing their energy toward the candle at the center of the circle:

> *As this candle burns down low,*
> *All of our good wishes glow.*
> *All the smoke that twirls above you*
> *Brings the blessings of those who love you.*

Chant until you can feel that the energy is raised and has been funneled into the candle. At the height of the chanting, put out the candle. Then present it to the mother. She may burn her magickally charged candle at any time to bring the love and blessings of her friends to her and her new child.

Another Candle Magick Spell

After you have built your cone of power, put the energy into your candle, and lit it, you can use this all-purpose incantation to send your magick on its way:

> *My goal in this flame I see.*
> *Bring my wish, my dream to me.*

An Incense Magick Spell

For this spell, which you can use to bless and safeguard your home and yourself, you will need a stick of incense. Light your incense and say the following chant:

> *Smoke and ember at the door,*
> *Bless this entrance evermore.*
> *Bless all those who come and go.*
> *With this sign, I make it so.*

As you chant these words, draw a pentacle deosil (clockwise) in the air with the stick of smoking incense. Visualize the smoke as a protective force encircling your home.

KNOT MAGICK

To do knot magick, you need a length of string or cord. Make sure your cord is long enough to easily tie nine knots. Use a string or cord in the color that corresponds to your magickal intent. This type of magick is great for either bringing items to you or sending items away from you. Knot magick is another type of magick that is easy to undo. All you have to do is untie the knots. You could even use it for weather magick to prevent rain for a short period of time, like the day you are holding a rummage sale to support your local animal shelter.

Spells for Knot Magick

Put the energy of your magickal intent into the string or cord. Envision your magick happening, and while you do this, tie nine knots in the cord as you say your spell. With each couplet, tie another knot. Tie the first knot on one end of the string. Then tie the second knot at the other end. The third knot goes in the middle, and the fourth knot goes between the first and the third knots. Refer to the following chart to see where each knot goes.

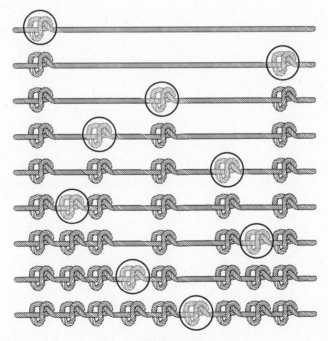

Knot magick.

Sometimes nine-knot spells, like the one here, are called witches' ladder spells. The following spell is a general blessing. It's great to use if you are moving into a new house or life situation. If you use thick, multicolored yarn, your finished collection of knots can be used as a decoration for the wall of your home:

> *By knot of one, the spell's begun.*
> *By knot of two, my magick is true.*
> *When I tie three, I call health to me.*
> *When I tie four, no evil comes through my door.*
> *By knot of five, I flourish and thrive.*
> *The magick of knot six, all my troubles soon will fix.*
> *The seventh knot tied safe and sound*
> *will bring good company around.*
> *Eighth knot on the string, great wisdom will bring.*
> *By knot of nine, success is mine.*

When you're finished, place the tied-up string on the wall to bless your home. If you want this magick to be permanent, you can bury the cord in the earth or you can burn it. But we think it is better to hang on to it. If you keep your knotted cord, you can undo the magick whenever you like by untying the knots in reverse order and chanting:

> *With each knot that I untie,*
> *Release the magick, let it fly.*
> *And it harm none, set it free,*
> *This is my will, so mote it be.*

You can also use knot magick, or the untying of knots in a spell, to rid yourself of bad habits. First, while concentrating on your magickal intent, tie your cord as in the witches' ladder spell above. Then undo each knot in the reverse order, while chanting to reinforce your magickal intent.

POTIONS, POWDERS, AND MORE

As you have probably noticed, witches use a huge variety of materials when working spells. Besides all the things we have discussed so far, you can also work with potions, powders, and even various kinds of paper.

Potions are probably among the first things that many people think of when they hear the word *witch*. When you hear the word *potion*, do you imagine a dark night, a bubbling cauldron of noxious brew, and three crones bent into the steam? Well, that sounds like a scene from *Macbeth* to us! Real witches mix real potions. They usually make them in their kitchens, and the ingredients are rarely so exotic as to include eye of newt. Potions are infusions of magickal herbs you can use as a tea or to anoint an object. Remember, never make a potion out of a poisonous plant if it is to be consumed.

Most potions are made by adding boiling water to magickally charged herbs and letting the herbs infuse for about 10 minutes, or by putting them into cold water and letting them sit in the sun all day to infuse naturally. If you heat your potion, it's best to cover the herbs while they are infusing so none of the vapor escapes. Another way to make a potion is to place a jar of water and herbs in the light of the full Moon and let it set overnight. Then, empower the solution and place it in a dark closet until the next full Moon, when it will be ready. Until then, remember to shake your potion gently once or twice every other day while it's brewing.

When the potion has steeped, strain out the herbs and your potion is all set to do its work. You could use a potion made from banishing herbs to clean your house of a negative influence. You could add a love potion to your bath. You could also rub it on your skin or spritz it on a poppet. You can also make love potions using a wine base instead of water. Here are two potions you may want to try.

Love Potion

You will need:

- 4 oz. distilled water

- 4 drops lavender oil

- 5 drops cinnamon oil

- 3 drops clove oil

- 1 pinch Dragon's blood powder

- 1 small rose quartz crystal

Combine the ingredients and place in a bottle; infuse with your intent. Let it sit for nine days. Each and every day at the same time, reinforce your intent into the potion. After the ninth day, spray the potion in the room before the object of your affection comes over. Or heat the potion in a room diffuser. You can also place a tablespoon or two in the washing machine and let your clothes become infused with the potion's energies. Wear your magickally infused clothes around your honey to enhance your personal charm.

Stay-Away Potion

This potion does just what its name implies. It will keep people you don't want hanging around from hanging around you.

You will need:

- 4 oz. distilled water

- 2 tsp. black pepper

- 2 tsp. salt

- 2 tsp. asafetida powder (an umami enhancer in Indian vegetarian cuisine)

Mix all the ingredients together and place your intent into the potion. Be specific about which people you want to have stay away. Let the potion sit for three days. Each day at the same time of day, reinforce your intent into the potion. After three days, take the potion outside and sprinkle it at the border of your property or where your walkway meets the public sidewalk. Refresh the potion and reinforce your intent every week until your problem goes away.

Powder Magick

After you have gained some experience with spells and working safely with herbs, you may want to try powder magick. (Always consider toxicity when working with herbs and never ingest an herb unless you know for certain it is safe. Never leave toxic herbs or substances out where they can be ingested by or harm any living thing.) To work powder magick, you mix up a powder and charge it with your magickal intent. Then you blow the powder, and with it your magick, into the air. Or you can bury the powder, sprinkle it on the ground or around a room, place it inside a poppet, or mix it into clay for a talisman. Magickal powders are made from finely ground herbs, a binder—such as benzoin, mastic, or orris root—and colored talc. You can also add glitter, or powdered silver or gold. Mix up a batch of your own custom-made powder.

Sweet Dreams Powder

♦ Finely ground chamomile

♦ Mugwort

♦ Lavender

♦ Sage

♦ Unscented blue talc for base

Use one part each of the herbs and four parts talc. If you can't find blue talc, use white and add a little food coloring. Use your completed dream powder as a body powder, dusting yourself lightly before bed. In summer if you are sweaty or have a sunburn, dust a little dream powder over your sheets, keeping most of the powder at the foot of your bed. Then brush off the powder and climb into bed. You should have sweet and prophetic dreams.

Paper Magick

You can work paper magick without much in the way of special supplies. Build a cone of power and put the energy into a piece of paper by writing your magickal intent on it. Use magickal symbols or a magickal alphabet if you like. Then light the paper on fire and watch it burn. As it burns, concentrate on your intent and see your magick rise up and go to work. You could use colored paper in a shade that corresponds with your magick. You can also use fancy paper such as rag or parchment, but keep in mind that both of these burn quite slowly. If you want to send your magick out quickly, buy some flash paper at your local metaphysical store. Flash paper has been specially treated to burn up in a flash. You light it and, poof, it is gone. Flash paper is great for magick that you want to send out with an extra kick and is a great way to work with the Element of Fire.

Celebrate Diana's Bow, the first sliver of waxing moonlight to appear in the night sky, by writing your intent for something new—a new project, a new pet, a new relationship—on a piece of flash paper and burning it. Draw Down the Moon and feel the Goddess energy infuse your intent for your new project with Diana's resourcefulness, strength, and single-minded purpose.

CHAPTER 22

DOING SPELLS

Putting spells together is one of the central arts of witchcraft. Writing spells gives you a great opportunity to use your knowledge and creativity. Crafting a spell can take time and thought, although sometimes you'll see what you want to do all in one flash. The more familiar you are with all the magickal substances—herbs, oils, and stones, to name a few—the easier it will be for you to tailor a spell to your specific intent and circumstances.

Remember, you resort to crafting a spell to attain your goal only after you have exhausted all the mundane actions available to you. If you haven't really tried to get what you want through nonmagickal channels, then you probably won't be able to focus your energy sufficiently, and it is unlikely that your magick will work.

WRITING SPELLS USING RHYMING AND WORDS OF POWER

It's nice to have a magick chant you can say when casting your spell. So even if you don't think you can do it, you should give rhyming a chance. As you write your spell, think about what it is you want to accomplish. (Even if you aren't using rhyme, you should write out what you want to say as part of the spell.) You might want to call an Element as part of your spell. A chant that draws on the Element of Fire for love and passion might sound like this:

> *Fire strong, Fire bright,*
> *Put love in my heart tonight.*
> *Passion true, let me burn,*
> *My beloved I'll not spurn.*
> *Fire, heat us with your power.*
> *Let love reign hour upon hour.*

After writing a chant like this one you may decide to reconsider. Maybe you want to add some emotional Water energy to your spell:

> *Fire, Fire warm my heart,*
> *Passion to me now impart.*
> *Water, sweetener of emotion,*
> *Bring me love and devotion.*
> *Passion and tenderness come to me.*
> *This is my will, so mote it be.*

Which Elements you work with is your choice. Know that once you have decided on your words and invested them with your energy and passion, they become your words of power—even if you think you can't write or that your rhymes sound silly. Your words represent your will and desire, because they come from your heart. When you repeat them over and over again, your energy will intensify; you will see your magick happen in your mind's eye, and your words will direct your power to manifest a change.

A STEP-BY-STEP GUIDE TO SPELL CASTING

Your spell is written. You've gathered your tools. Now you are ready to cast your spell and send out your magick. You can work your spell inside ritual or you can do magick by itself. If you plan on doing ritual, prepare your space. Get out all your tools, take your ritual bath, and dress in your ritual outfit. Cleanse and consecrate your space, pull up your magick circle, and start your ritual. Usually magick is done in ritual after you have called the God and Goddess and before you partake of cakes and wine.

If you are not going to do ritual, cleanse and consecrate your sacred space, pull up your magick circle, summon the Element you need for your spell (or the Elemental of that Element) or call deity, then do your magick.

If you have written a chant as part of your spell, you'll use it to help you build your cone of power. It's a good idea to have all the steps of your spell written out. Bring that paper into the circle with you so you can refer to it while you are working.

Doing Magick for Someone Else

You already know you should do magick for another person only if you have that person's permission. If you do magick for someone without permission, you are impinging on that person's free will and you will have to pay karmic consequences. If a person asks you to do magick, make sure the magick you have been asked to do is worth doing. You need to know if the person is sincere and if the magick is really for that person, or if he or she really intends it for someone else. You also need to be certain that the person has done all he or she can on the mundane level to achieve his or her goal.

When doing magick for someone else, keep in mind that it is never okay to accept money for your magickal work. People will want to pay you, but you cannot take their money. First of all, moneymaking is not what magick is for. If you do accept money for your magick, your magick will start to lose its spiritual value. Taking money for your magick can also create greed within you. In addition, you need to know that charging someone for magickal work is illegal in many states. The people you have helped may be very uncomfortable with the feeling that they owe you. What you can do is have them donate the money they would have given you to the charity of your choice. Alternatively, ask them to pass on your good deed by helping someone else. This way your magickal energy helps the person you did your working for and others as well.

How to Break a Spell

Some spells were just made to be broken! You can write a spell that undoes itself. Here's an example of a spell for enhancing karma that will break itself:

> *Listen to this spell I weave, take heed in what is told,*
> *For your hatred and unkind deeds will return to thee threefold.*
> *By the rise of the next full Moon a witch will sit and weep,*
> *For all the sorrow ye have sewn, thee will begin to reap.*
> *It's not too late to change your ways and break this painful spell,*
> *Replace the hatred in your heart so only love may dwell.*
> *So mote it be.*

Once the person in question has stopped acting and feeling hateful, the spell will break itself. This is also an example of a spell that will influence someone else's behavior. Notice that the spell itself does not mete out any punishment. It just serves as a reminder to the individual that there will be karmic payback for his or her negative actions.

One way to try to undo a spell you have cast is to take a cord and a pair of scissors, consecrate them, and empower them with your intent. As you cut the cord into little pieces, say the following chant:

> *Recall the magick of this spell,*
> *The intent that I sent out,*
> *From me to there and back again,*
> *This time I have no doubt.*
> *Break the spell and set it free,*
> *This now is my command:*
> *The energy cometh back to me,*
> *Return it to my hand.*

Cut up the entire cord. While cutting, hold all the pieces in one hand and don't let them drop. When you finish, take all the pieces and bury them in the earth to ground the energy you sent out.

MAGICK, SPELLS, AND ELECTRONIC DEVICES

Most twenty-first century witches own and use one or more electronic devices in their everyday lives. More and more, those devices are playing a part in the practice of magick. For many witches, electronic devices used in magick are controversial, but for many others, smart phones and tablets are finding a way into their magickal life. Electronic devices harness energy. Magick harnesses energy. Capturing that flow of energy may facilitate spells and magickal workings. Let's see how.

Electronic Devices in Ritual

If you do want to use an electronic device in magickal work, or to bring it into circle, you don't need to consecrate the device to your practice of magick or to the Goddess and God. All you need to do is to bless the device by asking for the blessings of the Goddess and God:

> *On this instrument that is part of myself I ask the Goddess and God to recognize the flow of electronic energy I carry with me in all of my life be not foreign to magick and not foreign to the Divine energy of the All.*

If you cast a hard circle (one you need to cut a door in to enter or exit), that circle is protective. Electronics in hard circles interfere with the flow of magickal energy from the Divine to the Earth and through your human bodies. The magick you do can get skewed, just by having the device in circle. If a phone begins beeping or buzzing unexpectedly, it interrupts the focus of those in circle and can disrupt your magick. For that reason, witches do not generally bring electronic devices into a hard circle, especially when high magick or formal ritual is being done. Some circles have a basket at the doorway for cell phones. For participants with special needs (a child or family member for whom you must be accessible), the phone can be placed out of circle. To exit, cut the energy upwards. All magickal work stops in circle until the person returns within. If you want to bring a cell phone into circle, ask the group, or the High Priestess, what is appropriate.

At large events, such as solstice festivals outdoors, witches may only call the quarters, creating a semi-permeable circle through which people can come and go. A semi-permeable circle does not require cutting a door to enter or exit. The circle consists of the people in it and the energy they generate. In this less formal setting, electronic devices may be permitted in some fashion. This doesn't mean, however, that you should start taking phone calls or begin texting in circle! Common sense and rules of etiquette apply. Follow any instructions given at the event regarding how you can bring and use electronics in circle.

As a solitaire you can decide how to incorporate electronics into your practice, both in and out of circle. Just like all of us do, witches go online and use social media; some write blogs and post videos or do podcasts. How we engage with digital media socially is a great cultural experiment of our time. It makes sense that digital technology will find its way into the practice of Wicca. Witches just need to pay attention to whether the energy is really doing what you intend it to do; that is, whether the electronic or digital media is enhancing or detracting from your magickal workings.

Ways to Use Electronic Devices in Magick

Some things to remember when using technology:

◆ It is important not to out people who still may be in the proverbial broom closet. Before you post a picture of your friend in a cool solstice outfit or make a comment on social media, remember that not all witches are open about their practice of Wicca. Ask permission. Think before you post or text. Be discreet and always respectful.

◆ Always ask permission before posting any photos or videos to social media. When in doubt, don't. Remember that formal rituals such as dedications and initiations are sacred and private events and should not be shared online or through social media.

◆ For less formal ritual gatherings, you might want to bring a remote witch into circle by using Skype, Facetime, or another video calling service.

◆ Many witches use the flashlight feature of their cell phones when working outdoors at night, or in lieu of using candles.

◆ Witches can use the compass feature to set up altars of the four directions or to prepare to cast a circle.

◆ Use apps to see heavenly bodies and constellations. The app uses the phone camera to create a virtual reality where you can see exactly where objects are in the sky just by moving the phone.

♦ The older generation does not use phones often to cast spells by text. But you can use letters, emojis, and numerological energy to create spells. The magickal energy put into the spell as you enter the coded message comes out when the recipient opens the text and deciphers the code.

♦ Voice-controlled smart speakers like the Echo Dot with Alexa, or Google Assist, amplify the flow of technological energy by entering the ears and mind and even the cells of the human body, filling it with information. Information is a flow as magick is a flow. Voice-assisted smart speakers may be helping to raise the flow of magickal energy in everyday life.

Right now, magick using electronic devices and digital technology is limited but that should (and will) change. So go ahead and follow that witchy Instagram, Pinterest your altar, track your cycles, and make your witchy playlists. Be respectful of others, and always act to hold Wiccan ritual sacred.

MORE SPELLS YOU CAN DO

Because witches are a creative bunch, there's no end to the number of spells, chants, talismans, amulets, and potions that you will encounter. You'll want to start creating your own, too. Or maybe you have already begun. Here are more spells. Use them if you like. Or use them as models to help you craft your own. And don't forget to keep your magickal record in your grimoire.

Crystal Talisman or Amulet

You can empower a crystal to either draw something you want toward you—money, love, or luck, for instance—or keep negative energies away from you. To do this, choose a crystal to match your intent (see Chapter 17). Cleanse the crystal of negative energy and then charge the crystal with your intent by chanting the following:

> *Air and Water, Earth and Fire,*
> *Hearken to my strong desire.*
> *Charge this crystal in its work for me.*
> *As I have said it, so mote it be.*

Envision your magick coming to pass while you chant. When you are finished, you can either carry the crystal with you or give it to someone else.

Empowering a Potion

When making a potion, say this chant while envisioning your magick coming to pass:

Strong the witch and strong the brew,
Here is magick made anew.
I charge this potion with my will,
Its magick purpose to fulfill.

Book Blessing

You can say this blessing over your grimoire or Book of Shadows:

My magick's my passion, the spirit's my guide.
The love for the Goddess I hold deep inside.
The book may she bless it with spiritual light.
And let only her children read of its rite.
For those of the Wicca truly can see,
That this is my will, so mote it be.

Healing Necklace

You will need three strands of embroidery thread, 2 or 3 feet long. Blue, green, and white are good colors for this purpose. You will also need a handful of pony beads in the same colors. Sit in your magick circle and tie the lengths of thread together at one end. Then begin braiding them. As you do so, string a bead every third time you cross the strings. While you create your charmed jewelry, softly repeat these words:

Braid by braid the magick grows.
Through each bead, the healing flows.
Let the wearer quickly find
Wholeness again in body and mind.

Strongly visualize the one who will wear the necklace—whether it be you or another. Continue braiding the threads and see that person as healthy and comfortable.

Money and Prosperity

This money-drawing spell is fun to do. You will need two nickels and some strong glue. Glue the two coins together, being careful not to glue yourself to the coins. As you do this, say:

> *As one coin to another clings,*
> *The energy of wealth it brings.*
> *The more I keep them close to me,*
> *The greater my good fortune be.*

Carry the glued-together coins in your pants pocket so they are near your root chakra— your internal wheel of energy associated with material needs (see Chapter 16). Or place them on your altar.

If you try this spell, make sure to record what you have done in your grimoire.

Or try the following spell for prosperity. Obtain a fresh, ripe pineapple. Cut off the top half of the pineapple. Peel, core, and cube it. Then carefully scoop out the insides of the bottom half. You want to leave the skin unbroken so you can use the bottom as a serving bowl. Core and cube the flesh. In a mixing bowl, stir the cubed pineapple with 1 teaspoon cinnamon, 1 teaspoon ground ginger, and 1 teaspoon allspice. As you stir, say:

> *May this sacred food be blessed,*
> *So to bring me all the best.*

Load the spiced pineapple back into the bowl you have created from the bottom half. Chill, then serve as dessert after a meal. It's nice to gaze at the pineapple's skin as you eat this fruit mixture. Allow yourself to take in the prosperous energy. Repeat this spell every few weeks to manifest your own prosperity.

Luck

We all could use a little good luck now and then. To enhance yours, make your own lucky anointing oil. To do this you will need:

♦ 2 oz. unscented almond oil

♦ 3 drops cinnamon essential oil

♦ 9 drops of rose or lotus oil

♦ 1 pinch dried vetivert

♦ 1 allspice berry

♦ 1 small peridot stone

Place the oils and spices in a jar or small bowl. When the moon is waxing, drop the stone into the oil and say:

> *Stone to oil and oil to me,*
> *Great will the change in my fortunes be.*
> *Lucky I am in all I do.*
> *This oil be so charged and this magick be true.*

Before you leave your home each day, anoint your feet with your lucky oil. You can also use this oil in small amounts on your purse or wallet. You can even apply it to lottery tickets, but do so sparingly; you wouldn't want to smear the ink! Your luck should noticeably improve within one cycle of the Moon.

Breaking Another Witch's Spell

If another witch has put a hex on you, here's how to undo it. You will need a length of silver cord and your bolline (magick knife used for cutting) or a pair of scissors. Tie one knot in each end of the cord. As you do this, visualize one knot representing you and the other the person who cast the hex. Cut the cord in the center, chant the following, and see the spell breaking:

From you to me this spell I break,
This was not right for you to make.
Its path I will abruptly end,
And back to you the spell I send.

FAIRY MAGICK

Be sure you really want to work with fairies. As we mentioned in Chapter 14, fairies can work wonderful magick for you, but they are also very mischievous and difficult to get rid of once they have infested the house. If you've decided you're ready to work with them, you will need—in addition to knowing your magickal intent—your magick tools and some *fairy dust*. Fairy dust is a superfine glitter, similar to embossing powder. You can buy it in small vials at most metaphysical shops. Some people keep the vials closed and wear them as magickal jewelry.

On a waxing Moon, sit in your magickal circle with your tools and fairy dust. Relax and visualize walking through the portal to the magickal Realm of Fairy. Walk through this wondrous place and drink in the magick. You may see fairies peering at you from their hiding places, flying overhead, or you may just hear them laugh. Get the feel of what it is like to be around fairies. When you're ready, come back through the portal and open your eyes in your magick circle. Now you can begin by chanting this verse:

To Fairy realms on moonlit night,
You lords and ladies of the Sidhe,
I search for you and do invite
Your presence in sacred space with me.
Bright ones, fair ones hear my voice,
Hearken to my magick call.
Come or not, it is your choice,
But magick touches one and all.

And if you choose to work with me,
Lending power to my spell,
I will sincerely grateful be

And also will reward you well.
Sweet milky drinks or honeyed-wine
Are offered up to pay your fee.
I invite your energies join with mine,
Wise ones of Fairy, come to me!

When you are finished, sit very still and quietly wait for them to appear. You may not see them at first, but you may feel their presence as an itch or a tickle in your hair. After they have arrived, do your intended magickal work. When you have finished, leave some sweet milk out for them, some fairy dust, or some wine mixed with honey.

CHAPTER 23

BEGIN YOUR YEAR-AND-A-DAY STUDY

You are about to become a scholar and a student of witchcraft. You will have to work hard—reading, listening, researching, and studying—to get a proper grounding in all the knowledge you must have to truly call yourself a witch. The seasonal program of study we have laid out below will guide you along your Wiccan path. It may look like a lot of work, but, rest assured, the path will be rewarding. If it takes you more than a year and a day to complete your studies, know that's okay. Be cool with yourself, and keep at it! A true Wicca practice is a life's work.

Some of the activities you will undertake are practices that you will engage in every day. Others are things you will do regularly, and still others are more like one time assignments—projects or investigations designed to start your exploration of a given area of Wiccan knowledge or practice. Take notes. Keep a running list in your grimoire of all the resources you have consulted. This way you will develop a wellspring of knowledge about the Craft you can return to at any time. Over the course of the year, you will be acquiring your major magickal tools—an athame, cauldron, chalice, pentagram, and wand, to start. You may not have to buy all of them. You can make or find some of them. Or perhaps someone will give you one of the magickal tools you seek. You'll also probably need candles, incense, and something to hold the burning incense. But don't get too far ahead of yourselves! Step on the path of your year-and-a-day studies for self-dedication to the Craft with a simple prayer. Take a deep breath:

> *Great breath of the Mother Goddess, help me to see All of your realms, open to me.*
> *Blessed be.*

SPRING

Traditionally a time to start new things, spring really is a time of new beginnings. Flowers are sprouting (or at least preparing to do so), trees are growing buds, and birds are preparing to nest. In the Wiccan religion, Imbolc, celebrated on February 2, is the time of renewed fertility of the earth. The soil is starting to warm, and seeds are just beginning to germinate. As such, this is a great time to start on your new path. While early February may not feel like spring, Nature really is getting ready to burst forth. Join in a celebration of the spring Sabbats of Imbolc, Ostara, or Beltane. Research the holidays and learn as much as you can about them.

Commitment, Dedication, Initiation

Some covens initiate new members at Imbolc. Try thinking of yourself as a seed newly planted and preparing to germinate in the warming Earth. The first thing you'll want to do in the spring is make a declaration of commitment to the Wiccan path. We explained about dedication and how to do a dedication ritual in Chapter 7. So, if you have not done so already, start planning your own dedication. Now, let us be the first to congratulate you and welcome you into the Craft! Every spring is a perfect time to renew your dedication to your Wicca practice. As you grow in the Craft, you may consider mentoring a young witch in the year-and-a-day process.

Begin Your Grimoire and Book of Shadows

This is also the time for you to start keeping your grimoire and your Book of Shadows. Every time you write in them, make sure to note the time of day, the phase of the Moon, and the sign of the Moon. Record spells and rituals that you do in your grimoire. You'll want to keep your Book of Shadows handy to write down all your thoughts and feelings as you enter into your Wiccan practice. Write in your books regularly during your whole year-and-a-day. Between the two books, you will be writing once or twice every two weeks. And make certain to record information, your thoughts, and your feelings after full Moon rituals and holidays.

Meditation and Divination

Many witchy activities require you to focus. Meditation is a great way to practice building up your powers of concentration. Make a commitment to meditate every day of spring. Choose a daily topic for your focus and write it on your calendar. Some ideas are the Goddess, the Wiccan Rede, Drawing Down the Moon, skyclad, Book of Shadows, the spring Sabbats (Imbolc, Ostara, Beltane), fairies, chalice, and more. Start off with 10-minute sessions and build up to 20 minutes. Write your essential thoughts in your journal, along with ideas for further exploration. As a witch, it is important to be comfortable and familiar with at least one form of divination. Divination will help you with day-to-day decisions by allowing you access to divine guidance. Divination techniques that are popular among Wiccans today include—pendulums, runes, and Tarot cards.

To make your pendulum, attach a fishing weight, a piece of jewelry, a spool of thread, or a crystal to the end of a string. Next decide what the pendulum's movements mean. Many witches make a card with the pendulum's answers that looks like this:

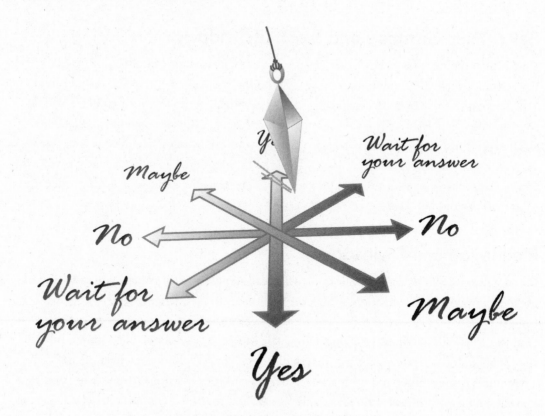

Hold the loose end of string in one hand and let your pendulum hang. Once it has become still, ask your question. Soon it will answer you by beginning to move again. Some witches use pendulums to help them choose among various items when out shopping.

Mark your spring calendar's days at random with each of the 25 rune symbols. On each assigned day, you may use the rune symbol as your daily subject for meditation. Or use the day to do more research on the rune symbol and its meaning. Do simple rune readings by drawing three runes from a velvet bag and meditating on their meaning for your day. Draw the daily rune symbols in your journal.

Tarot cards are another popular divination tool. A Tarot deck contains 78 cards—22 Major Arcana cards and 56 Minor Arcana cards. The cards of the Minor Arcana are a lot like regular playing cards. They have suits and either numbers or faces. The cards of the Major Arcana bear pictures that represent the significant issues or phases in an individual's spiritual development. Invest in a Tarot deck and a good Tarot book, such as *The Complete*

Idiot's Guide to Tarot, Second Edition, by Arlene Tognetti and Lisa Lenard. You can read Tarot cards as a means of looking into the future. Or you can use them to help you with a decision. You can also meditate on the images of the Major Arcana or use their energies.

Build Your Altar

Find out as much about your altar table as you can. Where did it come from? Did it have previous owners? Who were they and what were they like? What was the table used for? If your table (or other flat-topped object) is made of wood, find out what kind of tree the wood came from. Each tree has its own magickal energy, so if one is part of your altar, you'll want to know just what that vibe is. Here is a list of commonly accepted correspondences for the types of trees often used to make furniture.

Tree/Wood	Magickal Properties and Associations.
Ash	Protection, healing, abundance
Aspen	Knowledge, intuition, understanding
Beech	Letting go, renewal, positive outlook
Birch	Purification, protection, especially of the young
Cedar	Balance, spirituality, courage, dreams
Cherry	Success, efficiency, especially in business or manufacturing
Elder	Exorcism, healing, prosperity, joy, protection
Elm	Love, success, renewal of faith
Fir	Wisdom, regeneration
Locust	Healing, protection, cleansing
Maple	Luck, strength, love, family, long life
Oak	Health, strength, power, money, protection
Pear	Hope, lust, love, generosity, growth
Pine	Wisdom, longevity, grounding, fertility, blessing
Rosewood	Psychic powers, healing, divination, love
Walnut	Health, blessing, fertility, mental acumen

Once you have settled on your altar furniture and have determined that its energy is one you can work with, set up your altar. Place your altar in the East—the direction of Air and beginnings. Later you may move it so that it rests in the North.

SUMMER

Summertime! Long days filled with light, the abundance of fruits and vegetables, the lushness of Nature, and maybe even a vacation! On the Wiccan Wheel of the Year, the Lord and Lady are at the height of their strength now. While you are studying, make sure to get outside and enjoy all the best aspects of the season. Summer Sabbats are Summer Solstice and Lughnassad. Join in a summer Sabbat celebration, or create one of your own. Do research to learn as much as you can about these Sabbats.

Pick a Deity

Most witches are conversant in the myths and stories of the ancient Greeks and Romans, the Sumerians and Babylonians, Egyptians, the Celts, and the Nordic peoples. Commit to reading some about each of these ancient cultures. After you have completed your research and with the help of your magickal mentor, pick one deity you feel you relate to the best. Dedicate your altar space to this one deity. If you are open to it, the deity you have picked will teach you many things over the course of your year-and-a-day. (After a year and a day, you may rededicate your altar to another deity if you so choose.) If you have not set up your altar yet, get a picture or a small statue of your deity (or create one yourself) and bring it out when you do ritual.

Magickal Writing

A couple of times a week, practice writing in Theban script. Yup, it's another commitment! You really want to get proficient with your magickal writing and, if you keep working with this alphabet, pretty soon you will have it memorized. Theban script is the writing system many Gardnerian witches use.

Herbalism 101

With all the plants thriving and blooming, begin your study of herbs in summer. See if your local herb shop, metaphysical store, or community garden has any offerings for classes. If you have outdoor space or a sunny windowsill, start growing some herbs at this time. Besides cultivating herbs, you'll want to learn about wild crafting and harvesting them, too. Look for a mentor in magickal herbs who can pass along her knowledge to you and keep magickal traditions going.

Dance, Dance, Dance!

At least once a week for an hour, put on music and dance. If you are having trouble committing to a dance practice, meditate on Bastet, the Egyptian Goddess of pleasure, dancing, and other good things. You could even imagine her cat-headed form as you dance (or sway) to your music. And don't forget to write about your experiences in your Book of Shadows. Dance is an ancient part of Wiccan ritual, and greatly enhances the magick you do in circle.

FALL

As the hours of sunlight diminish, we naturally turn inward. In olden days, the harvesting of crops was a celebration and a preparation for the long, hard winter to come. Now, when night and day approach equal duration on Mabon, it's a time to accumulate and take stock. The Lord is preparing for his death at Samhain. And witches are preparing for this, more interior, season.

Deeper into Herbalism

During the fall, in addition to learning about the magickal uses of plants, study herbal healing. In the old days, witches were the healers of the community. So help keep this ancient tradition alive by learning about tinctures, poultices, plasters, and medicinal teas. If there is a class in your area that's not too expensive, sign up. If you have a mentor in magickal herbs, focus on healing arts now.

Astrology and Your Heavens

Fall, with its inward-turning gaze, is the perfect time to begin your study of astrology. If you are dressed warmly, fall is also a super time for looking at the night sky. The crisper, drier air allows the stars to shine bright and clear. And there's nothing like a starry night to inspire a sense of wonder and connection. Get a witches' calendar or almanac for the new calendar year and study it. Go online, and do your astrological birth chart, the chart of the position of the heavens at your birth. Learn to interpret your chart and make magickal connections.

Treasures from the Earth

Fall is also the time to begin your study of stones and crystals. Just like living beings, each crystal or stone has its own energy vibration. A knowledge and understanding of this energy can enhance your magick. Use crystal energy in healing work. Think of your learning in this area as a form of worship. By gaining an understanding of Nature's deep dwelling treasures, you are honoring Nature and the Earth herself. Visit a rock and mineral show, or an exhibit of stones at a natural history museum.

Music and You

The study of music can help you to hear the voice of Spirit. Witches need witches who can play instruments and sing! Music is an important part of ritual. It honors the Lord and Lady, engages our spirits, helps to reinforce ties of community, and, after you get over your initial shyness, it's fun to perform, too. Next season you *will* be performing!

The instrument you take up is entirely up to you. To make it easy on yourself, pick an instrument with a fixed pitch, such as piano, keyboard, recorder, or accordion. For those of you who consider yourself tone deaf, don't worry! Anybody can learn to play an instrument. You don't have to be a rock star, a diva, or a prodigy to become reasonably proficient.

Color Your Magick

The weather is cooling, and perhaps, where you live, the leaves are turning. Refine your color magick skills. Choose the color you are most drawn to, least drawn to, and feel most neutral about, and study their magickal associations and correspondences. Meditate on the colors and write about them in your journal. Look for the natural color palette of the fall season where you live. Make note of all the subtle, or not so subtle, gradations of tone and intensity. If you have paints, make some color studies of the seasonal palette. How is there magick in Nature's colors? Spend a day at a local art museum and meditate on the artists' uses of color.

WINTER

Winter is the time of the inward gaze and of nurturing your interior. Hibernation, darkness, and introspection reign now. Meditation and divination are natural pastimes during the long, cold nights. Rest and gather your energies for the busy spring to come. But winter is also a time that we need to act to keep our spirits up. You have accumulated a lot of knowledge and have developed some good habits and practices. You are about to complete your course of study. We hope you have enjoyed your journey!

Look Deep

The long, cold nights of winter are the time for you to take up scrying. Scrying is practiced by looking into a reflective surface. There you may see images of the future or ones that can help you in your spiritual development. Many witches use water for scrying. Others use crystal balls, specially prepared scrying glasses or mirrors, or pieces of obsidian. Try scrying with water. Fill a black cast-iron pan with water. Or fill your cauldron. Light a candle and pull up a white protective light all around you. Stare into the water. After some time, you may start to see swirls of color or a mist. Some of these may grow into images. Try scrying with a piece of dark, polished stone. Commit to practice scrying a few times every week and see what you can begin to see.

The Many Wiccan Traditions

Spend some time reading about the varied traditions of the Craft. If you're thinking of joining a coven, it's really important that you are comfortable with the tradition of that coven and that you know what you may be getting yourself into. Remember to consult at least two different sources on this topic.

The Wheel of the Year Has Turned!

Your year-and-a-day of study and exploration has drawn to a close. You are launched on your Wiccan path, and now it may be time to consider initiation into a coven, or self-initiation if you will continue as a solitaire. Keep learning, keep studying, and keep exploring your understanding of the Craft.

ATTEND A WICCAN CEREMONY

A handfasting is a Wiccan wedding ceremony, and is considered high ritual. Handfastings may occur at any time of year, though the timing may have magickal significance to the couple marrying. In your year-and-a-day of study and exploration, do your best to attend a handfasting ceremony and witness this happy ritual. Here are the parts of a handfasting ceremony:

♦ The place is blessed. Sacred space is created by casting a circle and sprinkling water from a symbolic branch, such as cedar, or sprinkling flowers, usually roses or gardenias. It can also be done by smudging the area and sprinkling salt water from a shell.

♦ The High Priestess comes to the altar, welcomes the guests, and asks for the attendance and blessings of the Lord and Lady. The Elemental powers are summoned by calling in the quarters. The couple comes to the altar and is blessed by the Priestess. The couple declares what they have brought into the sacred space and the meaning of their offering to their union.

♦ A blade is lowered into a chalice of wine to represent God and Goddess united. The couple shares bread and wine. The couple speaks their promises to each other for their marriage. They exchange tokens of their vows, usually rings, but not always.

♦ The Priestess blesses the couple's handfasting cord and drapes it around their clasped hands, usually in the infinity pattern. The cord is either tied at that time, or the couple pulls the cord in a way that creates a knot in the center, thus "tying the knot." Many Wiccan couples at this point jump a broom to seal their union. Jumping the broom at the end of the ritual symbolizes sweeping away everything negative in the past and starting anew.

♦ The circle is opened and all present celebrate with food and drink and music.

And like so many wonderful books, we end with a wedding! And a blessing:

> God and Goddess light your Wiccan path,
> By sunlight and by moonlight true.
> Blessing of the Divine All, blessed be!

RESOURCES

There's a great wealth of published material on Wicca, witchcraft, and related topics. Once you start investigating, you'll find books, videos, and CDs that will help guide you along your path. Use this list as a starting place. When you go looking for one of the titles listed here, browse the books in the surrounding area and see what else catches your eye and speaks to your heart.

SUGGESTED READING

Adler, Margot. *Drawing Down the Moon: Witches, Druids, Goddess-Worshippers, and Other Pagans in America Today.* New York: Arkana, 1997.

Berkowitz, Rita, and Deborah S. Romaine. *The Complete Idiot's Guide to Communicating with Spirits.* Indianapolis: Alpha Books, 2002.

Beyerl, Paul. *A Compendium of Herbal Magick.* Custer, WA: Phoenix Publishing, 1998.

———. *The Master Book of Herbalism.* Custer, WA: Phoenix Publishing, 1984.

Bonheim, Jalaja, ed. *Goddess.* New York: Stewart, Tabori, & Chang, 1997.

Briggs, Robin. *Witches and Neighbors: The Social and Cultural Context of European Witchcraft.* New York: Penguin, 1998.

Buckland, Raymond. *Buckland's Complete Book of Witchcraft.* St. Paul, MN: Llewellyn Publications, 1986.

Budapest, Zsuzsanna E. *Grandmother Moon: Lunar Magic in Our Lives: Spells, Rituals, Goddesses, Legends, and Emotions Under the Moon.* San Francisco: HarperSanFrancisco, 1991.

Bullfinch, Thomas. *The Age of Fable or Beauties of Mythology.* New York: Heritage Press, 1942.

Chearney, Lee Ann, ed. *The Quotable Angel.* New York: John Wiley & Sons, Inc., 1995.

Choquette, Sonia. *The Psychic Pathway: A Workbook for Reawakening the Voice of Your Soul.* New York: Crown, 1994.

Cunningham, Scott. *Cunningham's Encyclopedia of Crystal, Gem & Metal Magic.* St. Paul, MN: Llewellyn Publications, 1988.

———. *Cunningham's Encyclopedia of Magical Herbs.* St. Paul, MN: Llewellyn Publications, 1985.

———. *Wicca: A Guide for the Solitary Practitioner.* St. Paul, MN: Llewellyn Publications, 1988.

Curott, Phyllis. *Book of Shadows: A Modern Woman's Journey into the Wisdom of Witchcraft and the Magic of the Goddess.* New York: Broadway/Random House, 1998.

Eisler, Riane. *The Chalice and the Blade.* New York: Harper & Row, 1987.

Farrar, Janet, and Stewart Farrar. *The Witches' Goddess.* Custer, WA: Phoenix Publishing, 1987.

———. *The Witches' God.* Custer, WA: Phoenix Publishing, 1989.

Feldman, Gail, Ph.D., and Eve Adamson. *Releasing the Mother Goddess.* Indianapolis: Alpha Books, 2003.

Feldman, Gail, Ph.D., and Katherine A. Gleason. *Releasing the Goddess Within.* Indianapolis: Alpha Books, 2002.

Frazer, James G. *The Golden Bough: The Roots of Religion and Folklore.* New York: Avenel Books, 1981 (reprint of 1890 edition).

Gerwick-Brodeur, Madeline, and Lisa Lenard. *The Complete Idiot's Guide to Astrology, Third Edition.* Indianapolis: Alpha Books, 2003.

Gile, Robin, and Lisa Lenard. *The Complete Idiot's Guide to Palmistry, Second Edition.* Indianapolis: Alpha Books, 2005.

Graves, Robert. *The White Goddess.* New York: Noonday/FSG, 1948.

Grimassi, Raven. *The Wiccan Mysteries.* St. Paul, MN: Llewellyn Publications, 1997.

Hamilton, Edith. *Mythology: Timeless Tales of Gods and Heroes.* Boston: Little Brown, 1969.

Hopman, Ellen Evert, and Laurence Bond. *People of the Earth: The New Pagans Speak Out.* Rochester, VT: Destiny Books, 1996.

Hunter, Jennifer. *21st Century Wicca: A Young Witch's Guide to Living the Magical Life.* New York: Citadel Press, 1997.

Hutton, Ronald. *The Triumph of the Moon: A History of Modern Pagan Witchcraft.* New York: Oxford, 1999.

Illes, Judika. *The Element Encyclopedia of Witchcraft: The Complete A-Z for the Entire Magical World.* United Kingdom: Thorsons Element, 2005.

K, Amber. *Covencraft: Witchcraft for Three or More.* St. Paul, MN: Llewellyn Publications, 1998.

Lagerquist, Kay, and Lisa Lenard. *The Complete Idiot's Guide to Numerology, Second Edition.* Indianapolis: Alpha Books, 2004.

McCoy, Edain. *Entering the Summerland: Customs and Rituals of Transition into the Afterlife.* St. Paul, MN: Llewellyn Publications, 1996.

Melody. *Love Is in the Earth: A Kaleidoscope of Crystals* (updated). Wheat Ridge, CO: Earth-Love Publishing House, 1995.

Morrison, Dorothy. *Everyday Moon Magic.* St. Paul, MN: Llewellyn Publications, 2004.

———. *Everyday Sun Magic.* St. Paul, MN: Llewellyn Publications, 2005.

Penczak, Christopher. *City Magick*. York Beach, ME: Red Wheel/Weiser, 2001.

———. *Instant Magick*. St. Paul, MN: Llewellyn Publications, 2006.

Pliskin, Marci, and Shari L. Just. *The Complete Idiot's Guide to Interpreting Your Dreams, Second Edition*. Indianapolis: Alpha Books, 2004.

RavenWolf, Silver. *To Light a Sacred Flame: Practical Witchcraft for the Millennium*. St. Paul, MN: Llewellyn Publications, 1999.

———. *To Ride a Silver Broomstick: New Generation Witchcraft*. St. Paul, MN: Llewellyn Publications, 1999.

Rosean, Lexa. *Tarot Power: 22 Keys to Unlocking Magick, Spellcraft, and Meditation*. New York: Citadel Press, 2005.

Simms, Maria Kay. *The Witch's Circle: Rituals and Craft of the Cosmic Muse*. St. Paul, MN: Llewellyn Publications, 1994.

Starhawk. *The Spiral Dance: A Rebirth of the Ancient Religion of the Goddess: 20th Anniversary Edition*. San Francisco: HarperSanFrancisco, 1999.

Stone, Merlin. *When God Was a Woman*. New York: Harvest/HBJ, 1976.

Teish, Luisah. *Jambalaya: The Natural Woman's Book of Personal Charms and Practical Rituals*. New York: Harper & Row, 1985.

Tognetti, Arlene, and Lisa Lenard. *The Complete Idiot's Guide to Tarot, Second Edition*. Indianapolis: Alpha Books, 2003.

SUGGESTED VIEWING

Buckland, Raymond. *Witchcraft: Yesterday and Today.* 60 minutes. Llewellyn Worldwide, Ltd; 1990.

Farrar, Janet, and Stewart Farrar. *Discovering Witchcraft: A Journey Through the Elements.* 87 minutes. Sothis Films; 1998.

————. *Discovering Witchcraft: The Mysteries.* 60 minutes. Sothis Films; 1999.

SUGGESTED LISTENING

McKennitt, Loreena. *The Visit,* WEA/Warner, 1992.

On the Wings of Song and Robert Gass. *From the Goddess,* Spring Hill Music, 1989.

Reclaiming & Friends. *Chants: Ritual Music,* Serpentine Music Productions, 1987.

Rowland, Mike. *The Fairy Ring,* Emd/Narada, 1982.

Troika. *Goddess,* Emd/Narada, 1996.

Various artists. *The Best of Pagan Song,* Serpentine Music Productions, 2004.

SUGGESTED SURFING

The Witches' Voice: www.witchvox.com

Mystic Wicks: www.mysticwicks.com/

CREATING YOUR GRIMOIRE

Although there are no rules to follow when creating your grimoire, when you're just starting out you might be looking for some guidance. Remember that a grimoire is a how-to book that will allow you to recreate a meal you served or a ritual that was particularly successful (or unsuccessful!). It is the book you share with other witches when they say, "Can I have your formula for that heart-healing potion?" or, "I loved your incantation for Drawing Down the Moon. Would you mind if I used it, too?"

This is not the place for private reflection or comments about other witches in your coven. Those belong in your Book of Shadows. The Book of Shadows is your diary or journal. You might include your recipe for spiced cider in your grimoire, for example, but you would describe the party where you served it in your Book of Shadows.

Your grimoire does not have to be an expensive book. In fact, many witches find that a three-ring notebook is the perfect grimoire. You can rearrange pages, loan out recipes to friends, or take a spell into a circle just by removing one page. Other witches type everything into a computer and print what they need, and still others keep their magickal information on notecards in a box. If you put the printed page or notecard into a plastic sleeve, you save it from spilled wax or spaghetti sauce.

Here are some things you might want to include in your grimoire entries:

♦ Ritual preparations (bath, incense, etc.)

♦ Date and time

♦ Location and length of ritual

♦ Moon phase

♦ Weather

♦ Type and purpose of ritual

♦ Names of participants (or solitaire)

♦ Ritual clothing and jewelry worn

♦ Color of candles used

♦ Altar description

♦ Creating a circle

♦ Incantations used

♦ Deities invited

♦ Other spirits included

♦ Food served (with recipes)

♦ Magickal correspondences for spices and herbs used

♦ Outcome of ritual

Don't forget that a grimoire can also include photographs of events. A snapshot of a particularly memorable Samhain bonfire or a Beltane feast can help you remember the event. Plus, pictures of friends are a great way to bring a smile to your face when you need a lift.

You can copy the Magickal Record shown in Chapter 10 to get started in putting your own grimoire together. If, however, this format doesn't work for you, create your own Magickal Record template. Not every entry has to look the same or include the same information. It might be that you worked alone and didn't serve food. Or maybe you don't think the weather played a part. Only record what seems important to record.

Keeping a detailed grimoire makes it easier to be consistent in your spellcrafting. It will also help you in tracking your spiritual journey and in guiding other witches on their magickal paths.

INDEX

C

D

E

F

G

H

O

P

Q–R

S

T

· ·

U

X–Y

Z